MARRIAGE AND DIVORCE LAW

Global Perspectives

MARRIAGE AND DIVORCE LAW
Global Perspectives

BY

LEO TURNER

KNOWLEDGE BAKERS

KNOWLEDGE BAKERS

ISBN: 978-81-9755-940-2 (HB)

Published by : **Knowledge Bakers**
Pune, India
Email: info@knowledgebakers.com

PREFACE

Marriage and divorce laws are fundamental pillars of legal systems worldwide, shaping the rights, obligations, and protections afforded to individuals in intimate relationships. These laws not only regulate the formation and dissolution of marriages but also govern matters such as property division, child custody, spousal support, and domestic violence prevention. The legal landscape surrounding marriage and divorce is dynamic and varies significantly across jurisdictions, reflecting cultural norms, religious beliefs, and social attitudes towards marriage and family. As we embark on this exploration of marriage and divorce law from a global perspective, we delve into a realm where legal principles, cultural diversity, human rights, and social justice intersect, uncovering the complexities, challenges, and opportunities inherent in the regulation of intimate relationships.

This book, titled "Marriage and Divorce Law: Global Perspectives," is crafted to provide a comprehensive examination of marriage and divorce laws from diverse legal systems and cultural contexts around the world. Through collaboration with leading scholars, practitioners, and policymakers in family law and human rights, we aim to offer readers a nuanced and insightful journey through the complexities of marriage and divorce regulation.

As editors of this volume, we have curated a collection of chapters that cover a wide range of topics in marriage and divorce law, including legal frameworks, historical developments, case studies, comparative analyses, and emerging trends. Each chapter is designed to provide readers with a deep understanding of the legal, cultural, and societal factors that shape marriage and divorce laws in different countries and regions.

Furthermore, this book seeks to highlight the importance of promoting access to justice, gender equality, and human rights in the context of marriage and divorce. By examining the impact of legal reforms, judicial decisions, and international conventions on family law practices, we aim to inspire readers to advocate for fair, inclusive, and rights-based approaches to resolving marital disputes and protecting vulnerable individuals and families.

As we embark on this enlightening journey through the world of marriage and divorce law, we extend our gratitude to the contributors whose expertise and dedication have enriched this book. We hope that "Marriage and Divorce Law: Global Perspectives" serves as a valuable resource for legal professionals, policymakers, researchers, activists, and students alike, empowering them to navigate the complexities of family law regulation and contribute to the advancement of justice and equality in intimate relationships worldwide.

Leo Turner

CONTENTS

1

MARRIAGE: INTRODUCTION

Marriage, as a social institution, has been around for thousands of years. With things that are thousands of years old, it's easy to assume that they can only change slowly. But developments since the middle of the 20th century show that this assumption is wrong: in many countries marriages are becoming less common, people are marrying later, unmarried couples are increasingly choosing to live together, and in many countries we are seeing a 'decoupling' of parenthood and marriage. Within the last decades the institution of marriage has changed more than in thousands of years before.

The institution of marriage is an important part of societal structure, which exists in most parts of the world. While customs and traditions related to marriages vary, the common thread is the union of two individuals. Celebrations and coming together of families, friends and relatives is another thing that's common among marriages across the globe.

However, based on what part of the world you belong, marriages can have some very unique customs and traditions. Marriage laws also differ from country to country. And some of them are quite weird to say the least. To satisfy your curiosity, here's a quick look at some of the most weird marriage laws from around the world.

The word "marriage" derives from Middle English mariage, which first appears in 1250–1300 CE. This, in turn, is derived from Old French, marier (to marry), and ultimately Latin, marītāre, meaning to provide with a husband or wife and marītāri meaning to get married. The adjective marīt-us -a, -um meaning matrimonial or nuptial could also be used in the masculine form as a noun for "husband" and in the feminine form for "wife". The related word "matrimony" derives from the Old French word matremoine, which appears around 1300 CE and ultimately derives from Latin mātrimōnium, which combines the two concepts: mater meaning "mother" and the suffix -monium signifying "action, state, or condition".

Marriage, also called matrimony or wedlock, is a culturally and often legally recognized union between people called spouses. It establishes rights and obligations between them, as well as between them and their children, and between them and their in-laws. It is considered a cultural universal, but the definition of marriage varies between cultures and religions, and over time. Typically, it is an institution in which interpersonal relationships, usually sexual, are acknowledged or sanctioned. In some cultures, marriage is recommended or considered to be compulsory before pursuing any sexual activity. A marriage ceremony is called a wedding.

Individuals may marry for several reasons, including legal, social, libidinal, emotional, financial, spiritual, and religious purposes. Whom they marry may be influenced by gender, socially determined rules of incest, prescriptive marriage rules, parental choice, and individual desire. In some areas of the world, arranged marriage, child marriage, polygamy, and forced marriage are practiced. In other areas, such practices are outlawed to preserve women's rights or children's rights (both female and male) or as a result of international law.

Marriage has historically restricted the rights of women, who are sometimes considered the property of the husband. Around the world, primarily in developed democracies, there has been a general trend towards ensuring equal rights for women within marriage (including abolishing coverture, liberalizing divorce laws, and reforming reproductive and sexual rights) and legally recognizing the marriages of interfaith, interracial, and same-sex couples. Controversies continue regarding the legal status of married women, leniency towards violence within marriage, customs such as dowry and bride price, forced marriage, marriageable age, and criminalization of premarital and extramarital sex.

Marriage can be recognized by a state, an organization, a religious authority, a tribal group, a local community, or peers. It is often viewed as a contract. A religious marriage is performed by a religious institution to recognize and create the rights and obligations intrinsic to matrimony in that religion. Religious marriage is known variously as sacramental marriage in Catholicism, nikah in Islam, nissuin in Judaism, and various other names in other faith traditions, each with their own constraints as to what constitutes, and who can enter into, a valid religious marriage.

DEFINITIONS

Anthropologists have proposed several competing definitions of marriage in an attempt to encompass the wide variety of marital practices observed across cultures. Even within Western culture, "definitions of marriage have careened from one extreme to another and everywhere in between" (as Evan Gerstmann has put it).

Relation recognized by custom or law

In The History of Human Marriage (1891), Edvard Westermarck defined marriage as "a more or less durable connection between male and female lasting beyond the mere act of propagation till after the birth of the offspring." In The Future of Marriage in Western Civilization (1936), he rejected his earlier definition, instead provisionally defining marriage as "a relation of one or more men to one or more women that is recognized by custom or law".

LEGITIMACY OF OFFSPRING

The anthropological handbook Notes and Queries (1951) defined marriage as "a union between a man and a woman such that children born to the woman are the recognized legitimate offspring of both partners." In recognition of a practice by the Nuer people of Sudan allowing women to act as a husband in certain circumstances (the ghost marriage), Kathleen Gough suggested modifying this to "a woman and one or more other persons."

In an analysis of marriage among the Nayar, a polyandrous society in India, Gough found that the group lacked a husband role in the conventional sense; that unitary role in the west was divided between a non-resident "social father" of the woman's children, and her lovers who were the actual procreators. None of these men had legal rights to the woman's child. This forced Gough to disregard sexual access as a key element of marriage and to define it in terms of legitimacy of offspring alone: marriage is "a relationship established between a woman and one or more other persons, which provides a child born to the woman under circumstances not prohibited by the rules of relationship, is accorded full birth-status rights common to normal members of his society or social stratum."

Economic anthropologist Duran Bell has criticized the legitimacy-based definition on the basis that some societies do not require marriage for legitimacy. He argued that a legitimacy-based definition of marriage is circular in societies where illegitimacy has no other legal or social implications for a child other than the mother being unmarried.

Collection of rights

Edmund Leach criticized Gough's definition for being too restrictive in terms of recognized legitimate offspring and suggested that marriage be viewed in terms of the different types of rights it serves to establish. In a 1955 article in Man, Leach argued that no one definition of marriage applied to all cultures. He offered a list of ten rights associated with marriage, including sexual monopoly and rights with respect to children, with specific rights differing across cultures. Those rights, according to Leach, included:

1. "To establish a legal father of a woman's children.
2. To establish a legal mother of a man's children.
3. To give the husband a monopoly in the wife's sexuality.
4. To give the wife a monopoly in the husband's sexuality.
5. To give the husband partial or monopolistic rights to the wife's domestic and other labor services.
6. To give the wife partial or monopolistic rights to the husband's domestic and other labor services.
7. To give the husband partial or total control over property belonging or potentially accruing to the wife.
8. To give the wife partial or total control over property belonging or potentially accruing to the husband.
9. To establish a joint fund of property – a partnership – for the benefit of the children of the marriage.
10. To establish a socially significant 'relationship of affinity' between the husband and his wife's brothers."

Right of sexual access

In a 1997 article in Current Anthropology, Duran Bell describes marriage as "a relationship between one or more men (male or female) in severalty to one or more women that provides those men with a demand-right of sexual access within a domestic group and identifies women who bear the obligation of yielding to the demands of those specific men." In referring to "men in severalty", Bell is referring to corporate kin groups such as lineages which, in having paid bride price, retain a right in a woman's offspring even if her husband (a lineage member) deceases (Levirate marriage). In referring to "men (male or female)", Bell is referring to women within the lineage who may stand in as the "social fathers" of the wife's children born of other lovers. (See Nuer "ghost marriage".)

Types of Marriage

Monogamy

Monogamy is a form of marriage in which an individual has only one spouse during their lifetime or at any one time (serial monogamy).

Anthropologist Jack Goody's comparative study of marriage around the world utilizing the Ethnographic Atlas found a strong correlation between intensive plough agriculture, dowry and monogamy. This pattern was found in a broad swath of Eurasian societies from Japan to Ireland. The majority of Sub-Saharan African societies that practice extensive hoe agriculture, in contrast, show a correlation between "bride price" and polygamy. A further study drawing on the Ethnographic Atlas showed a statistical correlation between increasing size of the society, the belief in "high gods" to support human morality, and monogamy.

In the countries which do not permit polygamy, a person who marries in one of those countries a person while still being lawfully married to another commits the crime of bigamy. In all cases, the second marriage is considered legally null and void. Besides the second and subsequent marriages being void, the bigamist is also liable to other penalties, which also vary between jurisdictions.

Serial monogamy

Governments that support monogamy may allow easy divorce. In a number of Western countries, divorce rates approach 50%. Those who remarry do so usually no more than three times. Divorce and remarriage can thus result in "serial monogamy", i.e. having multiple marriages but only one legal spouse at a time. This can be interpreted as a form of plural mating, as are those societies dominated by female-headed families in the Caribbean, Mauritius and Brazil where there is frequent rotation of unmarried partners. In all, these account for 16 to 24% of the "monogamous" category.

Serial monogamy creates a new kind of relative, the "ex-". The "ex-wife", for example, remains an active part of her "ex-husband's" or "ex-wife's" life, as they may be tied together by transfers of resources (alimony, child support), or shared child custody. Bob Simpson notes that in the British case, serial monogamy creates an "extended family" – a number of households tied together in this way, including mobile children (possible exes may include an ex-wife, an ex-brother-in-law, etc., but not an "ex-child"). These "unclear families" do not fit the mould of the monogamous nuclear family. As a series of connected households, they come to resemble the polygynous model of separate households maintained by mothers with children, tied by a male to whom they are married or divorced.

Polygamy

Polygamy is a marriage which includes more than two spouses. When a man is married to more than one wife at a time, the relationship is called polygyny, and there is no marriage bond between the wives; and when a woman is married to more than one husband at a time, it is called polyandry, and there is no marriage bond between the husbands. If a marriage includes multiple husbands or wives, it can be called group marriage.

A molecular genetic study of global human genetic diversity argued that sexual polygyny was typical of human reproductive patterns until the shift to sedentary farming communities approximately 10,000 to 5,000 years ago in Europe and Asia, and more recently in Africa and the Americas. As noted above, Anthropologist Jack Goody's comparative study of marriage around the world utilizing the Ethnographic Atlas found that the majority of Sub-Saharan African societies that practice extensive hoe agriculture show a correlation between "Bride price" and polygamy. A survey of other cross-cultural samples has confirmed that the absence of the plough was the only predictor of polygamy, although other factors such as high male mortality in warfare (in non-state societies) and pathogen stress (in state societies) had some impact.

Marriages are classified according to the number of legal spouses an individual has. The suffix "-gamy" refers specifically to the number of spouses, as in bi-gamy (two spouses, generally illegal in most nations), and poly-gamy (more than one spouse).

Societies show variable acceptance of polygamy as a cultural ideal and practice. According to the Ethnographic Atlas, of 1,231 societies noted, 186 were monogamous; 453 had occasional polygyny; 588 had more frequent polygyny, and 4 had polyandry. However, as Miriam Zeitzen writes, social tolerance for polygamy is different from the practice of polygamy, since it requires wealth to establish multiple households for multiple wives. The actual practice of polygamy in a tolerant society may actually be low, with the majority of aspirant polygamists practicing monogamous marriage. Tracking the occurrence of polygamy is further complicated in jurisdictions where it has been banned, but continues to be practiced (de facto polygamy).

Zeitzen also notes that Western perceptions of African society and marriage patterns are biased by "contradictory concerns of nostalgia for traditional African culture versus critique of polygamy as oppressive to women or detrimental to development." Polygamy has been condemned as being a form of human rights abuse, with concerns arising over domestic abuse, forced marriage, and neglect. The vast majority of the world's countries, including virtually all of the world's developed nations, do not permit polygamy. There have been calls for the abolition of polygamy in developing countries.

Polygyny

Polygyny usually grants wives equal status, although the husband may have personal preferences. One type of de facto polygyny is concubinage, where only one woman gets a wife's rights and status, while other women remain legal house mistresses.

Although a society may be classified as polygynous, not all marriages in it necessarily are; monogamous marriages may in fact predominate. It is to this flexibility that Anthropologist Robin Fox attributes its success as a social support system: "This has often meant – given the imbalance in the sex ratios, the higher male infant mortality, the shorter life span of males, the loss of males in wartime, etc. – that often women were left without financial support from husbands. To correct this condition, females had to be killed at birth, remain single, become prostitutes, or be siphoned off into celibate religious orders.

Polygynous systems have the advantage that they can promise, as did the Mormons, a home and family for every woman."

Nonetheless, polygyny is a gender issue which offers men asymmetrical benefits. In some cases, there is a large age discrepancy (as much as a generation) between a man and his youngest wife, compounding the power differential between the two. Tensions not only exist between genders, but also within genders; senior and junior men compete for wives, and senior and junior wives in the same household may experience radically different life conditions, and internal hierarchy. Several studies have suggested that the wife's relationship with other women, including co-wives and husband's female kin, are more critical relationships than that with her husband for her productive, reproductive and personal achievement. In some societies, the co-wives are relatives, usually sisters, a practice called sororal polygyny; the pre-existing relationship between the co-wives is thought to decrease potential tensions within the marriage.

Fox argues that "the major difference between polygyny and monogamy could be stated thus: while plural mating occurs in both systems, under polygyny several unions may be recognized as being legal marriages while under monogamy only one of the unions is so recognized. Often, however, it is difficult to draw a hard and fast line between the two."

As polygamy in Africa is increasingly subject to legal limitations, a variant form of de facto (as opposed to legal or de jure) polygyny is being practiced in urban centers. Although it does not involve multiple (now illegal) formal marriages, the domestic and personal arrangements follow old polygynous patterns. The de facto form of polygyny is found in other parts of the world as well (including some Mormon sects and Muslim families in the United States). In some societies such as the Lovedu of South Africa, or the Nuer of the Sudan, aristocratic women may become female 'husbands.' In the Lovedu case, this female husband may take a number of polygamous wives. This is not a lesbian relationship, but a means of legitimately expanding a royal lineage by attaching these wives' children to it. The relationships are considered polygynous, not polyandrous, because the female husband is in fact assuming masculine gendered political roles.

Religious groups have differing views on the legitimacy of polygyny. It is allowed in Islam and Confucianism. Judaism and Christianity have mentioned practices involving polygyny in the past, however, outright religious acceptance of such practices was not addressed until its rejection in later passages. They do explicitly prohibit polygyny today.

Polyandry

Polyandry is notably more rare than polygyny, though less rare than the figure commonly cited in the Ethnographic Atlas (1980) which listed only those polyandrous societies found in the Himalayan Mountains. More recent studies have found 53 societies outside the 28 found in the Himalayans which practice polyandry. It is most common in egalitarian societies marked by high male mortality or male absenteeism. It is associated with partible paternity, the cultural belief that a child can have more than one father.

The explanation for polyandry in the Himalayan Mountains is related to the scarcity of land; the marriage of all brothers in a family to the same wife (fraternal polyandry) allows family land to remain intact and undivided. If every brother married separately and had children, family land would be split into unsustainable small plots. In Europe, this was prevented through the social practice of impartible inheritance (the dis-inheriting of most siblings, some of whom went on to become celibate monks and priests).

Plural marriage

Group marriage (also known as multi-lateral marriage) is a form of polyamory in which more than two persons form a family unit, with all the members of the group marriage being considered to be married to all the other members of the group marriage, and all members of the marriage share parental responsibility for any children arising from the marriage. No country legally condones group marriages, neither under the law nor as a common law marriage, but historically it has been practiced by some cultures of Polynesia, Asia, Papua New Guinea and the Americas – as well as in some intentional communities and alternative subcultures such as the Oneida Perfectionists in up-state New York. Of the 250 societies reported by the American anthropologist George Murdock in 1949, only the Kaingang of Brazil had any group marriages at all.

CHILD MARRIAGE

A child marriage is a marriage where one or both spouses are under the age of 18. It is related to child betrothal and teenage pregnancy.

Child marriage was common throughout history, even up until the 1900s in the United States, where in 1880 CE, in the state of Delaware, the age of consent for marriage was 7 years old. Still, in 2017, over half of the 50 United States have no explicit minimum age to marry and several states set the age as low as 14. Today it is condemned by international human rights organizations. Child marriages are often arranged between the families of the future bride and groom, sometimes as soon as the girl is born. However, in the late 1800s in England and the United States, feminist activists began calling for raised age of consent laws, which was eventually handled in the 1920s, having been raised to 16–18. Child marriages can also occur in the context of bride kidnapping.

In the year 1552 CE, John Somerford and Jane Somerford Brereton were both married at the ages of 3 and 2, respectively. Twelve years later, in 1564, John filed for divorce. While child marriage is observed for both boys and girls, the overwhelming majority of child spouses are girls. In many cases, only one marriage-partner is a child, usually the female, due to the importance placed upon female virginity. Causes of child marriage include poverty, bride price, dowry, laws that allow child marriages, religious and social pressures, regional customs, fear of remaining unmarried, and perceived inability of women to work for money.

Today, child marriages are widespread in parts of the world; being most common in South Asia and sub-Saharan Africa, with more than half of the girls in some countries in those regions being married before 18. The incidence of child marriage has been falling in most parts of the world. In developed countries, child marriage is outlawed or restricted.

Girls who marry before 18 are at greater risk of becoming victims of domestic violence, than those who marry later, especially when they are married to a much older man.

Same-sex and third-gender marriages

Several kinds of same-sex marriages have been documented in Indigenous and lineage-based cultures. In the Americas, We'wha (Zuni), was a lhamana (male individuals who, at least some of the time, dress and live in the roles usually filled by women in that culture); a respected artist, We'wha served as an emissary of the Zuni to Washington, where he met President Grover Cleveland. We'wha had at least one husband who was generally recognized as such.

While it is a relatively new practice to grant same-sex couples the same form of legal marital recognition as commonly granted to mixed-sex couples, there is some history of recorded same-sex unions around the world. Ancient Greek same-sex relationships were like modern companionate marriages, unlike their different-sex marriages in which the spouses had few emotional ties, and the husband had freedom to engage in outside sexual liaisons. The Codex Theodosianus (C. Th. 9.7.3) issued in 438 CE imposed severe penalties or death on same-sex relationships, but the exact intent of the law and its relation to social practice is unclear, as only a few examples of same-sex relationships in that culture exist. Same-sex unions were celebrated in some regions of China, such as Fujian. Possibly the earliest documented same-sex wedding in Latin Christendom occurred in Rome, Italy, at the San Giovanni a Porta Latina basilica in 1581.

Temporary marriages

Several cultures have practised temporary and conditional marriages. Examples include the Celtic practice of handfasting and fixed-term marriages in the Muslim community. Pre-Islamic Arabs practiced a form of temporary marriage that carries on today in the practice of Nikah mut'ah, a fixed-term marriage contract. The Islamic prophet Muhammad sanctioned a temporary marriage – sigheh in Iran and muta'a in Iraq – which can provide a legitimizing cover for sex workers. The same forms of temporary marriage have been used in Egypt, Lebanon and Iran to make the donation of a human ova legal for in vitro fertilisation; a woman cannot, however, use this kind of marriage to obtain a sperm donation. Muslim controversies related to Nikah Mut'ah have resulted in the practice being confined mostly to Shi'ite communities. The matrilineal Mosuo of China practice what they call "walking marriage".

COHABITATION

In some jurisdictions cohabitation, in certain circumstances, may constitute a common-law marriage, an unregistered partnership, or otherwise provide the unmarried partners with various rights and responsibilities; and in some countries, the laws recognize cohabitation in lieu of institutional marriage for taxation and social security benefits. This is the case, for example, in Australia. Cohabitation may be an option pursued as a form of resistance to traditional institutionalized marriage. However, in this context, some nations reserve the right to define the relationship as marital, or otherwise to regulate the relation, even if the relation has not been registered with the state or a religious institution.

Conversely, institutionalized marriages may not involve cohabitation. In some cases, couples living together do not wish to be recognized as married. This may occur because pension or alimony rights are adversely affected; because of taxation considerations; because of immigration issues, or for other reasons. Such marriages have also been increasingly common in Beijing. Guo Jianmei, director of the center for women's studies at Beijing University, told a Newsday correspondent, "Walking marriages reflect sweeping changes in Chinese society." A "walking marriage" refers to a type of temporary marriage formed by the Mosuo of China, in which male partners live elsewhere and make nightly visits. A similar arrangement in Saudi Arabia, called misyar marriage, also involves the husband and wife living separately but meeting regularly.

Partner selection

There is wide cross-cultural variation in the social rules governing the selection of a partner for marriage. There is variation in the degree to which partner selection is an individual decision by the partners or a collective decision by the partners' kin groups, and there is variation in the rules regulating which partners are valid choices.

The United Nations World Fertility Report of 2003 reports that 89% of all people get married before age forty-nine. The percent of women and men who marry before age forty-nine drops to nearly 50% in some nations and reaches near 100% in other nations.

In other cultures with less strict rules governing the groups from which a partner can be chosen the selection of a marriage partner may involve either the couple going through a selection process of courtship or the marriage may be arranged by the couple's parents or an outside party, a matchmaker.

Age difference

Some people want to marry a person that is older or younger than them. This may impact marital stability and partners with more than a 10-year gap in age tend to experience social disapproval In addition, older women (older than 35) have increased health risks when getting pregnant (which may only be an issue if the couple indeed intends on having children).

Social status and wealth

Some people want to marry a person with higher or lower status than them. Others want to marry people who have similar status. In many societies, women marry men who are of higher social status. There are marriages where each party has sought a partner of similar status. There are other marriages in which the man is older than the woman.Some persons also wish to engage in transactional relationship for money rather than love (thus a type of marriage of convenience). Such people are sometimes referred to as gold diggers. Separate property systems can however be used to prevent property of being passed on to partners after divorce or death. Higher income men are more likely to marry and less likely to divorce. High income women are more likely to divorce.

THE INCEST TABOO, EXOGAMY AND ENDOGAMY

Societies have often placed restrictions on marriage to relatives, though the degree of prohibited relationship varies widely. Marriages between parents and children, or between full siblings, with few exceptions, have been considered incest and forbidden. However, marriages between more distant relatives have been much more common, with one estimate being that 80% of all marriages in history have been between second cousins or closer. This proportion has fallen dramatically, but still, more than 10% of all marriages are believed to be between people who are second cousins or more closely related. In the United States, such marriages are now highly stigmatized, and laws ban most or all first-cousin marriage in 30 states. Specifics vary: in South Korea, historically it was illegal to marry someone with the same last name and same ancestral line.

An Avunculate marriage is a marriage that occurs between an uncle and his niece or between an aunt and her nephew. Such marriages are illegal in most countries due to incest restrictions. However, a small number of countries have legalized it, including Argentina, Australia, Austria, Malaysia, and Russia.

In various societies, the choice of partner is often limited to suitable persons from specific social groups. In some societies the rule is that a partner is selected from an individual's own social group – endogamy, this is often the case in class- and caste-based societies. But in other societies a partner must be chosen from a different group than one's own – exogamy, this may be the case in societies practicing totemic religion where society is divided into several exogamous totemic clans, such as most Aboriginal Australian societies. In other societies a person is expected to marry their cross-cousin, a woman must marry her father's sister's son and a man must marry his mother's brother's daughter – this is often the case if either a society has a rule of tracing kinship exclusively through patrilineal or matrilineal descent groups as among the Akan people of West Africa. Another kind of marriage selection is the levirate marriage in which widows are obligated to marry their husband's brother, mostly found in societies where kinship is based on endogamous clan groups.

Religion has commonly weighed in on the matter of which relatives, if any, are allowed to marry. Relations may be by consanguinity or affinity, meaning by blood or by marriage. On the marriage of cousins, Catholic policy has evolved from initial acceptance, through a long period of general prohibition, to the contemporary requirement for a dispensation. Islam has always allowed it, while Hindu texts vary widely.

Prescriptive marriage

In a wide array of lineage-based societies with a classificatory kinship system, potential spouses are sought from a specific class of relative as determined by a prescriptive marriage rule. This rule may be expressed by anthropologists using a "descriptive" kinship term, such as a "man's mother's brother's daughter" (also known as a "cross-cousin"). Such descriptive rules mask the participant's perspective: a man should marry a woman from his mother's lineage. Within the society's kinship terminology, such relatives are usually indicated by a specific term which sets them apart as potentially marriageable. Pierre Bourdieu notes, however, that very few marriages ever follow the rule, and that when they do so, it is for "practical kinship" reasons such as the preservation of family property, rather than the "official kinship" ideology.

Insofar as regular marriages following prescriptive rules occur, lineages are linked together in fixed relationships; these ties between lineages may form political alliances in kinship dominated societies. French structural anthropologist Claude Lévi-Strauss developed alliance theory to account for the "elementary" kinship structures created by the limited number of prescriptive marriage rules possible.

A pragmatic (or 'arranged') marriage is made easier by formal procedures of family or group politics. A responsible authority sets up or encourages the marriage; they may, indeed, engage a professional matchmaker to find a suitable spouse for an unmarried person. The authority figure could be parents, family, a religious official, or a group consensus. In some cases, the authority figure may choose a match for purposes other than marital harmony.

Forced marriage

A forced marriage is a marriage in which one or both of the parties is married against their will. Forced marriages continue to be practiced in parts of the world, especially in South Asia and Africa. The line between forced marriage and consensual marriage may become blurred, because the social norms of these cultures dictate that one should never oppose the desire of one's parents/relatives in regard to the choice of a spouse; in such cultures, it is not necessary for violence, threats, intimidation etc. to occur, the person simply "consents" to the marriage even if they don't want it, out of the implied social pressure and duty. The customs of bride price and dowry, that exist in parts of the world, can lead to buying and selling people into marriage.

In some societies, ranging from Central Asia to the Caucasus to Africa, the custom of bride kidnapping still exists, in which a woman is captured by a man and his friends. Sometimes this covers an elopement, but sometimes it depends on sexual violence. In previous times, raptio was a larger-scale version of this, with groups of women captured by groups of men, sometimes in war; the most famous example is The Rape of the Sabine Women, which provided the first citizens of Rome with their wives.

Other marriage partners are more or less imposed on an individual. For example, widow inheritance provides a widow with another man from her late husband's brothers.

In rural areas of India, child marriage is practiced, with parents often arranging the wedding, sometimes even before the child is born. This practice was made illegal under the Child Marriage Restraint Act of 1929.

Economic considerations

The financial aspects of marriage vary between cultures and have changed over time. In some cultures, dowries and bride wealth continue to be required today. In both cases, the financial arrangements are usually made between the groom (or his family) and the bride's family; with the bride often not being involved in the negotiations, and often not having a choice in whether to participate in the marriage.

In Early modern Britain, the social status of the couple was supposed to be equal. After the marriage, all the property (called "fortune") and expected inheritances of the wife belonged to the husband.

Dowry

A dowry is "a process whereby parental property is distributed to a daughter at her marriage (i.e. inter vivos) rather than at the holder's death (mortis causa)... A dowry establishes some variety of conjugal fund, the nature of which may vary widely. This fund ensures her support (or endowment) in widowhood and eventually goes to provide for her sons and daughters."

In some cultures, especially in countries such as Turkey, India, Bangladesh, Pakistan, Sri Lanka, Morocco, Nepal, dowries continue to be expected. In India, thousands of dowry-related deaths have taken place on yearly basis, to counter this problem, several jurisdictions have enacted laws restricting or banning dowry (see Dowry law in India). In Nepal, dowry was made illegal in 2009. Some authors believe that the giving and receiving of dowry reflects the status and even the effort to climb high in social hierarchy.

Direct Dowry contrasts with bride wealth, which is paid by the groom or his family to the bride's parents, and with indirect dowry (or dower), which is property given to the bride herself by the groom at the time of marriage and which remains under her ownership and control.

In the Jewish tradition, the rabbis in ancient times insisted on the marriage couple entering into a prenuptial agreement, called a ketubah. Besides other things, the ketubah provided for an amount to be paid by the husband in the event of a divorce or his estate in the event of his death. This amount was a replacement of the biblical dower or bride price, which was payable at the time of the marriage by the groom to the father of the bride. This innovation was put in place because the biblical bride price created a major social problem: many young prospective husbands could not raise the bride price at the time when they would normally be expected to marry.

So, to enable these young men to marry, the rabbis, in effect, delayed the time that the amount would be payable, when they would be more likely to have the sum. It may also be noted that both the dower and the ketubah amounts served the same purpose: the protection for the wife should her support cease, either by death or divorce. The only difference between the two systems was the timing of the payment. It is the predecessor to the wife's present-day entitlement to maintenance in the event of the breakup of marriage, and family maintenance in the event of the husband not providing adequately for the wife in his will. Another function performed by the ketubah amount was to provide a disincentive for the husband contemplating divorcing his wife: he would need to have the amount to be able to pay to the wife.

Morning gifts, which might also be arranged by the bride's father rather than the bride, are given to the bride herself; the name derives from the Germanic tribal custom of giving them the morning after the wedding night. She might have control of this morning gift during the lifetime of her husband, but is entitled to it when widowed. If the amount of her inheritance is settled by law rather than agreement, it may be called dower.

Depending on legal systems and the exact arrangement, she may not be entitled to dispose of it after her death, and may lose the property if she remarries. Morning gifts were preserved for centuries in morganatic marriage, a union where the wife's inferior social status was held to prohibit her children from inheriting a noble's titles or estates. In this case, the morning gift would support the wife and children. Another legal provision for widowhood was jointure, in which property, often land, would be held in joint tenancy, so that it would automatically go to the widow on her husband's death.

Islamic tradition has similar practices. A 'mahr', either immediate or deferred, is the woman's portion of the groom's wealth (divorce) or estate (death). These amounts are usually set on the basis of the groom's own and family wealth and incomes, but in some parts these are set very high so as to provide a disincentive for the groom exercising the divorce, or the husband's family 'inheriting' a large portion of the estate, especially if there are no male offspring from the marriage. In some countries, including Iran, the mahr or alimony can amount to more than a man can ever hope to earn, sometimes up to US$1,000,000 (4000 official Iranian gold coins). If the husband cannot pay the mahr, either in case of a divorce or on demand, according to the current laws in Iran, he will have to pay it by installments. Failure to pay the mahr might even lead to imprisonment.

BRIDEWEALTH

Bridewealth is a common practice in parts of Southeast Asia (Thailand, Cambodia), parts of Central Asia, and in much of sub-Saharan Africa. It is also known as brideprice although this has fallen in disfavor as it implies the purchase of the bride. Bridewealth is the amount of money or property or wealth paid by the groom or his family to the parents of a woman upon the marriage of their daughter to the groom. In anthropological literature, bride price has often been explained as payment made to compensate the bride's family for the loss of her labor and fertility. In some cases, bridewealth is a means by which the groom's family's ties to the children of the union are recognized.

Taxation

In some countries a married person or couple benefits from various taxation advantages not available to a single person. For example, spouses may be allowed to average their combined incomes. This is advantageous to a married couple with disparate incomes. To compensate for this, countries may provide a higher tax bracket for the averaged income of a married couple. While income averaging might still benefit a married couple with a stay-at-home spouse, such averaging would cause a married couple with roughly equal personal incomes to pay more total tax than they would as two single persons. In the United States, this is called the marriage penalty.

When the rates applied by the tax code are not based income averaging, but rather on the sum of individuals' incomes, higher rates will usually apply to each individual in a two-earner households in a progressive tax systems. This is most often the case with high-income taxpayers and is another situation called a marriage penalty.

Conversely, when progressive tax is levied on the individual with no consideration for the partnership, dual-income couples fare much better than single-income couples with similar household incomes. The effect can be increased when the welfare system treats the same income as a shared income thereby denying welfare access to the non-earning spouse. Such systems apply in Australia and Canada, for example.

Post-marital residence

In many Western cultures, marriage usually leads to the formation of a new household comprising the married couple, with the married couple living together in the same home, often sharing the same bed, but in some other cultures this is not the tradition. Among the Minangkabau of West Sumatra, residency after marriage is matrilocal, with the husband moving into the household of his wife's mother. Residency after marriage can also be patrilocal or avunculocal. In these cases, married couples may not form an independent household, but remain part of an extended family household.

Early theories explaining the determinants of postmarital residence connected it with the sexual division of labor. However, to date, cross-cultural tests of this hypothesis using worldwide samples have failed to find any significant relationship between these two variables. However, Korotayev's tests show that the female contribution to subsistence does correlate significantly with matrilocal residence in general. However, this correlation is masked by a general polygyny factor.

Although, in different-sex marriages, an increase in the female contribution to subsistence tends to lead to matrilocal residence, it also tends simultaneously to lead to general non-sororal polygyny which effectively destroys matrilocality. If this polygyny factor is controlled (e.g., through a multiple regression model), division of labor turns out to be a significant predictor of postmarital residence. Thus, Murdock's hypotheses regarding the relationships between the sexual division of labor and postmarital residence were basically correct, though the actual relationships between those two groups of variables are more complicated than he expected. There has been a trend toward the neolocal residence in western societies.

MARRIAGE LAWS

Marriage law refers to the legal requirements that determine the validity of a marriage, and which vary considerably among countries. See also Marriage Act.

Marriage laws refer to the legal requirements which determine the validity of a marriage, which vary considerably between countries. Article 16 of the Universal Declaration of Human Rights declares that "Men and women of full age, without any limitation due to race, nationality or religion, have the right to marry and to found a family. They are entitled to equal rights as to marriage, during marriage and at its dissolution. Marriage shall be entered into only with the free and full consent of the intending spouses."

Property regime

In many countries today, each marriage partner has the choice of keeping his or her property separate or combining properties. In the latter case, called community property, when the marriage ends by divorce each owns half. In lieu of a will or trust, property owned by the deceased generally is inherited by the surviving spouse.

In some legal systems, the partners in a marriage are "jointly liable" for the debts of the marriage. This has a basis in a traditional legal notion called the "Doctrine of Necessities" whereby, in a heterosexual marriage, a husband was responsible to provide necessary things for his wife. Where this is the case, one partner may be sued to collect a debt for which they did not expressly contract. Critics of this practice note that debt collection agencies can abuse this by claiming an unreasonably wide range of debts to be expenses of the marriage. The cost of defense and the burden of proof is then placed on the non-contracting party to prove that the expense is not a debt of the family. The respective maintenance obligations, both during and eventually after a marriage, are regulated in most jurisdictions; alimony is one such method.

Restrictions

Marriage is an institution that is historically filled with restrictions. From age, to race, to social status, to consanguinity, to gender, restrictions are placed on marriage by society for reasons of benefiting the children, passing on healthy genes, maintaining cultural values, or because of prejudice and fear. Almost all cultures that recognize marriage also recognize adultery as a violation of the terms of marriage.

Age

Most jurisdictions set a minimum age for marriage, that is, a person must attain a certain age to be legally allowed to marry. This age may depend on circumstances, for instance exceptions from the general rule may be permitted if the parents of a young person express their consent and/or if a court decides that said marriage is in the best interest of the young person (often this applies in cases where a girl is pregnant). Although most age restrictions are in place in order to prevent children from being forced into marriages, especially to much older partners - marriages which can have negative education and health related consequences, and lead to child sexual abuse and other forms of violence - such child marriages remain common in parts of the world. According to the UN, child marriages are most common in rural sub-Saharan Africa and South Asia. The ten countries with the highest rates of child marriage are: Niger (75%), Chad, Central African Republic, Bangladesh, Guinea, Mozambique, Mali, Burkina Faso, South Sudan, and Malawi.

KINSHIP

To prohibit incest and eugenic reasons, marriage laws have set restrictions for relatives to marry. Direct blood relatives are usually prohibited to marry, while for branch line relatives, laws are wary. Kinship relations through marriage is also called "affinity," relationships that arise in one's group of origin, can also be called one's descent group. Some cultures in kinship relationships may be considered to extend out to those who they have economic or political relationships with; or other forms of social connections. Within some cultures they may lead you back to gods or animal ancestors (totems). This can be conceived of on a more or less literal basis.

Race

Laws banning "race-mixing" were enforced in certain North American jurisdictions from 1691 until 1967, in Nazi Germany (The Nuremberg Laws) from 1935 until 1945, and in South Africa during most part of the Apartheid era (1949–1985). All these laws primarily banned marriage between persons of different racially or ethnically defined groups, which was termed "amalgamation" or "miscegenation" in the U.S. The laws in Nazi Germany and many of the U.S. states, as well as South Africa, also banned sexual relations between such individuals.

In the United States, laws in some but not all of the states prohibited the marriage of whites and blacks, and in many states also the intermarriage of whites with Native Americans or Asians. In the U.S., such laws were known as anti-miscegenation laws. From 1913 until 1948, 30 out of the then 48 states enforced such laws. Although an "Anti-Miscegenation Amendment" to the United States Constitution was proposed in 1871, in 1912–1913, and in 1928, no nationwide law against racially mixed marriages was ever enacted. In 1967, the Supreme Court of the United States unanimously ruled in Loving v. Virginia that anti-miscegenation laws are unconstitutional. With this ruling, these laws were no longer in effect in the remaining 16 states that still had them.

The Nazi ban on interracial marriage and interracial sex was enacted in September 1935 as part of the Nuremberg Laws, the Gesetz zum Schutze des deutschen Blutes und der deutschen Ehre (The Law for the Protection of German Blood and German Honour). The Nuremberg Laws classified Jews as a race and forbade marriage and extramarital sexual relations at first with people of Jewish descent, but was later ended to the "Gypsies, Negroes or their bastard offspring" and people of "German or related blood". Such relations were marked as Rassenschande (lit. "race-disgrace") and could be punished by imprisonment (usually followed by deportation to a concentration camp) and even by death.

South Africa under apartheid also banned interracial marriage. The Prohibition of Mixed Marriages Act, 1949 prohibited marriage between persons of different races, and the Immorality Act of 1950 made sexual relations with a person of a different race a crime.

Sex/gender

Same-sex marriage is legally performed and recognized (nationwide or in some jurisdictions) in Argentina, Australia, Austria, Belgium, Brazil, Canada, Colombia, Costa Rica, Denmark, Ecuador, Finland, France, Germany, Iceland, Ireland, Luxembourg, Malta, Mexico,[a] the Netherlands,[b] New Zealand,[c] Norway, Portugal, South Africa, Spain, Sweden, Taiwan, the United Kingdom,[d] the United States,[e] and Uruguay. Israel recognizes same-sex marriages entered into abroad as full marriages. Furthermore, the Inter-American Court of Human Rights has issued a ruling that is expected to facilitate recognition in several countries in the Americas.[f]

The introduction of same-sex marriage has varied by jurisdiction, being variously accomplished through legislative change to marriage law, a court ruling based on constitutional guarantees of equality, or by direct popular vote (via ballot initiative or referendum). The recognition of same-sex marriage is considered to be a human right and a civil right as well as a political, social, and religious issue. The most prominent supporters of same-sex marriage are human rights and civil rights organizations as well as the medical and scientific communities, while the most prominent opponents are religious groups. Various faith communities around the world support same-sex marriage, while many religious groups oppose it. Polls consistently show continually rising support for the recognition of same-sex marriage in all developed democracies and in some developing democracies.

The establishment of recognition in law for the marriages of same-sex couples is one of the most prominent objectives of the LGBT rights movement.

NUMBER OF SPOUSES

Polygyny is widely practiced in mostly Muslim and African countries. In the Middle Eastern region, Israel, Turkey and Tunisia are notable exceptions.

In most other jurisdictions, polygamy is illegal. For example, In the United States, polygamy is illegal in all 50 states.

In the late-19th century, citizens of the self-governing territory of what is present-day Utah were forced by the United States federal government to abandon the practice of polygamy through the vigorous enforcement of several Acts of Congress, and eventually complied. The Church of Jesus Christ of Latter-day Saints formally abolished the practice in 1890, in a document labeled 'The Manifesto' (see Latter Day Saint polygamy in the late-19th century). Among American Muslims, a small minority of around 50,000 to 100,000 people are estimated to live in families with a husband maintaining an illegal polygamous relationship.

Several countries such as India and Sri Lanka, permit only their Islamic citizens to practice polygamy. Some Indians have converted to Islam in order to bypass such legal restrictions. Predominantly Christian nations usually do not allow polygamous unions, with a handful of exceptions being the Republic of the Congo, Uganda, and Zambia.

State recognition

When a marriage is performed and carried out by a government institution in accordance with the marriage laws of the jurisdiction, without religious content, it is a civil marriage. Civil marriage recognizes and creates the rights and obligations intrinsic to matrimony in the eyes of the state. Some countries do not recognize locally performed religious marriage on its own, and require a separate civil marriage for official purposes. Conversely, civil marriage does not exist in some countries governed by a religious legal system, such as Saudi Arabia, where marriages contracted abroad might not be recognized if they were contracted contrary to Saudi interpretations of Islamic religious law.

In countries governed by a mixed secular-religious legal system, such as Lebanon and Israel, locally performed civil marriage does not exist within the country, which prevents interfaith and various other marriages that contradict religious laws from being entered into in the country; however, civil marriages performed abroad may be recognized by the state even if they conflict with religious laws. For example, in the case of recognition of marriage in Israel, this includes recognition of not only interfaith civil marriages performed abroad, but also overseas same-sex civil marriages.

In various jurisdictions, a civil marriage may take place as part of the religious marriage ceremony, although they are theoretically distinct. Some jurisdictions allow civil marriages in circumstances which are notably not allowed by particular religions, such as same-sex marriages or civil unions.

The opposite case may happen as well. Partners may not have full juridical acting capacity and churches may have less strict limits than the civil jurisdictions. This particularly applies to minimum age, or physical infirmities.

It is possible for two people to be recognized as married by a religious or other institution, but not by the state, and hence without the legal rights and obligations of marriage; or to have a civil marriage deemed invalid and sinful by a religion. Similarly, a couple may remain married in religious eyes after a civil divorce.

Most sovereign states and other jurisdictions limit legally recognized marriage to opposite-sex couples and a diminishing number of these permit polygyny, child marriages, and forced marriages. In modern times, a growing number of countries, primarily developed democracies, have lifted bans on, and have established legal recognition for, the marriages of interfaith, interracial, and same-sex couples. In some areas, child marriages and polygamy may occur in spite of national laws against the practice.

MARRIAGE LICENSE, CIVIL CEREMONY AND REGISTRATION

A marriage is usually formalized at a wedding or marriage ceremony. The ceremony may be officiated either by a religious official, by a government official or by a state approved celebrant. In various European and some Latin American countries, any religious ceremony must be held separately from the required civil ceremony. Some countries – such as Belgium, Bulgaria, France, the Netherlands, Romania and Turkey – require that a civil ceremony take place before any religious one. In some countries – notably the United States, Canada, the United Kingdom, the Republic of Ireland, Norway and Spain – both ceremonies can be held together; the officiant at the religious and civil ceremony also serving as agent of the state to perform the civil ceremony.

To avoid any implication that the state is "recognizing" a religious marriage (which is prohibited in some countries) – the "civil" ceremony is said to be taking place at the same time as the religious ceremony. Often this involves simply signing a register during the religious ceremony. If the civil element of the religious ceremony is omitted, the marriage ceremony is not recognized as a marriage by government under the law.

Some countries, such as Australia, permit marriages to be held in private and at any location; others, including England and Wales, require that the civil ceremony be conducted in a place open to the public and specially sanctioned by law for the purpose. In England, the place of marriage formerly had to be a church or register office, but this was extended to any public venue with the necessary licence. An exception can be made in the case of marriage by special emergency license (UK: licence), which is normally granted only when one of the parties is terminally ill. Rules about where and when persons can marry vary from place to place. Some regulations require one of the parties to reside within the jurisdiction of the register office (formerly parish).

Each religious authority has rules for the manner in which marriages are to be conducted by their officials and members. Where religious marriages are recognised by the state, the officiator must also conform with the law of the jurisdiction.

Common-law marriage

In a small number of jurisdictions marriage relationships may be created by the operation of the law alone. Unlike the typical ceremonial marriage with legal contract, wedding ceremony, and other details, a common-law marriage may be called "marriage by habit and repute (cohabitation)." A de facto common-law marriage without a license or ceremony is legally binding in some jurisdictions but has no legal consequence in others.

Civil unions

A civil union, also referred to as a civil partnership, is a legally recognized form of partnership similar to marriage. Beginning with Denmark in 1989, civil unions under one name or another have been established by law in several countries in order to provide same-sex couples rights, benefits, and responsibilities similar (in some countries, identical) to opposite-sex civil marriage. In some jurisdictions, such as Brazil, New Zealand, Uruguay, Ecuador, France and the U.S. states of Hawaii and Illinois, civil unions are also open to opposite-sex couples.

"Marriage of convenience"

Sometimes people marry to take advantage of a certain situation, sometimes called a marriage of convenience or a sham marriage. In 2003, over 180,000 immigrants were admitted to the U.S. as spouses of U.S. citizens; more were admitted as fiancés of US citizens for the purpose of being married within 90 days. These marriages had a diverse range of motives, including obtaining permanent residency, securing an inheritance that has a marriage clause, or to enroll in health insurance, among many others. While all marriages have a complex combination of conveniences motivating the parties to marry, a marriage of convenience is one that is devoid of normal reasons to marry. In certain countries like Singapore sham marriages are punishable criminal offences.

CONTEMPORARY LEGAL AND HUMAN RIGHTS CRITICISMS OF MARRIAGE

People have proposed arguments against marriage for reasons that include political, philosophical and religious criticisms; concerns about the divorce rate; individual liberty and gender equality; questioning the necessity of having a personal relationship sanctioned by government or religious authorities; or the promotion of celibacy for religious or philosophical reasons.

Power and gender roles

Historically, in most cultures, married women had very few rights of their own, being considered, along with the family's children, the property of the husband; as such, they could not own or inherit property, or represent themselves legally (see, for example, coverture). Since the late 19th century, in some (primarily Western) countries, marriage has undergone gradual legal changes, aimed at improving the rights of the wife. These changes included giving wives legal identities of their own, abolishing the right of husbands to physically discipline their wives, giving wives property rights, liberalizing divorce laws, providing wives with reproductive rights of their own, and requiring a wife's consent when sexual relations occur. In the 21st century, there continue to be controversies regarding the legal status of married women, legal acceptance of or leniency towards violence within marriage (especially sexual violence), traditional marriage customs such as dowry and bride price, forced marriage, marriageable age, and criminalization of consensual behaviors such as premarital and extramarital sex.

Feminist theory approaches opposite-sex marriage as an institution traditionally rooted in patriarchy that promotes male superiority and power over women. This power dynamic conceptualizes men as "the provider operating in the public sphere" and women as "the caregivers operating within the private sphere". "Theoretically, women ... [were] defined as the property of their husbands .... The adultery of a woman was always treated with more severity than that of a man." "[F]eminist demands for a wife's control over her own property were not met [in parts of Britain] until ... [laws were passed in the late 19th century]."

Traditional heterosexual marriage imposed an obligation of the wife to be sexually available for her husband and an obligation of the husband to provide material/financial support for the wife. Numerous philosophers, feminists and other academic figures have commented on this throughout history, condemning the hypocrisy of legal and religious authorities in regard to sexual issues; pointing to the lack of choice of a woman in regard to controlling her own sexuality; and drawing parallels between marriage, an institution promoted as sacred, and prostitution, widely condemned and vilified (though often tolerated as a "necessary evil"). Mary Wollstonecraft, in the 18th century, described marriage as "legal prostitution". Emma Goldman wrote in 1910: "To the moralist prostitution does not consist so much in the fact that the woman sells her body, but rather that she sells it out of wedlock". Bertrand Russell in his book Marriage and Morals wrote that: "Marriage is for woman the commonest mode of livelihood, and the total amount of undesired sex endured by women is probably greater in marriage than in prostitution." Angela Carter in Nights at the Circus wrote: "What is marriage but prostitution to one man instead of many?"

Some critics object to what they see as propaganda in relation to marriage – from the government, religious organizations, the media – which aggressively promote marriage as a solution for all social problems; such propaganda includes, for instance, marriage promotion in schools, where children, especially girls, are bombarded with positive information about marriage, being presented only with the information prepared by authorities.

The performance of dominant gender roles by men and submissive gender roles by women influence the power dynamic of a heterosexual marriage. In some American households, women internalize gender role stereotypes and often assimilate into the role of "wife", "mother", and "caretaker" in conformity to societal norms and their male partner. Author bell hooks states "within the family structure, individuals learn to accept sexist oppression as 'natural' and are primed to support other forms of oppression, including heterosexist domination." "The cultural, economic, political and legal supremacy of the husband" was "traditional ... under English law". This patriarchal dynamic is contrasted with a conception of egalitarian or Peer Marriage in which power and labour are divided equally, and not according to gender roles.

In the US, studies have shown that, despite egalitarian ideals being common, less than half of respondents viewed their opposite-sex relationships as equal in power, with unequal relationships being more commonly dominated by the male partner. Studies also show that married couples find the highest level of satisfaction in egalitarian relationships and lowest levels of satisfaction in wife dominate relationships. In recent years, egalitarian or Peer Marriages have been receiving increasing focus and attention politically, economically and culturally in a number of countries, including the United States.

Extra-marital sex

Different societies demonstrate variable tolerance of extramarital sex. The Standard Cross-Cultural Sample describes the occurrence of extramarital sex by gender in over 50 pre-industrial cultures. The occurrence of extramarital sex by men is described as "universal" in 6 cultures, "moderate" in 29 cultures, "occasional" in 6 cultures, and "uncommon" in 10 cultures. The occurrence of extramarital sex by women is described as "universal" in 6 cultures, "moderate" in 23 cultures, "occasional" in 9 cultures, and "uncommon" in 15 cultures. Three studies using nationally representative samples in the United States found that between 10 and 15% of women and 20–25% of men engage in extramarital sex.

Many of the world's major religions look with disfavor on sexual relations outside marriage. There are non-secular states that sanction criminal penalties for sexual intercourse before marriage. Sexual relations by a married person with someone other than his/her spouse is known as adultery. Adultery is considered in many jurisdictions to be a crime and grounds for divorce.

In some countries, such as Saudi Arabia, Pakistan, Afghanistan, Iran, Kuwait, Maldives, Morocco, Oman, Mauritania, United Arab Emirates, Sudan, Yemen, any form of sexual activity outside marriage is illegal.

In some parts of the world, women and girls accused of having sexual relations outside marriage are at risk of becoming victims of honor killings committed by their families. In 2011 several people were sentenced to death by stoning after being accused of adultery in Iran, Somalia, Afghanistan, Sudan, Mali and Pakistan. Practices such as honor killings and stoning continue to be supported by mainstream politicians and other officials in some countries. In Pakistan, after the 2008 Balochistan honour killings in which five women were killed by tribesmen of the Umrani Tribe of Balochistan, Pakistani Federal Minister for Postal Services Israr Ullah Zehri defended the barbaric practice; he said: "These are centuries-old traditions, and I will continue to defend them. Only those who indulge in immoral acts should be afraid."

SEXUAL VIOLENCE

An issue that is a serious concern regarding marriage and which has been the object of international scrutiny is that of sexual violence within marriage. Throughout much of the history, in most cultures, sex in marriage was considered a 'right', that could be taken by force (often by a man from a woman), if 'denied'. As the concept of human rights started to develop in the 20th century, and with the arrival of second-wave feminism, such views have become less widely held.

The legal and social concept of marital rape has developed in most industrialized countries in the mid- to late 20th century; in many other parts of the world it is not recognized as a form of abuse, socially or legally. Several countries in Eastern Europe and Scandinavia made marital rape illegal before 1970, and other countries in Western Europe and the English-speaking Western world outlawed it in the 1980s and 1990s. In England and Wales, marital rape was made illegal in 1991. Although marital rape is being increasingly criminalized in developing countries too, cultural, religious, and traditional ideologies about "conjugal rights" remain very strong in many parts of the world; and even in many countries that have adequate laws against rape in marriage these laws are rarely enforced.

Apart from the issue of rape committed against one's spouse, marriage is, in many parts of the world, closely connected with other forms of sexual violence: in some places, like Morocco, unmarried girls and women who are raped are often forced by their families to marry their rapist. Because being the victim of rape and losing virginity carry extreme social stigma, and the victims are deemed to have their "reputation" tarnished, a marriage with the rapist is arranged. This is claimed to be in the advantage of both the victim – who does not remain unmarried and doesn't lose social status – and of the rapist, who avoids punishment. In 2012, after a Moroccan 16-year-old girl committed suicide after having been forced by her family to marry her rapist and enduring further abuse by the rapist after they married, there have been protests from activists against this practice which is common in Morocco.

In some societies, the very high social and religious importance of marital fidelity, especially female fidelity, has as result the criminalization of adultery, often with harsh penalties such as stoning or flogging; as well as leniency towards punishment of violence related to infidelity (such as honor killings). In the 21st century, criminal laws against adultery have become controversial with international organizations calling for their abolition. Opponents of adultery laws argue that these laws are a major contributor to discrimination and violence against women, as they are enforced selectively mostly against women; that they prevent women from reporting sexual violence; and that they maintain social norms which justify violent crimes committed against women by husbands, families and communities. A Joint Statement by the United Nations Working Group on discrimination against women in law and in practice states that "Adultery as a criminal offence violates women's human rights". Some human rights organizations argue that the criminalization of adultery also violates internationally recognized protections for private life, as it represents an arbitrary interference with an individual's privacy, which is not permitted under international law.

Laws, human rights and gender status

The laws surrounding heterosexual marriage in many countries have come under international scrutiny because they contradict international standards of human rights; institutionalize violence against women, child marriage and forced marriage; require the permission of a husband for his wife to work in a paid job, sign legal documents, file criminal charges against someone, sue in civil court etc.; sanction the use by husbands of violence to "discipline" their wives; and discriminate against women in divorce.

Such things were legal even in many Western countries until recently: for instance, in France, married women obtained the right to work without their husband's permission in 1965, and in West Germany women obtained this right in 1977 (by comparison women in East Germany had many more rights). In Spain, during Franco's era, a married woman needed her husband's consent, referred to as the permiso marital, for almost all economic activities, including employment, ownership of property, and even traveling away from home; the permiso marital was abolished in 1975.

An absolute submission of a wife to her husband is accepted as natural in many parts of the world, for instance surveys by UNICEF have shown that the percentage of women aged 15–49 who think that a husband is justified in hitting or beating his wife under certain circumstances is as high as 90% in Afghanistan and Jordan, 87% in Mali, 86% in Guinea and Timor-Leste, 81% in Laos, 80% in Central African Republic. Detailed results from Afghanistan show that 78% of women agree with a beating if the wife "goes out without telling him [the husband]" and 76% agree "if she argues with him".

Throughout history, and still today in many countries, laws have provided for extenuating circumstances, partial or complete defenses, for men who killed their wives due to adultery, with such acts often being seen as crimes of passion and being covered by legal defenses such as provocation or defense of family honor.

Right and ability to divorce

While international law and conventions recognize the need for consent for entering a marriage – namely that people cannot be forced to get married against their will – the right to obtain a divorce is not recognized; therefore holding a person in a marriage against their will (if such person has consented to entering in it) is not considered a violation of human rights, with the issue of divorce being left at the appreciation of individual states.

In the EU, the last country to allow divorce was Malta, in 2011. Around the world, the only countries to forbid divorce are Philippines and Vatican City, although in practice in many countries which use a fault-based divorce system obtaining a divorce is very difficult. The ability to divorce, in law and practice, has been and continues to be a controversial issue in many countries, and public discourse involves different ideologies such as feminism, social conservatism, religious interpretations.

Dowry and bridewealth

In recent years, the customs of dowry and bride price have received international criticism for inciting conflicts between families and clans; contributing to violence against women; promoting materialism; increasing property crimes (where men steal goods such as cattle in order to be able to pay the bride price); and making it difficult for poor people to marry. African women's rights campaigners advocate the abolishing of bride price, which they argue is based on the idea that women are a form of property which can be bought. Bride price has also been criticized for contributing to child trafficking as impoverished parents sell their young daughters to rich older men. A senior Papua New Guinea police officer has called for the abolishing of bride price arguing that it is one of the main reasons for the mistreatment of women in that country. The opposite practice of dowry has been linked to a high level of violence (see Dowry death) and to crimes such as extortion.

Children born outside marriage

Historically, and still in many countries, children born outside marriage suffered severe social stigma and discrimination. In England and Wales, such children were known as bastards and whoresons.

There are significant differences between world regions in regard to the social and legal position of non-marital births, ranging from being fully accepted and uncontroversial to being severely stigmatized and discriminated.

The 1975 European Convention on the Legal Status of Children Born out of Wedlock protects the rights of children born to unmarried parents. The convention states, among others, that: "The father and mother of a child born out of wedlock shall have the same obligation to maintain the child as if it were born in wedlock" and that "A child born out of wedlock shall have the same right of succession in the estate of its father and its mother and of a member of its father's or mother's family, as if it had been born in wedlock."

While in most Western countries legal inequalities between children born inside and outside marriage have largely been abolished, this is not the case in some parts of the world.

The legal status of an unmarried father differs greatly from country to country. Without voluntary formal recognition of the child by the father, in most cases there is a need of due process of law in order to establish paternity. In some countries however, unmarried cohabitation of a couple for a specific period of time does create a presumption of paternity similar to that of formal marriage. This is the case in Australia. Under what circumstances can a paternity action be initiated, the rights and responsibilities of a father once paternity has been established (whether he can obtain parental responsibility and whether he can be forced to support the child) as well as the legal position of a father who voluntarily acknowledges the child, vary widely by jurisdiction.

A special situation arises when a married woman has a child by a man other than her husband. Some countries, such as Israel, refuse to accept a legal challenge of paternity in such a circumstance, in order to avoid the stigmatization of the child (see Mamzer, a concept under Jewish law). In 2010, the European Court of Human Rights ruled in favor of a German man who had fathered twins with a married woman, granting him right of contact with the twins, despite the fact that the mother and her husband had forbidden him to see the children.

The steps that an unmarried father must take in order to obtain rights to his child vary by country. In some countries (such as the UK – since 2003 in England and Wales, 2006 in Scotland, and 2002 in Northern Ireland) it is sufficient for the father to be listed on the birth certificate for him to have parental rights; in other countries, such as Ireland, simply being listed on the birth certificate does not offer any rights, additional legal steps must be taken (if the mother agrees, the parents can both sign a "statutory declaration", but if the mother does not agree, the father has to apply to court).

Children born outside marriage have become more common, and in some countries, the majority. Recent data from Latin America showed figures for non-marital childbearing to be 74% for Colombia, 69% for Peru, 68% for Chile, 66% for Brazil, 58% for Argentina, 55% for Mexico. In 2012, in the European Union, 40% of births were outside marriage, and in the United States, in 2013, the figure was similar, at 41%. In the United Kingdom 48% of births were to unmarried women in 2012; in Ireland the figure was 35%.

During the first half of the 20th century, unmarried women in some Western countries were coerced by authorities to give their children up for adoption. This was especially the case in Australia, through the forced adoptions in Australia, with most of these adoptions taking place between the 1950s and the 1970s. In 2013, Julia Gillard, then Prime Minister of Australia, offered a national apology to those affected by the forced adoptions.

Some married couples choose not to have children. Others are unable to have children because of infertility or other factors preventing conception or the bearing of children. In some cultures, marriage imposes an obligation on women to bear children. In northern Ghana, for example, payment of bridewealth signifies a woman's requirement to bear children, and women using birth control face substantial threats of physical abuse and reprisals.

Rights and obligations

A marriage bestows rights and obligations on the married parties, and sometimes on relatives as well, being the sole mechanism for the creation of affinal ties (in-laws). These may include, depending on jurisdiction:

- Giving one spouse or his/her family control over the other spouse's sexual services, labor, and property.
- Giving one spouse responsibility for the other's debts.

- Giving one spouse visitation rights when the other is incarcerated or hospitalized.
- Giving one spouse control over the other's affairs when the other is incapacitated.
- Establishing the second legal guardian of a parent's child.
- Establishing a joint fund of property for the benefit of children.
- Establishing a relationship between the families of the spouses.

These rights and obligations vary considerably between societies, and between groups within society. These might include arranged marriages, family obligations, the legal establishment of a nuclear family unit, the legal protection of children and public declaration of commitment.

A marriage, by definition, bestows rights and obligations on the married parties, and sometimes on relatives as well, being the sole mechanism for the creation of affinal ties (in-laws). Over 2.3 million weddings take place in the U.S each year. Historically, many societies have given sets of rights and obligations to husbands that have been very different from the sets of rights and obligations given to wives. In particular, the control of marital property, inheritance rights, and the right to dictate the activities of children of the marriage have typically been given to male marital partners.

However, these practices were curtailed to a great deal in many countries, especially Western countries, in the twentieth century, and more modern statutes tend to define the rights and duties of a spouse without reference to gender. In various marriage laws around the world, however, the husband continues to have authority; for instance, the Civil Code of Iran states at Article 1105: "In relations between husband and wife; the position of the head of the family is the exclusive right of the husband".

Common law marriage

In medieval Europe, marriage came under the jurisdiction of common law, which recognized as a valid marriage one where the parties stated that they took one another as wife and husband, even in absence of any witnesses.

The Council of Trent (convened 1545–1563) ruled that in the future a marriage was only valid in Roman Catholic countries if it was witnessed by a priest of the Roman Catholic Church or, if obtaining a priest were impractical, by other witnesses. This ruling was not accepted in the newly Protestant nations of Europe, nor by Protestants who lived in Roman Catholic countries or their colonies, nor by Eastern Orthodox Christians.

Common-law marriages were abolished in England and Wales by the Marriage Act 1753. The act required marriages to be performed by a priest of the Church of England unless the participants in the marriage were Jews or Quakers. The Act applied to Ireland after the Act of Union 1800, but the requirement for a valid marriage to be performed by a Church of England priest created special problems in predominantly Roman Catholic Ireland. The law did not provide an exception. The Act did not apply to Scotland because, by the Acts of Union 1707, Scotland retained its own legal system. To get around the requirements of the Marriage Act, such as minimum-age requirements, couples would go to Gretna Green in southern Scotland, to get married under Scottish law (such as Lydia Bennet and George Wickham in Pride and Prejudice).

The Marriage Act 1753 also did not apply to Britain's overseas colonies of the time, so common-law marriages continued to be recognized in the what became the United States and Canada. In the United States, common-law marriages are still recognized in Alabama, Colorado, Iowa, Kansas, Montana, Rhode Island, South Carolina, Texas, Utah and the District of Columbia, and in several Canadian provinces.

All countries in Europe have now abolished "marriage by habit and repute", with Scotland being the last to do so in 2006.

Australia has recognised de facto relationships since the Family Law Act of 2009.

MARRIAGE RESTRICTIONS

Marriage is an institution that is historically filled with restrictions. From age, to gender, to social status, various restrictions are placed on marriage by communities, religious institutions, legal traditions and states.

Marriage age

The minimum age at which a person is able to lawfully marry, and whether parental or other consents are required, vary from country to country. In the U.S the minimum age is 18 except for Nebraska (19) and Mississippi (21). In England and Wales the general age at which a person may marry is 18, but 16- or 17-year-olds may get married with their parents' or guardians' consent. If they are unable to obtain this, they can gain consent from the courts, which may be granted by the Magistrates' Courts, or the County or High Court family divisions.

Gender restrictions

Legal, social, and religious restrictions apply in all countries on the genders of the couple. In response to changing social and political attitudes, some jurisdictions and religious denominations now recognize marriages between people of the same sex. Other jurisdictions have instead "civil unions" or "domestic partnerships", while additional others explicitly prohibit same-sex marriages.

In 1989, Denmark became the first country in the modern era to give same-sex couples the right to formalize their relation as a registered partnership. As of 2015, twenty eight countries have come to recognize same-sex marriages for civil purposes, namely the Netherlands, Belgium, Spain, Canada, South Africa, Norway, Sweden, Portugal, Iceland, Argentina, Denmark, Brazil, France, Uruguay, New Zealand, United Kingdom, Luxembourg, Finland, Ireland, Malta, Costa Rica, Taiwan, Colombia and the United States. Denmark gave same-sex couples the right to marry in 2013, and this right extends to a right to get married in the Church of Denmark, although individual priests have the right to refuse to perform such marriages. On June 26, 2015, Supreme Court of the United States ruled that the ban on same-sex marriages were de jure unconstitutional, which de facto legalized the same-sex marriage process in the United States.

Europe

To avoid the use of the term "marriage", some governments provide civil unions, which, depending on the jurisdiction, are open to same-sex couples only, opposite-sex couples only, or both same-sex and opposite-sex couples, to confer all or a portion of the benefits of married status . Civil unions (and registered/domestic partnerships) are currently recognized and accepted in approximately 30 out of 193 countries worldwide and in some U.S. states . In some countries where it has been adopted, applications for marriage licenses have far exceeded governmental estimates of demand. Some jurisdictions, such as the nations of Israel, Aruba, and the Netherlands Antilles, as well as the U.S. state of New Mexico recognize same-sex marriages lawfully entered into elsewhere, while not permitting them to be performed locally.

In addition to civil authorities, some religious denominations ceremonially perform civil unions and same-sex marriages, and recognize them as essentially equivalent to other marriages. For example, Lutheran churches in Netherlands, New Zealand, Sweden and some Lutheran churches of the Evangelical Church in Germany allow blessing ceremonies for same-sex couples, as do Unitarian Universalist churches.

FURTHER RELIGIOUS CONFLICTS

These developments have created a political and religious reaction in some countries, including in England, where the Church of England, after long debate, officially banned blessings of gay couples by Church of England clergy, and in the United States, which continues to experience conflicts, based upon religious grounds.

Kinship restrictions

Kinship is two people that are related by blood or adoption, such as brother, sister, mother, father, aunt, uncle etc. No European country prohibits marriage between first cousins. The U.S. is the only western country with cousin marriage restrictions. Societies have often placed restrictions on marriage to relatives, though the degree of prohibited relationship varies widely. In most societies, marriage between brothers and sisters has been forbidden, with ancient Egyptian, Hawaiian, and Inca royalty being prominent exceptions. In many societies, marriage between first cousins is preferred, while at the other extreme, the medieval Catholic Church prohibited marriage even between distant cousins.

In the United Kingdom, the Deceased Wife's Sister's Marriage Act 1907 removed the previous prohibition for a man to marry the sister of his deceased wife. In Australia, marriage with an ancestor or descendant is prohibited, as is a marriage between a brother and a sister, whether of whole blood or half-blood and even if the brother or sister has been adopted.

All mainstream religions prohibit some marriages on the basis of the consanguinity (lineal descent) and affinity (kinship by marriage) of the prospective marriage partners, though the standards vary.

Social restrictions

In the Indian Hindu community, especially in the Brahmin caste, marrying a person of the same gotra was prohibited, since persons belonging to the same gotra are said to have identical patrilineal descent. In ancient India, when gurukuls existed, the shishyas (pupils) were advised against marrying any of guru's children, as shishyas were also considered the guru's children and it would be considered marriage among siblings. However, there were exceptions, including Arjuna's son Abhimanyu's marriage to Uttra, the dance student of Arjuna in Mahabharata. The Hindu Marriage Act, 1955 brought reforms in the area of same-gotra marriages, which were banned prior to the act's passage. Now the Indian constitution allows any consenting adult heterosexual couple (women 18 or older and men 21 or older) from any race, religion, caste, or creed to marry.

Many societies have also adopted other restrictions on whom one can marry, such as prohibitions of marrying persons with the same surname, or persons with the same sacred animal. Anthropologists refer to these sorts of restrictions as exogamy. One example is South Korea's general taboo against a man marrying a woman with the same family name. The most common surname in South Korea is Kim (almost 20%); however, there are several branches (or clans) in the Kim surname. (Korean family names are divided into one or more clans.) Only intra-clan marriages are prohibited, as they are considered one type of endogamy. Thus, many "Kim-Kim" couples can be found.

Societies have also at times required marriage from within a certain group. Anthropologists refer to these restrictions as endogamy. An example of such restrictions would be a requirement to marry someone from the same tribe. Racist laws adopted by some societies in the past—such as Nazi-era Germany, apartheid-era South Africa, and most of the United States in the nineteenth and the first half of the 20th century—and which prohibited marriage between persons of different races could also be considered examples of endogamy.

In modern Israel, the status of marriage is the same as it was historically under the Ottoman Empire and the British mandate, where civil marriage does not exist and authority for marriage is given by the state solely to the recognized religious denominations (Orthodox Judaism, Islam, Druze, and ten Christian denominations (primarily Orthodox Christianity and Catholicism, but also including the Episcopal Church).

Israeli couples who wish to contract a marriage that are not allowed under the auspices of any of these religious denominations (including same-sex marriages, marriages involving Israelis of Jewish descent who are not recognized by the state as Jewish and marriages between non-Jewish Arab citizens of Israel and Israeli Jews) or simply wish to get legally married outside the auspices of one of these institutions cannot do so in Israel itself.

However, Israel does recognize civil marriages between Israeli citizens that are contracted abroad, including same-sex marriage, so couples in these situations will often hold a non-binding ceremony in Israel and fly abroad (often to nearby Cyprus) to contract a legal marriage that is then recognized in Israel.

In the U.S., many laws banning interracial marriage, which were state laws, were gradually repealed between 1948 and 1967. The U.S. Supreme Court declared all such laws unconstitutional in the case of Loving v. Virginia in 1967.

Polygamy

Polygamy—being married to more than one spouse—is illegal in many countries. While accepted by some societies, it is far less common than monogamy.

Polygamy is normally not permitted in most western countries, although some recognize bona fide polygamous marriages that were performed in other countries. In North America, only British Columbia and Saskatchewan allows and sanctions polygamous relationships under legal jurisdictional statute. Polygamy is practiced illegally by some groups in the United States and Canada, primarily by certain Mormon fundamentalist sects that separated from the mainstream Latter Day Saints movement after the practice was renounced in 1890.

Many societies, even some with a cultural tradition of polygamy, recognize monogamy as the only valid form of marriage. For example, People's Republic of China shifted from allowing polygamy to supporting only monogamy in the Marriage Act of 1953 after the Communist revolution.

In Islam, polygamy is permitted by the Quran (4:3) which states "If you fear you might fail to give orphan women their due rights if you were to marry them, then marry other women of your choice—two, three, or four. But if you are afraid you will fail to maintain justice (between your wives) then content yourselves with one or those bondwomen(slaves) in your possession. This way you are less likely to commit injustice (to the orphan girls in your care)." [This verse is from a para which is setting out rules for adoption of orphans.]

Africa has the highest rate of polygamy in the world. In Senegal, for example, nearly 47 percent of marriages are multiple. In India, only Muslims are allowed to practice polygamy.

State recognition

In many jurisdictions, a civil marriage may take place as part of the religious marriage ceremony, although they are theoretically distinct. In most American states, a wedding must be officiated by the justice of the peace in order for it to be recognized. However, priests, ministers, rabbis, and many other religious authorities can act as viable agents of the state. In some countries, such as France, Spain, Germany, Turkey, Argentina, Japan and Russia, it is necessary to be married by government authority separately from any religious ceremony, with the state ceremony being the legally binding one. In those cases, the marriage is usually legalized before the ceremony. Some jurisdictions allow civil marriages in circumstances which are notably not allowed by particular religions, such as same-sex marriages or civil unions.

Marriage relationships may also be created by the operation of the law alone, as in common-law marriage, sometimes called "marriage by habit and repute." This is a judicial recognition that two people who have been living as domestic partners are subject to the rights and obligations of a legal marriage, even without formally marrying. However, in the UK at least, common-law marriage has been abolished and there are no rights available unless a couple marries or enters into a civil partnership. In all cases, a married person cannot become eligible for common law timeframe until divorced from any previous spouse.

In some cases couples living together do not wish to be recognised as married, such as when pension or alimony rights are adversely affected, or because of taxation consideration, or because of immigration issues, and for many other reasons. Usually, consent forms the basis of such relationships that are not really marital, with authoritative property laws being inapplicable.

The status in the eyes of one authority may not be the same as for another. For example, a marriage may be recognised civilly, but not by a church, and vice versa. Normally a marriage entered into in one country will be recognised in other countries. Sometimes, however, a religious ceremony or a marriage entered into in one country is not recognized by another, such as a same-sex marriage.

INTERNATIONAL RECOGNITION

Some countries give legal recognition to marriages performed in another country under the Hague Convention on Marriages (1978). For this to apply, both the country of marriage and the country where recognition is sought need to be members of this convention.

If the country of marriage is not a member of the Hague Convention on Marriages (1978), then the marriage documents will need to be certified following the Apostille convention. This certification is usually performed in the country of marriage by the embassy of the country whose recognition is sought.

License

A marriage license is a document issued, either by a church or state authority, authorizing a couple to marry. The procedure for obtaining a license varies between jurisdictions and has changed over time.

- Marriages are becoming less common
- In many countries marriage rates are declining

The proportion of people who are getting married is going down in many countries across the world.

The chart here shows this trend for a selection of countries. It combines data from multiple sources, including statistical country offices and reports from the UN, Eurostat and the OECD.

Marriage rates in the US over the last century

For the US we have data on marriage rates going back to the start of the 20th century. This lets us see when the decline started, and trace the influence of social and economic changes during the process.

- In 1920, shortly after the First World War, there were 12 marriages annually for every 1,000 people in the US. Marriages in the US then were almost twice as common as today.
- In the 1930s, during the Great Depression, the rate fell sharply. In the 1930s marriages became again more common and in 1946 – the year after the Second World War ended – marriages reached a peak of 16.4 marriages per 1,000 people.
- Marriage rates fell again in the 1950s and then bounced back in the 1960s.
- The long decline started in the 1970s. Since 1972, marriage rates in the US have fallen by almost 50%, and are currently at the lowest point in recorded history.

HOW DID MARRIAGE RATES CHANGE AROUND THE WORLD?

The chart also shows that in comparison to other rich countries, the US has had particularly high historical marriage rates. But in terms of changes over time, the trend looks similar for other rich countries. The UK and Australia, for example, have also seen marriage rates declining for decades, and are currently at the lowest point in recorded history.

For non-rich countries the data is sparse, but available estimates from Latin America, Africa and Asia suggest that the decline of marriages is not exclusive to rich countries. Over the period 1990 – 2010 there was a decline in marriage rates in the majority of countries around the world.

But there's still a lot of cross-country variation around this general trend, and in some countries changes are going in the opposite direction. In China, Russia and Bangladesh, for example, marriages are more common today than a couple of decades ago.

In many rich countries there are statistical records going back several generations, allowing us to estimate marriage rates by age and year of birth. The chart here uses those records to give marriage rates by age and year of birth for five cohorts of men in England and Wales.

For instance, you can look at 30-year-olds, and see what percentage of them in each cohort was married. Of those men who were born in 1940, about 83% were married by age 30. Among those born in 1980 only about 25% were married by age 30.

The trend is stark. English men in more recent cohorts are much less likely to have married, and that's true at all ages.

There are two causes for this: an increasing share of people in younger cohorts are not getting married; and younger cohorts are increasingly choosing to marry later in life

Average age at marriage

People are marrying later

In many countries, declining marriage rates have been accompanied by an increase in the age at which people are getting married. This is shown in the chart here, where we plot the average age of women at first marriage.

The increase in the age at which people are getting married is stronger in richer countries, particularly in North America and Europe. In Sweden, for example, the average age of marriage for women went up from 28 in 1990 to 34 years in 2017.

In Bangladesh and several countries in sub-Saharan Africa, the average age at marriage is low and has remained unchanged for several years. In Niger, where child marriage is common, the average age at marriage for women has remained constant, at 17 years, since the early 1990s. But these countries are the exceptions. The age at which women marry is increasing in many countries in all regions, from Norway to Japan to Chile.

Share of women married by age and year of birth

- More people marrying later means that a greater share of young people being unmarried.
- According to the British census of 1971 about 85% of women between the age of 25 and 29 were married, as this chart shows. By 2011 that figure had declined to 58%.
- For older people the trend is reversed – the share of older women who never got married is declining. In the 1971 census the share of women 60-64 who had ever been married was lower than it is for women in that age-bracket in the decades since.

- You can create similar charts for both men and women across all countries, using the UN World Marriage Data site here. This lets you explore in more detail the distribution of marriages by age across time, for both men and women.

There has been a 'decoupling' of parenthood and marriage

The share of children born outside of marriage has increased substantially in almost all OECD countries

An arrangement where two or more people are not married but live together is referred to as cohabitation. In recent decades cohabitation has become increasingly common around the world. In the US, for example, the US Census Bureau estimates that the share of young adults between the age of 18 and 24 living with an unmarried partner went up from 0.1% to 9.4% over the period 1968-2018; and according to a recent survey from Pew Research, today most Americans favor allowing unmarried couples to have the same legal rights as married couples.

The increase in cohabitation is the result of the two changes that we discussed above: fewer people are choosing to marry and those people who do get married tend to do so when they are older, and often live with their partner before getting married. In the UK, for example, 85% of people who get married cohabited first.

Long-run data on the share of people living in cohabitation across countries is not available, but some related datapoints are: In particular, the proportion of births outside marriage provide a relevant proxy measure, allowing comparisons across countries and time; if more unmarried people are having children, it suggests that more people are entering long-term cohabiting relationships without first getting married. It isn't a perfect proxy – as we'll see below, rates of single parenting have also changed, meaning that rates of births outside marriage will not match perfectly with cohabitation rates – but it provides some information regarding the direction of change.

- The chart here shows the percentage of all children who were born to unmarried parents.
- As we can see, the share of children born outside of marriage has increased substantially in almost all OECD countries in recent decades. The exception is Japan, where there has been only a very minor increase.
- In 1970, most OECD countries saw less than 10% of children born outside of marriage. In 2014, the share had increased to more than 20% in most countries, and to more than half in some.
- The trend is not restricted to very rich countries. In Mexico and Costa Rica, for example, the increase has been very large, and today the majority of children are born to unmarried parents.

- Globally, the percentage of women in either marriage or cohabitation is decreasing, but only slightly
- In recent decades there has been a decline in global marriage rates, and at the same time that there has been an increase in cohabitation. What's the combined effect if we consider marriage and cohabitation together?
- The chart below plots estimates and projections, from the UN Population Division, for the percentage of women of reproductive age (15 to 49 years) who are either married or living with an unmarried partner.
- Overall, the trend shows a global decline – but only a relatively small one, from 69% in 1970 to 64% projected for 2020. At any given point in the last five decades, around two-thirds of all women were married or cohabitated.
- There are differences between regions. In East Asia the share of women who are married or in a cohabiting union increased, in South America the share is flat, and in North America and North Europe it declined.
- Single parenting is common, and in many countries it has increased in recent decades
- This chart shows the share of households of a single parent living with dependent children.

There are large differences between countries. In Colombia there has been an upward trend, and according to the most recent estimates, 13% of all households are a single parent with one or more dependent children. In India, on the other hand, the corresponding figure is 5%, with no clear trend up or down.

The causes and situations leading to single parenting are varied, and unsurprisingly, single-parent families are very diverse in terms of socio-economic background and living arrangements, across countries, within countries, and over time. However, there are some common patterns:

1. Women head the majority of single-parent households, and this gender gap tends to be stronger for parents of younger children. Across OECD countries, about 12% of children aged 0-5 years live with a single parent; 92% of these live with their mother.
2. Single-parent households are among the most financially vulnerable groups. This is true even in rich countries. According to Eurostat data, across European countries 47% of single-parent households were "at risk of poverty or social exclusion" in 2017, compared with 21% of two-parent households.
3. Single parenting was probably more common a couple of centuries ago. But single parenting back then was often caused by high maternal mortality rather than choice or relationship breakdown; and it was also typically short in duration, since remarriage rates were high.

SAME-SEX MARRIAGE HAS BECOME POSSIBLE IN MANY COUNTRIES

Marriage equality is increasingly considered a human and civil right, with important political, social, and religious implications around the world.

- In 1989, Denmark became the first country to recognize a legal relationship for same-sex couples, establishing 'registered partnerships' granting those in same-sex relationships most of the rights given to married heterosexuals.
- It took more than a decade for same-sex marriage to be legal anywhere in the world. In December 2000, the Netherlands became the first country to establish same-sex marriage by law.
- In the first two decades of the 21st century attitudes and legislation changed quickly in many countries: by December 2019 same-sex marriages were legally recognised in 30 countries.

Where are same-sex marriages legal?

This map shows in green all the countries where same-sex marriage is legal. Also shown are those countries where same-sex couples have other rights such as legal recognition of civil unions.

- More than half of the countries that allow same-sex marriage are in Western Europe. But there are several Western European countries that still do not allow them. In Italy, Switzerland and Greece same-sex marriage is not legal, although in these countries there are alternative forms of recognition for same-sex couples.
- Across all of Asia and Africa, the most populated regions in the world, same-sex marriage is only legal in two countries: Taiwan and South Africa.

Are same-sex marriages increasing in countries where they are legal?

The Netherlands became the first country in the world to open up marriage for same-sex couples in December 2000. In 2001 a total of 2,414 same-sex couples got married. In the two years that followed the number of same-sex marriages decreased, and after that it stabilized at a roughly constant level.

In other countries we see a similar pattern – many same-sex marriages take place immediately after marriage equality laws are introduced. The chart here shows this for the US, plotting estimates of the cumulative number of same-sex married couple households, using data from the American Community Survey.

Same-sex marriage in the US expanded from one state in 2004 to all fifty states in 2015, and the largest year-on-year growth was observed precisely during this period, from 2012 to 2015.10

How common is marriage among LGBT couples?

- There are very few nationally representative surveys that specifically interview lesbian, gay, bisexual or transgender (LGBT) adults. One important exception is a survey from Gallup in the US, with data for the period 2015-2017.
- For LGBT Americans, same-sex cohabitation is becoming less common, but same-sex marriages are becoming more so.
- In 2017, 10.2% of LGBT adults in the US were married to a same-sex spouse. That is up from 7.9% in the months prior to the Supreme Court decision in 2015, but only marginally higher than the 9.6% measured in the first year after the ruling.

Some perspective on the progress made regarding marriage equality

The rate of adoption of marriage equality legislation over time gives us some perspective on just how quickly things have changed. In the year 2000 same-sex marriage was not legal in any country – 20 years later it was legal in 30 countries.

Changes in attitudes towards homosexuality are one of the key factor that have enabled the legal transformations that are making same-sex marriage increasingly possible.

As the second chart here shows, the share of countries where same-sex sexual acts are considered a criminal offence has gone down from 77% in 1960, to 34% in 2019.

Despite these positive trends, much remains to be done to improve the rights of LGBTQ people. In some countries people are imprisoned and even killed simply because of their sexual orientation or gender identity; and even in countries where same-sex sexual activity is legal, these groups of people face violence and discrimination.

Marriage trends show that social institutions can, and often do change quickly

Across the world, fewer people are choosing to marry, and those who do marry are, on average, doing so later in life. The underlying drivers of these trends include the rise of contraceptives, the increase of female participation in labor markets (as we explain in our article here), and the transformation of institutional and legal environments, such as new legislation conferring more rights on unmarried couples.

These changes have led to a broad transformation of family structures. In the last decades, many countries have seen an increase in cohabitation, and it is becoming more common for children to live with a single parent, or with parents who are not married.

These changes have come together with a large and significant shift in people's perceptions of the types of family structures that are possible, acceptable and desirable. Perhaps the clearest example of this is the rise of same-sex marriage.

The de-institutionalization of marriage and the rise of new family models since the middle of the 20th century show that social institutions that have been around for thousands of years can change very rapidly.

Marriage Equality around the World

The Human Rights Campaign Foundation tracks developments in the legal recognition of same-sex marriage around the world. Working with our network of alumni and partners, we lift up the voices of local advocates and share tools, resources, and lessons learned to empower movements for marriage equality.

Current State of Marriage Equality

There are currently 31 countries where same-sex marriage is legal: Argentina, Australia, Austria, Belgium, Brazil, Canada, Chile, Colombia, Costa Rica, Denmark, Ecuador, Finland, France, Germany, Iceland, Ireland, Luxembourg, Malta, Mexico, the Netherlands, New Zealand, Norway, Portugal, South Africa, Spain, Sweden, Switzerland, Taiwan, the United Kingdom, the United States of America and Uruguay.

Processes of Legalization

- 22 countries have legalized same-sex marriage nationally through legislation. Among these, Australia, Ireland and Switzerland legalized same-sex marriage through legislation only after nation-wide votes.
- 7 countries have legalized same-sex marriage nationally through court decisions — Austria, Brazil, Colombia, Costa Rica, Ecuador, Mexico, South Africa, Taiwan and the United States of America.
- 2 countries, South Africa and Taiwan, enacted legislation legalizing same-sex marriage after courts mandated them to do so.

Countries that Legalized Marriage Equality in 2021

Chile: On December 9 the president of Chile signed into law a marriage equality bill that passed in the Senate on December 7 and the lower house on Nov. 23. Same sex civil unions had been legal since 2015.

Switzerland: On December 16, 2020, the Swiss Parliament overwhelmingly passed legislation extending marriage to same-sex couples. A public referendum held in September 2021 overwhelmingly confirmed support for marriage equality by 64%.

Countries that Legalized Marriage Equality in 2020

Costa Rica: The Supreme Court of Costa Rica ruled in November 2018 in support of the historic January 2018 advisory opinion of the InterAmerican Court of Human Rights that marriage equality was consistent with Costa Rica's obligations under the American Convention on Human Rights. The Supreme Court set May 26, 2020 as the deadline for the National Assembly to enact such legislation, but it did not meet that deadline, and marriage equality came into effect on that date.

Countries that Legalized Marriage Equality in 2019

Austria: The Constitutional Court of Austria ruled on December 4, 2017 that denial of marriage equality was discriminatory, legalizing same-sex marriage. Marriage equality took effect January 1, 2019.

Taiwan: The Taiwan Constitutional Court ruled in 2017 that marriage could not be restricted to opposite-sex couples and gave parliament two years to enact legislation legalizing same-sex marriage. Parliament passed legislation to legalize same-sex marriage which went into effect May 24, 2019, making Taiwan the first country to enact marriage equality in Asia.

Ecuador: Legalized after Ecuador's Constitutional Court found on June 12, 2019 that its ban was unconstitutional, marriage equality took effect in Ecuador on July 8, 2019.

International Institutions & Marriage Equality

The Inter-American Court of Human Rights is an independent judicial institution of the Organization of American States. In 2018, it issued an advisory opinion to Costa Rica that signatories of the American Convention on Human Rights are obliged to make same-sex marriage legal. The Court's guidance applies to 20 signatory countries and has proven a powerful tool in advocating for marriage equality in these countries.

The European Court of Justice (ECJ) serves as a high court in the European Union. In 2018, the ECJ determined that all EU countries were required to recognize the same-sex marriages of EU and non-EU citizens for purposes of immigration, regardless of whether same-sex marriage is legal in those countries. In recognition of this decision, the Supreme Administrative Court of Bulgaria affirmed in 2019 that the country would recognize such same-sex marriages for the purposes of immigration.

Places to Watch for Marriage Equality in 2022

This list includes a few of the many countries where HRC Global is tracking developments in support of marriage equality.

- Andorra
- Bermuda
- Cuba
- Czech Republic
- India

- Japan
- Philippines
- Thailand

Methodology

This page is based on a review of legislation and judicial decisions recognizing same-sex marriage. It does not identify countries that recognize other kinds of relationships between same-sex couples, such as civil unions, registered partnerships or domestic partnerships.

We note that processes for obtaining a marriage license for same-sex couples in some countries differ across localities, such as in Mexico where, in light of a constitutional court ruling, some states have enacted marriage equality while, in other states, same-sex couples must seek an amparo from a federal court to obtain a license.

Same-sex married couples in many countries do not share all of the same rights and benefits as different-sex married couples, such as the right to adoption. In some countries, same-sex couples also experience additional restrictions. For example, in Taiwan same-sex marriage is only available to Taiwanese citizens or a citizen of a foreign country that recognizes same-sex marriage who seeks to marry a Taiwanese citizen.

2

DIVORCE: INTRODUCTION

Divorce (also known as dissolution of marriage) is the process of terminating a marriage or marital union. Divorce usually entails the canceling or reorganizing of the legal duties and responsibilities of marriage, thus dissolving the bonds of matrimony between a married couple under the rule of law of the particular country or state. Divorce laws vary considerably around the world, but in most countries, divorce requires the sanction of a court or other authority in a legal process, which may involve issues of distribution of property, child custody, alimony (spousal support), child visitation / access, parenting time, child support, and division of debt. In most countries, monogamy is required by law, so divorce allows each former partner to marry another person.

Divorce is different from annulment, which declares the marriage null and void, with legal separation or de jure separation (a legal process by which a married couple may formalize a de facto separation while remaining legally married) or with de facto separation (a process where the spouses informally stop cohabiting). Reasons for divorce vary, from sexual incompatibility or lack of independence for one or both spouses to a personality clash to infidelity.

The only countries that do not allow divorce are the Philippines and the Vatican City. In the Philippines, divorce for non-Muslim Filipinos is not legal unless the husband or wife is an undocumented immigrant and satisfies certain conditions. The Vatican City is a state ruled by the head of the Catholic Church, a religion that does not allow for divorce. Countries that have relatively recently legalized divorce are Italy (1970), Portugal (1975, although from 1910 to 1940 it was possible both for the civil and religious marriage), Brazil (1977), Spain (1981), Argentina (1987), Paraguay (1991), Colombia (1991; from 1976 was allowed only for non-Catholics), Andorra (1995), Ireland (1996), Chile (2004) and Malta (2011).

The topic of divorce would seem to require no introduction. Divorce refers to the often messy and painful end of a marriage. For better or for worse, divorce is a very common event these days. Most everyone has been touched by it, either by going through it themselves as a spouse or a child, or knowing someone who has gone through it as a spouse or as a child. Despite widespread familiarity with the effects of divorce, the details of the divorce process are less well known. In this section, we discuss the important concepts and procedures involved in the divorce process with the sincere hope that educating people regarding this information will help minimize pain.

Grounds for divorce vary widely from country to country. Marriage may be seen as a contract, a status, or a combination of these. Where it is seen as a contract, the refusal or inability of one spouse to perform the obligations stipulated in the contract may constitute a ground for divorce for the other spouse. In contrast, in some countries (such as Sweden, Finland, Australia, New Zealand), divorce is purely no fault. This means it does not matter what the reasons are that a party or parties want to separate. They can separate of their own free will without having to prove someone is at fault for the divorce. Many jurisdictions offer both the option of a no fault divorce as well as an at fault divorce. This is the case, for example, in many US states (see Grounds for divorce (United States)) or the Czech Republic.

Though divorce laws vary between jurisdictions, there are two basic approaches to divorce: fault based and no-fault based. However, even in some jurisdictions that do not require a party to claim fault of their partner, a court may still take into account the behavior of the parties when dividing property, debts, evaluating custody, shared care arrangements and support. In some jurisdictions, one spouse may be forced to pay the attorney's fees of another spouse.

Laws vary as to the waiting period before a divorce is effective. Also, residency requirements vary. However, issues of division of property are typically determined by the law of the jurisdiction in which the property is located.

In Europe, divorce laws differ from country to country, reflecting differing legal and cultural traditions. In some countries, particularly (but not only) in some former communist countries, divorce can be obtained only on one single general ground of "irretrievable breakdown of the marriage" (or a similar formulation). Yet, what constitutes such a "breakdown" of the marriage is interpreted very differently from jurisdiction to jurisdiction, ranging from very liberal interpretations (e.g. Netherlands) to quite restrictive ones (e.g., in Poland, there must be an "irretrievable and complete disintegration of matrimonial life," but there are many restrictions to granting a divorce). Separation constitutes a ground of divorce in some European countries (in Germany, e.g., a divorce is granted on the basis of a 1-year separation if both spouses consent, or 3-year separation if only one spouse consents). Note that "separation" does not necessarily mean separate residences – in some jurisdictions, living in the same household but leading a separate life (e.g., eating, sleeping, socializing, etc. separately) is sufficient to constitute de facto separation; this is explicitly stated, e.g., in the family laws of Latvia or the Czech Republic.

Divorce laws are not static; they often change reflecting evolving social norms of societies. In the 21st century, many European countries have made changes to their divorce laws, in particular by reducing the length of the necessary periods of separation, e.g., Scotland in 2006 (1 or 2 years from the previous 2 or 5 years); France in 2005 (2 years from the previous 6 years), Switzerland in 2005 (2 years from the previous 4 years), Greece in 2008 (two years from the previous four years). Some countries have completely overhauled their divorce laws, such as Spain in 2005, and Portugal in 2008. A new divorce law also came into force in September 2007 in Belgium, creating a new system that is primarily no-fault. Bulgaria also modified its divorce regulations in 2009. Also in Italy, new laws came into force in 2014 and 2015 with significant changes in Italian law in matter of divorce: apart from shortening of the period of obligatory separation (6 months for uncontested divorces and 1 year for contested ones from the previous 3 years), are allowed other forms of getting a divorce – as an alternative to court proceedings, i.e. the negotiations with the participation of an advocate or agreement made before the registrar of Public Registry Office. Austria by contrast is a European country where the divorce law still remains conservative.

The liberalization of divorce laws is not without opposition, particularly in the United States. Indeed, in the US, certain conservative and religious organizations are lobbying for laws which restrict divorce. In 2011, in the US, the Coalition for Divorce Reform was established, describing itself as an organization "dedicated to supporting efforts to reduce unnecessary divorce and promote healthy marriages."

The magisterium of the Roman Catholic Church founds the concept of marriage on natural moral law, elaborated by St. Thomas Aquinas, supplemented by the revealed Divine law. The doctrine of the Doctor Angelicus has been partially shared by the Eastern Orthodox Church in the course of history.

LAW

Types

In some jurisdictions, the courts will seldom apply principles of fault, but might willingly hold a party liable for a breach of a fiduciary duty to his or her spouse (for example, see Family Code Sections 720 and 1100 of the California Family Code). Grounds for divorce differs from state to state in the U.S. Some states have no-fault divorce; some states require a declaration of fault on the part of one partner or both; some states allow either method.

In most jurisdictions, a divorce must be certified (or ordered by a Judge) by a court of law to come into effect. The terms of the divorce are usually determined by the courts, though they may take into account prenuptial agreements or post-nuptial agreements, or ratify terms that the spouses may have agreed to privately (this is not true in the United States, where agreements related to the marriage typically have to be rendered in writing to be enforceable). In the absence of agreement, a contested divorce may be stressful to the spouses.

In some other countries,[where?] when the spouses agree to divorce and to the terms of the divorce, it can be certified by a non-judiciary administrative entity. The effect of a divorce is that both parties are free to marry again if a filing in an appellate court does not overturn the decision.

Contested divorce

Contested divorces mean that one of several issues are required to be heard by a judge at trial level—this is more expensive, and the parties will have to pay for a lawyer's time and preparation. In such a divorce the spouses are not able to agree on issues for instance child custody and division of marital assets. In such situations, the litigation process takes longer to conclude. The judge controls the outcome of the case. Less adversarial approaches to divorce settlements have recently emerged, such as mediation and collaborative divorce settlement, which negotiate mutually acceptable resolution to conflicts. This principle in the United States is called 'Alternative Dispute Resolution' and has gained popularity.

At-fault divorce

Before the late 1960s, nearly all countries that permitted divorce required proof by one party that the other party had committed an act incompatible with the marriage. This was termed "grounds" for divorce (popularly called "fault") and was the only way to terminate a marriage. In the United States, no-fault divorce is available in all 50 states, as is the case with Australia, New Zealand, Canada and other Western countries.

Fault-based divorces can be contested; evaluation of offenses may involve allegations of collusion of the parties (working together to get the divorce), or condonation (approving the offense), connivance (tricking someone into committing an offense), or provocation by the other party. Contested fault divorces can be expensive, and not usually practical as eventually most divorces are granted. Comparative rectitude is a doctrine used to determine which spouse is more at fault when both spouses are guilty of breaches.

The grounds for a divorce which a party could raise and need to prove included 'desertion,' 'abandonment,' 'cruelty,' or 'adultery.' The requirement of proving a ground was revised (and withdrawn) by the terms of 'no-fault' statutes, which became popular in many Western countries in the late 1960s and early 1970s. In 'no-fault' jurisdictions divorce can be obtained either on a simple allegation of 'irreconcilable differences,' 'irretrievable break-down,' or 'incompatibility' with respect to the marriage relationship, or on the ground of de facto separation.

Summary divorce

A summary (or simple) divorce, available in some jurisdictions[which?], is used when spouses meet certain eligibility requirements or can agree on key issues beforehand.

Key factors:

- Short duration of marriage (less than five years)
- Absence of children (or, in some jurisdictions, prior allocation of child custody and of child-support direction and amount)
- Absence or minimal value of real property at issue and any associated encumbrances such as mortgages
- Absence of agreed-as-marital property above a given value threshold (around $35,000 not including vehicles)
- Absence, with respect to each spouse, of claims to personal property above a given value threshold, typically the same as that for total marital property, with such claims including claims to exclusive previous ownership of property described by the other spouse as marital

No-fault divorce

Most Western jurisdictions have a no-fault divorce system, which requires no allegation or proof of fault of either party. The barest of assertions suffice. For example, in countries that require "irretrievable breakdown," the mere assertion that the marriage has broken down will satisfy the judicial officer. In other jurisdictions requiring irreconcilable differences, the mere allegation that the marriage has been irreparable by these differences is enough for granting a divorce. Courts will not inquire into facts. A "yes" is enough, even if the other party vehemently says "no."

The application can be made by either party or by both parties jointly.

In jurisdictions adopting the 'no-fault' principle regarding whether to grant a divorce, some courts may still take into account the fault of the parties when determining some aspects of the content of the divorce decree, e.g., its terms for the division of property and debts and the absence, or amount, of spousal support. Provisions related to child custody are determined using a different fundamental standard: the child's or children's best interests; At the same time, some behaviors that may constitute marital fault (e.g., violence, cruelty, endangerment, neglect, or substance abuse) may also qualify as factors to be considered when determining child custody, they do so for the independent reason that they provide evidence as to what arrangement is in the child's or children's best interests in the future.

Uncontested divorce

It is estimated that upwards of 95% of divorces in the U.S. are "uncontested", because the two parties are able to come to an agreement (either with or without lawyers/mediators/collaborative counsel) about the property, children, and support issues. When the parties can agree and present the court with a fair and equitable agreement, approval of the divorce is almost guaranteed. If the two parties cannot come to an agreement, they may ask the court to decide how to split property and deal with the custody of their children. Though this may be necessary, the courts would prefer parties to come to an agreement prior to entering court.

Where the issues are not complex and the parties are cooperative, a settlement often can be directly negotiated between them. In the majority of cases, forms are acquired from their respective state websites and a filing fee is paid to the state. Most U.S. states charge between $175 and $350 for a simple divorce filing. Collaborative divorce and mediated divorce are considered uncontested divorces.

In the United States, many state court systems are experiencing an increasing proportion of pro se (i.e., litigants represent themselves without a lawyer) in divorce cases. In San Diego, for example, the number of divorce filings involving at least one self-representing litigant rose from 46% in 1992 to 77% in 2000, and in Florida from 66% in 1999 to 73% in 2001. Urban courts in California report that approximately 80% of the new divorce filings are filed pro se.

Collaborative divorce

Collaborative divorce is a method for divorcing couples to come to an agreement on divorce issues. In a collaborative divorce, the parties negotiate an agreed resolution with the assistance of attorneys who are trained in the collaborative divorce process and in mediation and often with the assistance of a neutral financial specialist or divorce coaches. The parties are empowered to make their own decisions based on their own needs and interests, but with complete information and full professional support.

Once the collaborative divorce starts, the lawyers are disqualified from representing the parties in a contested legal proceeding, should the collaborative law process end prematurely. Most attorneys who practise collaborative divorce claim that it can be more cost-effective than other divorce methods, e.g., going to court.

Electronic divorce

Portugal, for example, allows two persons to file an electronic request for no-fault collaborative divorce in a non judiciary administrative entity. In specific cases, with no children, real property, alimony, or common address, can be completed within one hour.

Mediated divorce

Divorce mediation is an alternative to traditional divorce litigation. In a divorce mediation session, a mediator facilitates the discussion between the two parties by assisting with communication and providing information and suggestions to help resolve differences. At the end of the mediation process, the separating parties have typically developed a tailored divorce agreement that can be submitted to the court. Mediation sessions can include either party's attorneys, a neutral attorney, or an attorney-mediator who can inform both parties of their legal rights, but does not provide advice to either, or can be conducted with the assistance of a facilitative or transformative mediator without attorneys present at all. Some mediation companies, such as Wevorce, also pair clients with counselors, financial planners and other professionals to work through common mediation sticking points.

Divorce mediators may be attorneys who have experience in divorce cases, or they may be professional mediators who are not attorneys, but who have training specifically in the area of family court matters. Divorce mediation can be significantly less costly, both financially and emotionally, than litigation. The adherence rate to mediated agreements is much higher than that of adherence to court orders. An article in the Jerusalem Post by Hadassah Fidler explained that mediated divorces have become a lot more popular, to the extent that some countries (such as Israel) have instituted a new law which will require divorcing couples to consider mediation before applying to court.[48

DIVORCE IS COMMON

The first thing to know about divorce is that it is common and nothing to be ashamed of. According to recent statistics, the rate of divorce in the United States (0.40%) is approximately half the rate of marriage (0.78%), suggesting that approximately 50% of all marriages - an enormous number! - are ending in divorce. While the actual meaning of these figures is arguable (given that it may be unfair to try to predict who will divorce in the future based on who is divorcing today), there is no disputing the fact that a great number of Americans have divorced and will divorce in the future. Divorce is so common it has become an industry unto itself with lawyers and matchmaking companies being just a few of the groups deriving economic benefit from the process. Under the social pressure of so many divorces, the stigma that used to be attached to divorce is largely gone. It continues to be painful to divorce, but with so much company, it is no longer a lonely isolated place.

Divorce is an ancient institution

The second thing to know about divorce is that it is an old and venerable institution. People have been getting divorces as long as people have been getting married. The ease with which a divorce can be obtained, the social stigma attached to divorce, and the amount of control religious and political powers have exercised over divorce have varied significantly over time and cultures. On the one hand, some accounts suggest that Islamic law at one point allowed a man to divorce his wife by simply stating the phrase "I divorce you" three times. On the other hand, other accounts suggest that the sixteenth century

English king Henry XIII went so far as to cause the Anglican Church to be created (or at least become fully recognized) so as to gain permission for a divorce which the Catholic Church had denied him.

Less than 50 years ago, divorce was only widely available in the United States on a "fault" basis; it could only be obtained by demonstrating to the state's approval that one of the partners was acting badly enough to warrant release of the other partner. Acceptable grounds for fault divorce varied from state to state, but usually included abuse, adultery, and abandonment. The difficulty of gaining divorce, and a cultural climate that stigmatized divorce combined to keep divorce rates low. Since the 1960s most states have adopted "no-fault" divorce laws that allow couples to divorce without proving wrongdoing. Due in part to this reform and probably to other cultural changes, the divorce rate has risen, and being divorced is no longer looked down upon.

Divorce doesn't have to be awful

The third thing to know about divorce is that it isn't always awful. With the availability of no-fault divorce options, the process of divorce is no longer necessarily adversarial. Partners are now free to proceed with divorce as calmly and rationally as they can manage. Certainly divorce is frequently born out of marital conflict and proceeds as a knockdown, drag-out fight for possessions, child custody and pride. But modern divorce can also take place amicably, consciously and without a court battle. Marriage therapy can help conflicted partners to repair their marriage, or, if that is not possible, to separate on as positive terms as is possible. Arbitration is available to help partners successfully divide their possessions without recourse to the courts. The quality of the divorce any given couple will end up experiencing will be deeply influenced by the quality of relationships the partners can maintain with each other, and with professional helpers they work with during the separation process.

DIVORCE IS A LEGAL PROCESS SEPARATELY FROM AN EMOTIONAL ONE

The fourth thing to know about divorce is that it is at once an emotional journey, and a legal process, and that it is best to keep these two aspects of divorce separate when that is possible. Marriage is a legal contract recognized by the state conferring rights, privileges and responsibilities. From a legal perspective, divorce is a process of disengaging partners from the legal marriage contract and making sure that those things the spouses are responsible for (including children and property) are properly accounted and cared for. The very rational and purposeful legal process of divorce contrasts mightily with the chaotic and emotional aspects of divorce which involve coming to grips with rather massive life changes as significant and shattering as any family death and which may involve significant grief, anger, sadness and pain. We'll be dealing with the emotional and legal aspects of divorce separately in this document.

Divorce is not the end of the world

The final thing to know up front about divorce is that divorce is not the end of the world. Divorce is a crisis involving a very real end, but it is also a very real new beginning. Divorce is the end of a chapter of life, but not the end of life itself (even though it may feel that way). In the midst of the divorce crisis are seeds of opportunities for remaking life into something again enjoyable new and creatively good. It is important to keep this hopeful and true message in mind as the process unfolds.

Divorce rates increased after 1970 – in recent decades the trends very much differ between countries

Trends in the rate of divorces relative to the size of the population

When we zoom out and look at the large-scale picture at the global or regional level since the 1970s, we see an overall increase in divorce rates. The UN in its overview of global marriage patterns notes that there is a general upward trend: "at the world level, the proportion of adults aged 35-39 who are divorced or separated has doubled, passing from 2% in the 1970s to 4% in the 2000s."

But, when we look more closely at the data we can also see that this misses two key insights: there are notable differences between countries; and it fails to capture the pattern of these changes in the period from the 1990s to today.

As we see in the chart, for many countries divorce rates increased markedly between the 1970s and 1990s. In the US, divorce rates more than doubled from 2.2 per 1,000 in 1960 to over 5 per 1,000 in the 1980s. In the UK, Norway and South Korea, divorce rates more than tripled. Since then divorce rates declined in many countries.

The trends vary substantially from country to country. In the chart the US stands out as a bit of an outlier, with consistently higher divorce rates than most other countries, but also an earlier 'peak'. South Korea had a much later 'peak', with divorce rates continuing to rise until the early 2000s. In other countries – such as Mexico and Turkey – divorces continue to rise. As the OECD Family Database notes, between 1995 and 2017 (or the nearest available estimate), divorce rates increased in 18 OECD countries, but fell in 12 others.

The pattern of rising divorce rates, followed by a plateau or fall in some countries (particularly richer countries) might be partially explained by the differences in divorce rates across cohorts, and the delay in marriage we see in younger couples today.

Economists Betsey Stevenson and Justin Wolfers looked in detail at the changes and driving forces in marriage and divorce rates in the US.14 They suggest that the changes we see in divorce rates may be partly reflective of the changes in expectations within marriages as women entered the workforce. Women who married before the large rise in female employment may have found themselves in marriages where expectations were no longer suited. Many people in the postwar years married someone who was probably a good match for the postwar culture, but ended up being the wrong partner after the times had changed. This may have been a driver behind the steep rise in divorces throughout the 1970s and 1980s.

THE SHARE OF MARRIAGES ENDING IN DIVORCE

Trends in crude divorce rates give us a general overview of how many divorces happen each year, but need to be interpreted with caution. First, crude rates mix a large number of cohorts – both older and young couples; and second, they do not account for how the number of marriages is changing.

To understand how patterns of divorce are changing it is more helpful to look at percentage of marriages that end in divorce, and look in more detail at these patterns by cohort.

Let's take a look at a country where divorce rates been declining in recent decades.

Here we see that for all three lines, the overall pattern is similar:

- The share of marriages that end in divorce increased through the 1960s to the 1990s.
- In 1963, only 1.5% of couples had divorced before their fifth anniversary, 7.8% had divorced before their tenth, and 19% before their twentieth anniversary. By the mid-1990s this had increased to 11%, 25% and 38%, respectively.
- Since then, divorces have been on the decline. The percentage of couples divorcing in the first five years has halved since its 1990s peak. And the percentage who got divorced within the first 10 years of their marriage has also fallen significantly.

Divorces by age and cohort

What might explain the recent reduction in overall divorce rates in some countries?

The overall trend can be broken down into two key drivers: a reduction in the likelihood of divorce for younger cohorts; and a lengthening of marriage before divorce for those that do separate.

We see both of these factors in the analysis of divorce rates in the US from Stevenson and Wolfers. This chart maps out the percentage of marriages ending in divorce: each line represents the decade they got married (those married in the 1950s, 60s, 70s, 80s and 1990s) and the x-axis represents the years since the wedding.

We see that the share of marriages ending in divorce increased significantly for couples married in 1960s or 70s compared to those who got married in the 1950s. The probability of divorce within 10 years was twice as high for couples married in the 1960s versus those who got married in the 1950s. For those married in the 1970s, it was more than three times as likely.

You might have heard the popularised claim that "half of marriages end in divorce". We can see here where that claim might come from – it was once true: 48% of American couples that married in the 1970s were divorced within 25 years.

But since then the likelihood of divorce has fallen. It fell for couples married in the 1980s, and again for those in the 1990s. Both the likelihood of divorce has been falling, and the length of marriage has been increasing.

Share of marriages ending in divorce in the US, by year of marriage

This is also true for marriages in the UK. This chart shows the cumulative share of marriages that ended in divorce: each line represents the year in which couples were married. A useful way to compare different age cohorts is by the steepness of the line: steeper lines indicate a faster accumulation of divorces year-on-year, particularly in the earlier stages of marriages.

You might notice that the divorce curves for couples in the 1960s are shallower and tend to level out in the range of 20% to 30%. Divorce rates then became increasingly steep throughout the 1970s; 80s and 90s, and eventually surpass cumulative rates from the 1960s. But, since the 1990s, these curves appear to be falling once again, mirroring the findings from the US.

We don't know yet how long the marriages of younger couples today will last. It will take several decades before we have the full picture on more recent marriages and their eventual outcomes.

Marriages in many countries are getting longer

As we saw from data on divorce rates, in some countries – particularly richer countries such as the UK, US and Germany – divorce rates have been falling since the 1990s. This can be partially explained by a reduction in the share of marriages ending in divorce, but also by the length of marriages before their dissolution.

How has the length of marriages changed over time?

In the chart here we see the duration of marriages before divorce across a number of countries where this data is available. An important point to note here is that the definitions are not consistent across countries: some countries report the median length of marriage; others the mean. Since the distribution of marriage lengths is often skewed, the median and mean values can be quite different. As the UK Office for National Statistics notes:

"The median duration of marriage at divorce in this release is represented by the middle value when the data are arranged in increasing order. The median is used, rather than the mean, because the duration of marriage for divorces is not symmetrically distributed. Therefore, the median provides a more accurate reflection of this distribution. The mean would be affected by the relatively small number of divorces that take place when duration of marriage exceeds 15 years."

So, we have to keep this in mind and be careful if we make cross-country comparisons. On the chart shown we note for each country whether the marriage duration is given as the median or mean value.

But, we can gain insights for single countries over time. What we see for a number of countries is that the average duration of marriage before divorce has been increasing since the 1990s or early 2000s. If we take the UK as an example: marriages got notably shorter between the 1970s to the later 1980s, falling from around 12 to 9 years. But, marriages have once again increased in length, rising back to over 12 years.

This mirrors what we saw in data on the share of marriages ending in divorce: divorce rates increased significantly between the 1960s/70s through the 1990s, but have seen a fall since then.

We see a similar pattern in the United States, New Zealand, Australia, and Singapore. However, there is still a significant amount of heterogeneity between countries.

POLYGAMY AND DIVORCE

Polygamy is a significant structural factor governing divorce in countries where this is permitted. Little-to-no analysis has been completed to explicitly explain the link between marital instability and polygamy which leads to divorce. The frequency of divorce rises in polygamous marriages compared to monogamous relationships. Within polygamous unions, differences in conjugal stability are found to occur by wife order. There are 3 main mechanisms through which polygamy affects divorce: economic restraint, sexual satisfaction, and childlessness. Many women escape economic restraint through divorcing their spouses when they are allowed to initiate a divorce.

Causes

An annual study in the UK by management consultants Grant Thornton, estimates the main proximal causes of divorce based on surveys of matrimonial lawyers.

The main causes in 2004 were:

- Adultery; Extramarital sex; Infidelity – 27%
- Domestic violence – 17%
- Midlife crisis – 13%
- Addictions, e.g. alcoholism and gambling – 6%
- Workaholism – 6%
- Other factors - 31%

According to this survey, husbands engaged in extramarital affairs in 75% of cases, wives in 25%. In cases of family strain, wives' families were the primary source of strain in 78%, compared to 22% of husbands' families. Emotional and physical abuse were more evenly split, with wives affected in 60% and husbands in 40% of cases. In 70% of workaholism-related divorces it was husbands who were the cause, and in 30%, wives. The 2004 survey found that 93% of divorce cases were petitioned by wives, very few of which were contested. 53% of divorces were of marriages that had lasted 10 to 15 years, with 40% ending after 5 to 10 years. The first 5 years are relatively divorce-free, and if a marriage survives more than 20 years it is unlikely to end in divorce.

Social scientists study the causes of divorce in terms of underlying factors that may possibly motivate divorce. One of these factors is the age at which a person gets married; delaying marriage may provide more opportunity or experience in choosing a compatible partner. Wage, income, and sex ratios are other such underlying factors that have been included in analyses by sociologists and economists.

The elevation of divorce rates among couples who cohabited prior to marriage is called the "cohabitation effect." Evidence suggests that although this correlation is partly due to two forms of selection (a) that persons whose moral or religious codes permit cohabitation are also more likely to consider divorce permitted by morality or religion and (b) that marriage based on low levels of commitment is more common among couples who cohabit than among couples who do not, such that the mean and median levels of commitment at the start of marriage are lower among cohabiting than among non-cohabiting couples), the cohabitation experience itself exerts at least some independent effect on the subsequent marital union.

In 2010, a study by Jay Teachman published in Journal of Marriage and Family found that women who have cohabited or had premarital sex with men other than their husbands have an increased risk of divorce, and that this effect is strongest for women who have cohabited with multiple men prior to marriage. To Teachman, the fact that the elevated risk of divorce is only experienced when the premarital partner(s) is someone other than the husband indicates that premarital sex and cohabitation are now a normal part of the courtship process in the United States. This study only considers data on women in the 1995 National Survey of Family Growth in the United States. Divorce is sometimes caused by one of the partners finding the other unattractive.

Recent studies show that the cohabitation effect on divorce varies across different cultures and periods. Another article published in Journal of Marriage and Family found that when cohabitation was uncommon in pre-reform China, premarital cohabitation increased the likelihood of subsequent divorce, but this association disappeared when cohabitation became prevalent.

EFFECTS

Some of the effects associated with divorce include academic, behavioral, and psychological problems. Although this may not always be true, studies suggest that children from divorced families are more likely to exhibit such behavioral issues than non-divorced families.

Divorce and relationships

Research done at Northern Illinois University on Family and Child Studies suggests that divorce of couples experiencing high conflict can positively affect families by reducing conflict in the home. There are, however, many instances when the parent-child relationship may suffer due to divorce. Financial support is many times lost when an adult goes through a divorce. The adult may be obligated to obtain additional work to maintain financial stability. This can lead to a negative relationship between the parent and child; the relationship may suffer due to a lack of attention towards the child and minimal parental supervision

Studies have also shown that parental skills decrease after a divorce occurs; however, this effect is only a temporary change. "Many researchers have shown that a disequilibrium, including diminished parenting skills, occurs in the year following the divorce but that by two years after the divorce re-stabilization has occurred and parenting skills have improved."

Some couples choose divorce even when one spouse's desire to remain married is greater than the other spouse's desire to obtain a divorce. In economics, this is known as the Zelder Paradox and is more familiar with marriages that have produced children and less common with childless couples.

Research has also found that recent divorcees report significantly higher hostility levels after the divorce than before, and that this effect applies equally to both male and female divorcees.

In an American Psychological Association study of parents' relocation after a divorce, researchers found that a move has a long-term effect on children. In the first study conducted amongst 2,000 college students on the effects of parental relocation relating to their children's well-being after divorce, researchers found major differences. In divorced families in which one parent moved, the students received less financial support from their parents compared with divorced families in which neither parent moved. These findings also imply other negative outcomes for these students, such as more distress related to the divorce and did not feel a sense of emotional support from their parents. Although the data suggests negative outcomes for these students whose parents relocate after divorce, there is insufficient research that can alone prove the overall well-being of the child A newer study in the Journal of Family Psychology found that parents who move more than an hour away from their children after a divorce are much less well off than those parents who stayed in the same location

Effects on children

Psychological

Divorce is associated with diminished psychological well-being in children and adult offspring of divorced parents, including greater unhappiness, less satisfaction with life, weaker sense of personal control, anxiety, depression, and greater use of mental health services. A preponderance of evidence indicates that there is a causal effect between divorce and these outcomes.

A study in Sweden led by the Centre for Health Equity Studies (Chess) at Stockholm University/Karolinska Institutet, is published in the Journal of Epidemiology & Community Health found that children living with just one parent after divorce suffer from more problems such as headaches, stomach aches, feelings of tension and sadness than those whose parents share custody.

Children of divorced parents are also more likely to experience conflict in their own marriages, and are more likely to experience divorce themselves. They are also more likely to be involved in short-term cohabiting relationships, which often dissolve before marriage. There are many studies that show proof of an intergenerational transmission of divorce, but this does not mean that having divorced parents will absolutely lead a child to divorce. There are two key factors that make this transmission of divorce more likely. First, inherited biological tendencies or genetic conditions may predispose a child to divorce as well as the "model of marriage" presented by the child's parents.

According to Nicholas Wall, former President of the Family Division of the English High Court, "People think that post-separation parenting is easy – in fact, it is exceedingly difficult, and as a rule of thumb my experience is that the more intelligent the parent, the more intractable the dispute. There is nothing worse, for most children, than for their parents to denigrate each other. Parents simply do not realize the damage they do to their children by the battles they wage over them. Separating parents rarely behave reasonably, although they always believe that they are doing so, and that the other party is behaving unreasonably."

Children involved in high-conflict divorce or custody cases can experience varying forms of psychological distress due to conflict between their parents. Legal professionals recognize that alienating behaviors are common in child custody cases, but are cautious about accepting the concept of parental alienation.

Research shows that children can be affected 2–4 years before the separation or divorce even occurs. This can be due to parental conflict and anticipation of a divorce, and decreased parental contact. Many couples believe that by separating, or becoming legally divorced that they are helping their children, and in situations of extreme parental conflict or abuse it most likely will be beneficial.

Exposure to marital conflict and instability, most often has negative consequences for children. Several mechanisms are likely to be responsible. First, observing overt conflict between parents is a direct stressor for children. Observational studies reveal that children react to inter-parental conflict with fear, anger, or the inhibition of normal behavior. Preschool children – who tend to be egocentric – may blame themselves for marital conflict, resulting in feelings of guilt and lowered self-esteem. Conflict between parents also tends to spill over and negatively affect the quality of parents' interactions with their children. Researchers found that the associations between marital conflict and children's externalizing and internalizing problems were largely mediated by parents' use of harsh punishment and parent–child conflict. Furthermore, modeling verbal or physical aggression, parents "teach" their children that disagreements are resolved through conflict rather than calm discussion. As a result, children may not learn the social skills (such as the ability to negotiate and reach compromises) that are necessary to form mutually rewarding relationships with peers.

Girls and boys deal with divorce differently. For instance, girls who initially show signs of adapting well, later suffer from anxiety in romantic relationships with men. Studies also showed that girls who were separated from their fathers at a younger age tended to be angrier toward the situation as they aged. Anger and sadness were also observed as common feelings in adolescents who had experienced parental divorce.

ACADEMIC AND SOCIOECONOMIC

Frequently, children who have experienced a divorce have lower academic achievement than children from non-divorced families In a review of family and school factors related to adolescents' academic performance, it noted that a child from a divorced family is two times more likely to drop out of high school than a child from a non-divorced family. These children from divorced families may also be less likely to attend college, resulting in the discontinuation of their academic career.

Many times academic problems are associated with those children from single-parent families. Studies have shown that this issue may be directly related to the economical influence of divorce. A divorce may result in the parent and children moving to an area with a higher poverty rate and a poor education system all due to the financial struggles of a single parent.

Children of divorced parents also achieve lower levels of socioeconomic status, income, and wealth accumulation than children of continuously married parents. These outcomes are associated with lower educational achievement.

Young men or women between the ages of 7 and 16 who had experienced the divorce of their parents were more likely than youths who had not experienced the divorce of their parents to leave home because of friction, to cohabit before marriage, and to parent a child before marriage.

Divorce often leads to worsened academic achievement in children ages 7–12, the most heightened negative effect being reading test scores. These negative effects tend to persist, and even escalate after the divorce or separation occurs.

Children of divorced or separated parents exhibit increased behavioral problems and the marital conflict that accompanies parents' divorce places the child's social competence at risk.

Divorce of elderly couples

In the United States of America, since the mid-1990s, the divorce rate has increased to over 50% among baby boomers. More and more seniors are staying single; an analysis of census data conducted at Bowling Green State University predicted that divorce numbers would continue to rise. Baby boomers who remain unmarried are five times more likely to live in poverty than those who are married. They are also three times as likely to receive food stamps, public assistance or disability payments.

Sociologists believe that the rise in the number of older Americans who are not married is a result of factors such as longevity and economics. Women, especially, are becoming more and more financially independent which allows them to feel more secure with being alone, in addition to changing perceptions of being divorced or single. This has resulted in less pressure for baby boomers to marry or stay married.

Asia

Japan

In Japan, divorces were on an upward trend from the 1960s until 2002 when they hit a peak of 290,000 divorces. While divorce rates have increased since the 1900s, they have also slightly declined since 2002. In fact, in 2020 there were approximately 193,300 divorces. This is a significant decrease from the prior year, 2019, which recorded 208,489 divorces.

There are several types of divorces in Japan; Divorce by Agreement, Divorce by Conciliation, and Divorce by Judgement. Divorce by Agreement (rikon), occurs when both parties mutually agree to separate and do not need to go to court. This is the most common type of divorce in Japan. Divorce by Conciliation (chotei rikon) is sought out when individuals are unable to agree on terms or separate. Thus, these cases go to court in hope to come to a mutual agreement for both parties. Lastly, Divorce by Judgement (saiban rikon) occurs when individuals are unable to reach an agreement in court during conciliation. Divorce by judgement is uncommon in Japan.

India

India has one of the lowest divorce rates in the world with around 1% of marriages ending in divorces. That being said, a lot of individuals split without choosing to go through the process of divorce. In fact, a large number of marriages are not registered and thus, a dissolution in such partnership would not be shown in the divorce statistics. Additionally, divorce is still stigmatized and seen as taboo amongst many families in India.

The Hindu Marriage Act is an Act of the Parliament of India enacted in 1955. Three other important acts were also enacted as part of the Hindu Code Bills during this time: the Hindu Succession Act (1956), the Hindu Minority and Guardianship Act (1956), the Hindu Adoptions and Maintenance Act (1956). Divorce under various acts in India: The Parsi Marriage and Divorce Act, 1936 The dissolution of Muslim Marriage Act, 1939 The Parsi Marriage and Divorce Act, 1936 The Special Marriage Act, 1956 The Foreign Marriage Act, 1969 Dissolution of Muslim Marriages Act, 1939 The Dissolution of Marriage and Judicial separation (under the Indian Divorce Act, 1869).

Due to the existence of diverse religious faiths in India, the Indian Judiciary has implemented laws separately for couples belonging to different religious beliefs. Mutual consent divorce procedure is relatively easier and fast while contested divorce procedure takes longer and depends on the religions of the couples.

Taiwan

Taiwan's divorce rate in 2020 stood at 2.19 divorces per 1,000 residents. This is the lowest recorded divorce rate in the past 10 years. Many divorces in Taiwan are not done in court if there is a mutual agreement. If one of the parties does not consent to the divorce, then the other spouse may file for divorce under a valid reason of bigamy, infidelity, ill treatment or desertion. Before 2020, adultery in Taiwan was considered a crime and punishable by law.

China

China currently holds one of the highest divorce rates in the Asia Pacific region. Compared to 2000, China's divorce rates have gone up substantially from a 0.96 crude divorce rate to 3.09 rate in 2020. While China's divorce rate has been increasing since 2000, the highest recorded crude divorce rate in the past 20 years was in 2019 with 3.36 divorces. However, since 2019, China's recorded divorce rate has gone down.

China has no-fault divorce which was implemented through the New Marriage Law in 1950. This allows individuals to divorce without showing any evidence of wrongdoing. China is one of the only Asian countries which permits no-fault divorce.

South Korea

The crude divorce rate in South Korea in 2020 was 2.1. Compared to prior years, the number of divorces recorded depicts that there are less filed divorces each year. Both the number of marriages and divorces decreased from 2019 by 10.7% and 3.9% respectively.

The highest proportion of divorces in 2020 was amongst those who have been married for 20 years or more followed by those who have been married for four years or less. Such findings may suggest that divorce has become more socially accepted in South Korea and the stigma behind separating has lessened.

Singapore

Singapore has a crude divorce rate of 1.7 divorce per 1,000 residents. Singapore has seen a decrease in divorce rates compared to previous years. In fact, 2020 marks the lowest number of divorces recorded. In 2020, there were 6,700 divorces compared to 2015 - 2019 which recorded an average number of 7,536 marital dissolutions. Additionally, most divorces were initiated by women.

Singapore requires you to be married for three years before filing for divorce. That being said, if one has suffered exceptional hardship, they are eligible to file for divorce before the three years. Additionally, to get a divorce, there must be proof of an "irretrievable breakdown" of one of the four factors which include adultery, unreasonable behaviour, desertion and separation.

Indonesia

In 2020 there were around 291,000 divorces recorded in Indonesia. These numbers are lower than the previous year - reportedly due to the pandemic and a longer process of the dissolution process. Divorces are settled in religious courts, if they are Muslim, or through 'talaq' where a married man can pronounce divorce to his wife. There are six grounds of divorce, with an additional two for Moslem marriages, which include:

1. One of the spouse has committed adultery, is an alcoholic, is addicted to drugs, is a gambler or other vices which are difficult to cure;
2. One of the spouse has deserted the other spouse for two consecutive years – without consent and without legitimate reasons;
3. One of the spouse has been sentenced to imprisonment for five years or more;
4. One of the spouses has resorted to cruelty or severe ill-treatment, endangering the life of the other spouse;
5. One of the spouse has developed a disability or disease, preventing from him or her from fulfilling the duties of husband or wife;
6. The spouses have irreconcilable differences as evidenced by frequent disagreements.
7. The husband has violated taklik talak (a promise that the husband expressly made and written onto the marriage certificate).
8. One party convert from Islam into another faith.

EUROPE

Divorce has increased across Europe in the past decade - the rate varies between European countries. One study estimated that legal reforms accounted for about 20% increase of the divorce rates in Europe between 1960 and 2002. In 2019, Luxembourg had the highest divorce rate per 100 marriages followed by Portugal, Finland, and Spain. Countries in Europe with some of the lowest number of divorces per 100 marriages are Ireland and Malta.

Serbia

On average, for every three new marriages in Serbia, one divorce occurs. In 2019, 35,570 marriages were concluded in Serbia, 10,899 marriages were divorced, and the number of divorces per 1,000 inhabitants was 1.6%.

United Kingdom

In 2015, the highest divorces rates in the UK were recorded all beside the sea, with Blackpool in the top position. The UK divorce rate is estimated at 42% and in 2019, around 107,599 divorces were reported. The highest number of divorce applications are reportedly made on Divorce Day, which is always the first Monday of the new year.

North America

United States

The crude divorce rate in 2022 in the United States is 2.3 divorces. This is significantly lower than prior years, such as those in 2001 where 4.1 divorces were recorded. These recent findings suggest a downward trend of the number of people dissolving their marriage. However, divorce rates range from state to state. It's important to look back on why prior years had such a high divorce rate amongst Americans.

The National Center for Health Statistics reports that wives, with children present, filed for divorce in approximately two-thirds of cases from 1975 to 1988 in the U.S. For example, 71.4% of the cases were filed by women in 1975 and 65% were filed by women in 1988. It is estimated that upwards of 95% of divorces in the U.S. are "uncontested", because the two parties are able to come to an agreement without a hearing (either with or without lawyers/mediators/collaborative counsel) about the property, children, and support issues.

In 2000, the divorce rate reached its peak at 40% but has since slowly declined. In 2001, marriages between people of different faiths were three times more likely to get divorced than those of the same faith. In fact, in a 1993 study, members of two mainline Protestant religions had a 20% chance of being divorced in 5 years; a 33% for a Catholic and Evangelical, and a 40% chance for a Jew and a Christian.

Couples with different ethnicities and races also had distinctive divorce statistics. In 2008, a study by Jenifer L. Bratter and Rosalind B. King on the Education Resources Information Center, found that unions between White males and non-White females as well as between Hispanics and non-Hispanic individuals, have similar or lower risks of divorce than White marriages. Unions between a White male and Black female last longer than White-White pairings or White-Asian pairings. Conversely, a White female with a Black male and White female with an Asian male are more prone to divorce than White-White pairings.

Additionally, as found in 2010, success in marriage has been associated with a higher education and older age. For example, 81% of college graduates who were over 26 years old, who wed in the 1980s, were still married 20 years later. Additionally, 65% of college graduates under 26, who married in the 1980s, were still married 20 years later. Furthermore, 49% of high school graduates under 26 years old, who married in the 1980s, were still married 20 years later. Conversely, 2.9% of adults aged 35–39 and without a college degree got divorced in the year 2009 - compared with 1.6% with a college education.

Another study looking at population differences found that a 1% increase in the unemployment rate correlated with a 1% decrease in the divorce rate. This was found to be presumably true for individuals who were financially challenged when trying to afford the legal proceedings. Nevertheless, another study from 1900 to 2008 found that there was a significant increase in the risk of divorce following a layoff and being unemployed.

Oceania

Australia

The crude divorce rate in Australia in 2020 was 1.9 divorces. This rate has remained somewhat consistent throughout the past few years and is the same as the previous year. However, as divorces are granted after 12 months of separation, splits during COVID may not be reflected in the current divorce rate. The divorce rate has decreased substantially over the past 20 years with 2.6 divorces recorded in 2000. In order to apply for divorce, one must be separated for at least 12 months.

New Zealand

New Zealand's divorce rate in 2020 was 7.6 divorces per 1,000 residents. This rate marks a decrease from previous years - such as those in 1983 with a crude divorce rate of 13.3. In fact, this rate has decreased significantly from the previous year, 2019, with a divorce rate of 8.4. Before filing for divorced, one must be separated for at least two years. After this time, one is eligible to submit an application. If it is a joint application, divorce will take effect after one month. If one applies as a sole application, then the other spouse has the opportunity to defend it within a certain time period. Additionally, if individuals appear in court together and the judge files the divorce order, then the divorce will effective immediately.

Social attitudes

Attitudes toward divorce vary substantially across the world. Divorce is considered socially unacceptable by most of the population in certain Sub-Saharan African countries such as Ghana, Uganda, Nigeria and Kenya, South Asian countries like India and Pakistan and South-East Asian countries such as the Philippines and Indonesia.

The majority of the population considers divorce acceptable in Eastern Europe, East Asia, Latin America and the United States. In developed regions such as Western Europe and Japan, more than 80% of the population consider divorce socially acceptable. Divorce is also widely accepted in certain Muslim majority countries such as Jordan, Egypt and Lebanon, at least when men initiate it.

In same-sex married couples (United States)

All U.S. states permit same-sex marriage. For same-sex couples in the United States, divorce law is in its infancy.

Rights of spouses to custody of children

Upon dissolution of a same-sex marriage, legal questions remain as to the rights of spouses to custody of the biological children of their spouses. Unresolved legal questions abound in this area.

Child custody policies include several guidelines that determine with whom the child lives following divorce, how time is divided in joint custody situations, and visitation rights. The most frequently applied custody guideline is the best interests of the child standard, which takes into account the parents' preferences, the child's preferences, the interactions between parents and children, children's adjustment, and all family members' mental and physical health.

HISTORY

Greco-Roman culture

The ancient Athenians liberally allowed divorce, but the person requesting divorce had to submit the request to a magistrate, and the magistrate could determine whether the reasons given were sufficient.

Divorce was rare in early Roman culture but as their empire grew in power and authority Roman civil law embraced the maxim, "matrimonia debent esse libera" ("marriages ought to be free"), and either husband or wife could renounce the marriage at will. The Christian emperors Constantine and Theodosius restricted the grounds for divorce to grave cause, but this was relaxed by Justinian in the 6th century.

Mali Empire

In post-classical Mali, laws relating to divorced women were documented in the Timbuktu manuscripts.

MEDIEVAL EUROPE

After the fall of the Roman Empire, familial life was regulated more by ecclesiastical authority than civil authority. The Catholic and Orthodox Church had, among others, a differing view of divorce.

The Orthodox Church recognized that there are rare occasions when it is better that couples do separate. For the Orthodox, to say that marriage is indissoluble means that it should not be broken, the violation of such a union, perceived as holy, being an offense resulting from either adultery or the prolonged absence of one of the partners. Thus, permitting remarriage is an act of compassion of the Church towards sinful man.

Under the influence of the Catholic Church, the divorce rate had been greatly reduced by the 9th or 10th century, which considered marriage a sacrament instituted by Jesus Christ and indissoluble by mere human action.

Although divorce, as known today, was generally prohibited in Catholic lands after the 10th century, separation of husband and wife and the annulment of marriage were well-known. What is today referred to as "separate maintenance" (or "legal separation") was termed "divorce a mensa et thoro" ("divorce from bed-and-board"). The husband and wife physically separated and were forbidden to live or cohabit together, but their marital relationship did not fully terminate. Civil courts had no power over marriage or divorce. The grounds for annulment were determined by a Catholic church authority and applied in ecclesiastical courts. Annulment was for canonical causes of impediment existing at the time of the marriage. "For in cases of total divorce, the marriage is declared null, as having been absolutely unlawful ab initio." The Catholic Church held that the sacrament of marriage produced one person from two, inseparable from each other: "By marriage, the husband and wife are one person in law: that is, the very being of legal existence of the woman is suspended during the marriage or at least incorporated and consolidated into that of the husband: under whose wing, protection and cover, she performs everything." Since husband and wife became one person upon marriage, recognition of that oneness could be rescinded only on the grounds that the unity never existed to begin with, i.e., that the proclamation of marriage was erroneous and void from the start.

Secularisation in Europe

After the Reformation, marriage came to be considered a contract in the newly Protestant regions of Europe, and on that basis, civil authorities gradually asserted their power to decree a "divortium a vinculo matrimonii", or "divorce from all the bonds of marriage".

Since no precedents existed defining the circumstances under which marriage could be dissolved, civil courts heavily relied on the previous determinations of the ecclesiastic courts and freely adopted the requirements set down by those courts. As the civil courts assumed the power to dissolve marriages, courts still strictly construed the circumstances under which they would grant a divorce, and considered divorce to be contrary to public policy. Because divorce was considered to be against the public interest, civil courts refused to grant a divorce if evidence revealed any hint of complicity between the husband and wife to divorce, or if they attempted to manufacture grounds for a divorce. Divorce was granted only because one party to the marriage had violated a sacred vow to the "innocent spouse". If both husband and wife were guilty, "neither would be allowed to escape the bonds of marriage".

Eventually, the idea that a marriage could be dissolved in cases in which one of the parties violated the sacred vow gradually allowed expansion of the grounds upon which divorce could be granted from those grounds which existed at the time of the marriage to grounds which occurred after the marriage, but which exemplified violation of that vow, such as abandonment, adultery, or "extreme cruelty". An exception to this trend was the Anglican Church, which maintained the doctrine of marital indissolubility.

During the English Civil War, the Puritans briefly passed a law that divested marriage of all sacrament, leaving it as a secular contract that could be broken. John Milton wrote four divorce tracts in 1643–1645 that argued for the legitimacy of divorce on grounds of spousal incompatibility. His ideas were ahead of their time; arguing for divorce at all, let alone a version of no-fault divorce, was extremely controversial and religious figures sought to ban his tracts. In 1670 a precedent was first set with an Act of Parliament allowing Lord John Manners to divorce his wife, Lady Anne Pierrepont, and until the passage of the Matrimonial Causes Act 1857, divorce could only be obtained through a specific Act of Parliament.

The move towards secularisation and liberalisation was reinforced by the individualistic and secular ideals of the Enlightenment. The Enlightened absolutist, King Frederick II ("the Great") of Prussia decreed a new divorce law in 1752, in which marriage was declared to be a purely private concern, allowing divorce to be granted on the basis of mutual consent. This new attitude heavily influenced the law in neighbouring Austria under Emperor Joseph II, where it was applied to all non-Catholic Imperial subjects. Divorce was legalised in France after the French revolution on a similar basis, although the legal order of the ancien regime was reinstated at the Bourbon restoration of 1816. The trend in Europe throughout the 19th century, was one of increased liberalisation; by the mid-19th century, divorce was generally granted by civil courts in the case of adultery.

In Britain, before 1857 wives were regarded as under the economic and legal protection of their husbands, and divorce was almost impossible. It required a very expensive private Act of Parliament costing perhaps £200, of the sort only the richest could possibly afford. It was very difficult to secure divorce on the grounds of adultery, desertion, or cruelty. The first key legislative victory came with the Matrimonial Causes Act 1857, which passed over the strenuous opposition of the highly traditional Church of England. The new law made divorce a civil affair of the courts, rather than a Church matter, with a new civil court in London handling all cases. The process was still quite expensive, at about £40, but now became feasible for the middle class. A woman who obtained a judicial separation took the status of a feme sole, with full control of her own civil rights. Additional amendments came in 1878, which allowed for separations handled by local justices of the peace. The Church of England blocked further reforms until the final breakthrough came with the Matrimonial Causes Act 1973.

In Spain, the 1931 Constitution of the Second Spanish Republic for the first time recognised a right to divorce. The first law to regulate divorce was the Divorce Act of 1932, which passed the Republican Parliament despite the opposition of the Catholic Church and a coalition of the Agrarian Minority and Minority Basque-Navarre Catholic parties. The dictatorship of General Franco abolished the law. After the restoration of democracy, a new divorce law was passed in 1981, again over the opposition of the Catholic Church and part of the Christian Democrat party, then a part of the ruling Union of Democratic Center. During the first socialist government of Felipe González Márquez, the 1981 law was amended to expedite the process of separation and divorce of marriages, which was again opposed by the Church, which called it "express divorce".

In Italy, the first divorce law was introduced on 1 December 1970, despite the opposition of the Christian Democrats, and entered into force on 18 December 1970. In the following years, the Christian Democrats, supported also by parties opposed to the law, promoted a recall referendum. In 1974, in a referendum, the majority of the population voted against a repeal of the divorce law. A feature of the 1970 divorce law was the long period of marital separation of five years required. This period was reduced to three in 1987 and to a year in 2015, in the case of judicial separation, and six months in the case of separation by mutual agreement.

Divorce rates increased markedly during the 20th century in developed countries, as social attitudes towards family and sex changed dramatically. Divorce has become commonplace in some countries, including the United States, Canada, Australia, Germany, New Zealand, Scandinavia, and the United Kingdom.

Japan

In the Edo Period (1603–1868), husbands could divorce their wives by writing letters of divorce. Frequently, their relatives or marriage arrangers kept these letters and tried to restore the marriages. Wives could not divorce their husbands. Some wives were able to gain sanctuary in certain Shinto "divorce temples". After a wife had spent three years in a temple, her husband was required to divorce her. In 19th century Japan, at least one in eight marriages ended in divorce.

There are four types of divorce in Japan: divorce by agreement in which the divorce is mutual; divorce by mediation, which happens in family court; divorce by decision of family court that takes place when a couple cannot complete a divorce through mediation; and divorce by judgment of a district court.

India

On a national level, the Special Marriage Act, passed in 1954, is an inter-religious marriage law permitting Indian nationals to marry and divorce irrespective of their religion or faith. The Hindu Marriage Act, in 1955 which legally permitted divorce to Hindus and other communities who chose to marry under these acts. The Indian Divorce Act 1869 is the law relating to the divorce of person professing the Christian religion. Divorce can be sought by a husband or wife on grounds including adultery, cruelty, desertion for two years, religious conversion, mental abnormality, venereal disease, and leprosy.

Divorce is also available based on mutual consent of both the spouses, which can be filed after at least one year of separated living. Mutual consent divorce can not be appealed, and the law mandates a minimum period of six months (from the time divorce is applied for) for divorce to be granted. Contested divorce is when one of the spouse is not willing to divorce the other spouse, under such condition the divorce is granted only on certain grounds according to the Hindu marriage act of 1955. While a Muslim husband can unilaterally bring an end to the marriage by pronouncing talaq, Muslim women must go to court, claiming any of the grounds provided under the Dissolution of Muslim Marriage Act.

In the first major family law reform in the last decade, the Supreme Court of India banned the Islamic practice of "Triple Talaq" (divorce by uttering of the "Talaq" word thrice by the husband). The landmark Supreme Court of India judgment was welcomed by women activists across India.

Official figures of divorce rates are not available, but it has been estimated that 1 in 100 or another figure of 11 in 1,000 marriages in India end up in divorce.

Various communities are governed by specific marital legislation, distinct to Hindu Marriage Act, and consequently have their own divorce laws:

- The Parsi Marriage and Divorce Act, 1936
- The Dissolution of Muslim Marriage act, 1939
- The Foreign Marriage Act, 1969
- The Muslim Women (Protection of Rights on Divorce) Act, 1986

An amendment to the marriage laws to allow divorce based on "irretrievable breakdown of marriage" (as alleged by one of the spouses) is under consideration in India. In June 2010, the Union Cabinet of India approved the Marriage Laws (Amendment) Bill 2010, which, if cleared by Parliament, would establish "irretrievable breakdown" as a new ground for divorce. Under the proposed amendment, the court before proceeding to the merits of the case must be satisfied by the evidences produced that parties have been living apart for a continuous period of not less than three years immediately preceding the presentation of the petition.

ISLAMIC LAW

Divorce in Islam can take a variety of forms, some initiated by the husband and some initiated by the wife. The main traditional legal categories are talaq (repudiation), khul (mutual divorce/annulment), judicial divorce and oaths. The theory and practice of divorce in the Islamic world have varied according to time and place. Historically, the rules of divorce were governed by sharia, as interpreted by traditional Islamic jurisprudence, and they differed depending on the legal school. Historical practice sometimes diverged from legal theory. In modern times, as personal status (family) laws were codified, they generally remained "within the orbit of Islamic law", but control over the norms of divorce shifted from traditional jurists to the state.

Philippines

Divorce as a means of terminating marriage is illegal for all Filipinos except Filipino Muslims. There is only civil annulment after a lengthy legal separation. The process is costly and long, and there are many legally married couples in extramarital relations, even without a divorce law.

Code of Muslim Personal Laws of the Philippines, known as Presidential Decree (PD) No. 1083, Title II- Marriage and Divorce, Chapter 3-Divorce allows for divorce recognized by the state. There are two sharia courts in the Philippine judicial system that hear these cases.

On July 27, 2010, Gabriela Women's Party filed in Congress House Bill No 1799, or the Divorce Bill of the Philippines, as one of many attempts to introduce pro-divorce legislation. Senator Pia Cayetano has filed a separate divorce bill in the Senate. During that time, the Philippines, along with Malta and the Vatican, are the three most conservative countries on the issue of divorce. The bill did not pass any level of legislation because of this.

In 2013, the divorce bill was refiled, however, did not pass any level of legislation as well.

In a latest attempt, the divorce bill was refiled again in 2017. On February 22, 2018, the House of Representatives committee on population and family relations approved a bill seeking to legalize divorce, the first time in Philippine history for such a measure to pass the committee level of legislation. The majority of the members of the House of Representatives (lower house of Congress), both majority and minority blocs, are in favor of divorce, however, divorce continues to be a divisive issue in the Senate (upper house of Congress), as stark opposition is present among male senators.

Religion and divorce

In some countries (commonly in Europe and North America), the government defines and administers marriages and divorces. While ceremonies may be performed by religious officials on behalf of the state, a civil marriage and thus, civil divorce (without the involvement of a religion) is also possible. Due to differing standards and procedures, a couple can be legally unmarried, married, or divorced by the state's definition, but have a different status as defined by a religious order. Other countries use religious law to administer marriages and divorces, eliminating this distinction. In these cases, religious officials are generally responsible for interpretation and implementation.

Islam allows, yet generally advises against divorce, and it can be initiated by either the husband or the wife.

Dharmic religions allow divorce under some circumstances.

Christian views on divorce vary: Catholic teaching allows only annulment, while most other denominations discourage it except in the event of adultery. For example, the Allegheny Wesleyan Methodist Connection, in its 2014 Discipline, teaches:

We believe that the only legitimate marriage is the joining of one man and one woman (Gen. 2:24; Rom. 7:2; 1 Cor. 7:10; Eph. 5:22, 23). We deplore the evils of divorce and remarriage. We regard adultery as the only scripturally justifiable grounds for divorce; and the party guilty of adultery has by his or her act forfeited membership in the church. In the case of divorce for other cause, neither party shall be permitted to marry again during the lifetime of the other; and violation of this law shall be punished by expulsion from the church (Matt. 5:32; Mark 10:11, 12). In the carrying out of these principles, guilt shall be established in accordance with judicial procedures set forth in The Discipline.

Jewish views of divorce differ, with Reform Judaism considering civil divorces adequate; Conservative and Orthodox Judaism, on the other hand, require that the husband grant his wife a divorce in the form of a get.

The Millet System, where each religious group regulates its own marriages and divorces, is still present in varying degrees in some post–Ottoman countries like Iraq, Syria, Jordan, Lebanon, Israel, the Palestinian Authority, Egypt, and Greece. Several countries use sharia (Islamic law) to administrate marriages and divorces for Muslims. Thus, Marriage in Israel is administered separately by each religious community (Jews, Christians, Muslims, and Druze), and there is no provision for interfaith marriages other than marrying in another country. For Jews, marriage and divorce are administered by Orthodox rabbis. Partners can file for divorce either in rabbinical court or Israeli civil court.

Gender and divorce

According to a study published in the American Law and Economics Review, women have filed slightly more than two-thirds of divorce cases in the United States. This trend is mirrored in the UK where a recent study into web search behavior found that 70% of divorce inquiries were from women. These findings also correlate with the Office for

National Statistics publication "Divorces in England and Wales 2012 which reported that divorce petitions from women outnumber those from men by 2 to 1.

Regarding divorce settlements, according to the 2004 Grant Thornton survey in the UK, women obtained a better or considerably better settlement than men in 60% of cases. In 30% of cases the assets were split 50–50, and in only 10% of cases did men achieve better settlements (down from 24% the previous year). The report concluded that the percentage of shared residence orders would need to increase in order for more equitable financial divisions to become the norm.

Some jurisdictions give unequal rights to men and women when filing for divorce.

For couples to Conservative or Orthodox Jewish law (which by Israeli civil law includes all Jews in Israel), the husband must grant his wife a divorce through a document called a get. Granting the 'get' obligates him to pay the woman a significant sum of money(10,000-$20,000) as stated on the religious prenuptial contract, which can be in addition to whatever prior settlement he had reached as far as continuous child support and funds he had to pay by court order in the civil divorce. If the man refuses, (and agreeing on condition he will not have to pay the money is still called refusing), the woman can appeal to a court or the community to pressure the husband. A woman whose husband refuses to grant the get or a woman whose husband is missing without sufficient knowledge that he died, is called an agunah, is still married, and therefore cannot remarry. Under Orthodox law, children of an extramarital affair involving a married Jewish woman are considered mamzerim and cannot marry non-mamzerim.

3

MARRIAGE AND DIVORCE LAWS IN THE UNITED STATES

Marriage in the United States is a legal, social, and religious institution. The marriage age in the United States is set by each state and territory, either by statute or the common law applies. An individual can marry in the United States as of right, without parental consent or other authorisation, on reaching 18 years of age in all states except in Nebraska, where the general marriage age is 19, and Mississippi where the general marriage age is 21. In Puerto Rico the general marriage age is also 21. In all these jurisdictions, these are also the ages of majority. In Alabama, however, the age of majority is 19, while the general marriage age is 18. Most states also set a lower age at which underage persons are able to marry with parental and/or judicial consent. Marriages where one partner is less than 18 years of age are commonly referred to as child or underage marriages.

Marriage laws have changed considerably in the United States over time, including the removal of bans on interracial marriage and same-sex marriage. In 2009, there were 2,077,000 marriages, according to the U.S. Census Bureau. The median age for the first marriage has increased in recent years. The median age in the early 1970s was 23 for men and 21 for women; and it rose to 28 for men and 26 for women by 2009 and by 2017, it was 29.5 for men and 27.4 for women.

Marriages vary considerably in terms of religion, socioeconomic status, age, commitment, and so forth. Reasons for marrying may include a desire to have children, love, or economic security. Marriage has been in some instances used for the sole purpose of gaining a green card and/or facilitating full citizenship; the Immigration Marriage Fraud Amendments of 1986 are among laws that can be used to set aside sham marriages, and a marriage visa can be obtained in advance of entry of the non-national where there is a long-term, committed relationship demonstrable. In 2003, 184,741 immigrants were admitted as spouses of US citizens.

Marriages can be terminated by annulment, divorce or death of a spouse. Divorce (known as dissolution of marriage in some states) laws vary by state, and address issues such as how the two spouses bifurcate their property, how children will be cared for, and support obligations of one spouse toward the other. Since the late 1960s, divorce has become more prevalent. In 2005, it was estimated that 20% of marriages would end in divorce within five years. Divorce rates in 2005 were four times the divorce rates in 1955, and a quarter of children less than 16 years old are raised by a stepparent. Marriages that end in divorce last for a median of 8 years for both men and women.

As a rough rule, marriage has more legal ramifications than other types of bonds between consenting adults. A civil union is "a formal union between two people of the same or of different genders which results in, but falls short of, marriage-like rights and obligations," according to one view. Domestic partnerships are a version of civil unions. Registration and recognition are functions of states, localities, or employers; such unions may be available to couples of the same sex and, sometimes, opposite sex. Cohabitation to a certain extent is an expectation of marriage, in which context it means living together, a term also applied to when two unmarried people live together and have an intimate or loving relationship.

INTERJURISDICTIONAL RECOGNITION

All U.S. jurisdictions recognize all validly contracted out-of-state marriages under their laws of comity and choice of law/conflict of laws rules - including marriages that cannot be legally contracted domestically. Likewise, an invalidly contracted out-of-state marriage will not be valid domestically, even if it could have been validly contracted domestically. For example, California allows first cousins to marry but Nevada does not. If two first cousins attempt to marry in Nevada, that marriage will not be valid in either Nevada or California, notwithstanding it could be legally contracted in California. But if they attempt to marry in California, their attempt will be successful and the marriage will be valid in both California and Nevada, notwithstanding the marriage could not be legally contracted in Nevada. This may lead to jurisdiction shopping.

History of Marriage in US

The marriage between Luisa de Abrego, a free black domestic servant from Seville and Miguel Rodríguez, a white Segovian conquistador in 1565 in St. Augustine (Spanish Florida), is the first known and recorded Christian marriage anywhere in what is now the continental United States.

When the country was founded in the 1770s, marriage between whites and non-whites was in many states forbidden due to the racist attitudes of the time. Nine states, including the most recent two, never passed any law clearly forbidding such a marriage. In 1948, the California Supreme Court became the first state high court to declare the state's ban on interracial marriage unconstitutional. In 1967, the U.S. Supreme Court unanimously rendered unenforceable remaining interracial marriage laws – these had been applicable in sixteen states forming the south-east of the United States – in Loving v. Virginia. It struck down the law directly in that state. In 2000, Alabama became the last state to adapt its laws to the Supreme Court's decision, when 60% of voters endorsed a ballot initiative that removed anti-miscegenation language from the state constitution.

Expectations of a marriage partner have changed over time. Second U.S. President John Adams wrote in his diary that the ideal spouse was willing to "palliate faults and mistakes, to put the best construction upon words and actions, and to forgive injuries." A 1940 paper by a sociology professor at the University of Pennsylvania reported that male students resisted the idea of marrying a girl who they suspected had sex with another man. The sexual revolution in 1960s United States altered this norm for many.

Over the last 50 years, Americans increasingly choose not to marry. The proportion of Americans age 25–50 who had never married rose from 9% in 1970 to 35% in 2018. They also increasingly find themselves in a household without a partner: the proportion of Americans age 25–54 who were not currently living with a partner (whether married or unmarried) rose from 29% in 1990 to 38% in 2019.

DEMOGRAPHICS

Marital status by age group in 2004

In 2004 the U.S. Census Bureau measured the marital status of U.S. residents, showing several trends. While about 96% of residents in their 70s and 80s were married at least once, many were widowed due to the death of their spouses. In addition, a large portion of middle-aged Americans are either divorced, legally separated, or informally separated. Of those who were "separated or divorced," approximately 74% were legally divorced, 15% were "separated," and 11% were listed as having an "absent spouse."

Marital status in the U.S. in the year 2000

The four maps on the right shows the pattern of married, widowed, separated, and divorced households in the United States in the year 2000. The map on the bottom left shows that the west coast had the highest percentages of households to go through divorce. According to the map bottom right of the census chart the south east coast and New Orleans had the highest percentage of separated houses in the U.S. The northeast had the highest percentages of marriages. The highest percentages of widowed households was in the Midwest.

Trends and census data of 2006–2010

As of 2006, 55.7% of Americans age 18 and over were married. According to the 2008–2010 American Community Survey 3-Year Estimates, 51.5% of males and 47.7% of females over the age of 15 were married. The separation rate was 1.8% for males and 2.5% for females.

African Americans have married the least of all of the predominant ethnic groups in the U.S. with a 29.9% marriage rate, but have the highest separation rate which is 4.5%. Native Americans have the second lowest marriage rate with 37.9%. Hispanics have a 45.1% marriage rate, with a 3.5% separation rate.

In the United States, the two ethnic groups with the highest marriage rates included Asians with 58.5% and Whites with 52.9%. Asians have the lowest rate of divorce among the main groups with 1.8%. Whites, African Americans, and Native Americans have the highest rates of being widowed ranging from 5%–6.5%. They also have the highest rates of divorce among the three, ranging from 11%–13% with Native Americans having the highest divorce rate.

The median age for Americans' first marriage has risen in recent years, with the median age at first marriage in the early 1970s being 21 for women and 23 for men, and in 2009, it had risen to 26 for women and 28 for men.

In 2009, 2,077,000 marriages occurred in the United States. From that point on, though, a Pew study found that the number of new marriages declined 5% in just one year (that is, from 2009 to 2010).

According to the 2010 U.S. Census Bureau, the average family income is higher than previous years at $62,770. The percentage of family households below the poverty line in 2011 was 15.1%, higher than in 2000 when it was 11.3%. According to a report in 2013, the percentage of heterosexual couples who marry has fallen dramatically, but couples who marry are more likely to have college degrees and higher income than those who do not marry. Some sociologists suggest that marriage in twenty-first century America has become a luxury good.

SOCIOLOGY OF MARRIAGE

Types of marriage

Monogamy is when one person marries one other person and is the most common and accepted form of marriage in the United States. Serial monogamy is when individuals are permitted to marry again, often on the death of the first spouse or after divorce; they cannot have more than one spouse at one time because that would be polygamy which in countries with marital monogamy like the US is called bigamy. Polygamy is a form of marriage in which someone marries multiple people at a given time, and is illegal throughout the U.S. under the Edmunds Act. Part of the function of looking at marriage from a sociological perspective is to give insight into the reasons behind various marital arrangements.

Reasons for marriage

There are several reasons that Americans marry. The desire to have children is one; having a family is a high priority among many Americans. People also desire love, companionship, commitment, continuity, and permanence. There are some reasons for marriage that are ephemeral. These reasons include social legitimacy, social pressure, the desire for a high social status, economic security, rebellion or revenge, or validation of an unplanned pregnancy.

LAW

Marriage laws are established by individual states. There are two methods of receiving state recognition of a marriage: common-law marriage and obtaining a marriage license. Common-law marriage is no longer permitted in most states. Though federal law does not regulate state marriage law, it does provide for rights and responsibilities of married couples that differ from those of unmarried couples. Reports published by the General Accounting Office in 1997 and 2004 identified over 1000 such laws.

Marriage as a fundamental right

The United States Supreme Court has in at least 15 cases since 1888 ruled that marriage is a fundamental right. These cases are:

1. Maynard v. Hill, 125 U.S. 190 (1888) Marriage is "the most important relation in life" and "the foundation of the family and society, without which there would be neither civilization nor progress."
2. Meyer v. Nebraska, 262 U.S. 390 (1923) The right "to marry, establish a home and bring up children" is a central part of liberty protected by the Due Process Clause.
3. Skinner v. Oklahoma ex rel. Williamson, 316 U.S. 535 (1942) Marriage is "one of the basic civil rights of man" and "fundamental to the very existence and survival of the race."
4. Griswold v. Connecticut, 381 U.S. 479 (1965) "We deal with a right of privacy older than the Bill of Rights—older than our political parties, older than our school system. Marriage is a coming together for better or for worse, hopefully enduring, and intimate to the degree of being sacred. It is an association that promotes a way of life, not causes; a harmony in living, not political faiths; a bilateral loyalty, not commercial or social projects. Yet it is an association for as noble a purpose as any involved in our prior decisions."
5. Loving v. Virginia, 388 U.S. 1 (1967) "The freedom to marry has long been recognized as one of the vital personal rights essential to the orderly pursuit of happiness by free men."
6. Boddie v. Connecticut, 401 U.S. 371 (1971) "[M]arriage involves interests of basic importance to our society" and is "a fundamental human relationship."
7. Cleveland Board of Education v. LaFleur, 414 U.S. 632 (1974) "This Court has long recognized that freedom of personal choice in matters of marriage and family

life is one of the liberties protected by the Due Process Clause of the Fourteenth Amendment."

8. Moore v. City of East Cleveland, 431 U.S. 494 (1977) "[W]hen the government intrudes on choices concerning family living arrangements, this Court must examine carefully the importance of the governmental interests advanced and the extent to which they are served by the challenged regulation."
9. Carey v. Population Services International, 431 U.S. 678 (1977) "[I]t is clear that among the decisions that an individual may make without unjustified government interference are personal decisions relating to marriage, procreation, contraception, family relationships, and child rearing and education."
10. Zablocki v. Redhail, 434 U.S. 374 (1978) "[T]he right to marry is of fundamental importance for all individuals."
11. Turner v. Safley, 482 U.S. 78 (1987) "[T]he decision to marry is a fundamental right" and an "expression[ ] of emotional support and public commitment."
12. Planned Parenthood of Southeastern Pennsylvania v. Casey, 505 U.S. 833 (1992) "Our law affords constitutional protection to personal decisions relating to marriage, procreation, contraception, family relationships, child rearing, and education. [...] These matters, involving the most intimate and personal choices a person may make in a lifetime, choices central to personal dignity and autonomy, are central to the liberty protected by the Fourteenth Amendment. At the heart of liberty is the right to define one's own concept of existence, of meaning, of the universe, and of the mystery of human life."
13. M.L.B. v. S.L.J., 519 U.S. 102 (1996) "Choices about marriage, family life, and the upbringing of children are among associational rights this Court has ranked as 'of basic importance in our society,' rights sheltered by the Fourteenth Amendment against the State's unwarranted usurpation, disregard, or disrespect."
14. Lawrence v. Texas, 539 U.S. 558 (2003) "[O]ur laws and tradition afford constitutional protection to personal decisions relating to marriage, procreation, contraception, family relationships, and education. ... Persons in a homosexual relationship may seek autonomy for these purposes, just as heterosexual persons do."
15. Obergefell v. Hodges, 576 U.S. ___ (2015) "[T]he right to marry is a fundamental right inherent in the liberty of the person, and under the Due Process and Equal Protection Clauses of the Fourteenth Amendment couples of the same-sex may not be deprived of that right and that liberty."

Age of marriage

The age at which a person can marry varies by state. The marriage age is generally 18 years, with the exception of Nebraska (19) and Mississippi (21). In addition, all states, except Delaware, allow minors to marry in certain circumstances, such as parental consent, judicial consent, pregnancy, or a combination of these situations. Most states allow minors aged 16 and 17 to marry with parental consent alone. 30 states have set an absolute minimum age by statute, which varies between 13 and 18, while in 20 states there is no statutory minimum age if other legal conditions are met. In states with no set minimum age, the traditional common law minimum age is 14 for boys and 12 for girls – ages which have been confirmed by case law in some states. Over the past 15 years, more than 200,000 minors married in the US, and in Tennessee a 10-year-old girl was married in 2001, before the state finally set a minimum age of 17 in 2018.

RESTRICTIONS AND EXPANSIONS OF MARRIAGE

Marriage has been restricted over the course of the history of the United States according race, sexual orientation, number of parties entering into the marriage, and familial relationships.

Common-law marriage

Eight states and the District of Columbia recognize common-law marriages. Once they meet the requirements of the respective state, couples in those recognized common-law marriages are considered legally married for all purposes and in all circumstances. Common-law marriage can be contracted in Colorado, Iowa, Kansas, Montana, Rhode Island, South Carolina, Texas, Utah, and the District of Columbia. Common-law marriage may also be valid under military law for purposes of a bigamy prosecution under the Uniform Code of Military Justice.

All U.S. jurisdictions recognize common-law marriages that were validly contracted in the originating jurisdiction, because they are valid marriages in the jurisdiction where they were contracted, because of the Full Faith and Credit Clause. However, absent legal registration or similar notice of the marriage, the parties to a common law marriage or their eventual heirs may have difficulty proving their relationship to be marriage. Some states provide for registration of an informal or common-law marriage based on the declaration of each of the spouses on a state-issued form.

Marriage law and race

Anti-miscegenation laws which prohibited interracial marriage date back to Colonial America. The earliest were established in Maryland and Virginia in the 1660s. After independence, seven of the original colonies and many new states, particularly those in the West and the South, also implemented anti-miscegenation laws. Despite a number of repeals in the 19th century, in 1948, 30 out of 48 states enforced prohibitions against interracial marriage. A number of these laws were repealed between 1948 and 1967. In 1948, the California Supreme Court ruled the Californian anti-miscegenation statute unconstitutional in Perez v. Sharp. Many other states repealed their laws in the following decade, with the exception of states in the South. In 1967, the U.S. Supreme Court declared all anti-miscegenation laws unconstitutional in Loving v. Virginia.

As at September 9, 2019, eight states required couples to declare their racial background when applying for a marriage license, without which they cannot marry. The states are Connecticut, Delaware, Kentucky, Louisiana, Minnesota, Virginia, New Hampshire and Alabama. As at September 9, 2019, the Virginia law was being challenged in court.

Marriage law and sexual orientation

For much of the United States's history, marriage was restricted to heterosexual couples. Marriage licenses were issued to gay male couples Michael McConnell and Jack Baker in 1970 and Billie Ert and Antonio Molina in 1972, but both marriages were declared invalid by courts afterwards. In 1993, three same-sex couples challenged the legality Hawaii's statute prohibiting gay marriage in the lawsuit Baehr v. Miike. The case brought same-sex marriage to national attention and spurred the creation of the Defense of Marriage Act (DOMA) in 1996, which denied federal recognition of same-sex marriages and defined marriage to be between one man and one woman. In 2013, the United States Supreme Court ruled that Section 3 of DOMA was unconstitutional in the case of United States v. Windsor.

In 2004, Massachusetts became the first state to issue marriage licenses to same-sex couples. In reaction, many states took measures to define marriage as existing between one man and one woman. By 2012, 31 states had amended their constitutions to prevent same-sex marriage, and 6 had legalized it. Bolstered by the repeal of DOMA, an additional 30 states legalized same-sex marriage between 2012 and 2015. On June 26, 2015, the U.S. Supreme Court declared all state bans on same-sex marriage unconstitutional in Obergefell v. Hodges.

Polygamy

Polygamy (or bigamy) is illegal in all 50 states, as well as the District of Columbia, Guam, and Puerto Rico. Bigamy is punishable by a fine, imprisonment, or both, according to the law of the individual state and the circumstances of the offense. Because state laws exist, polygamy is not actively prosecuted at the federal level, but the practice is considered "against public policy" and, accordingly, the U.S. government does not recognize bigamous marriages for immigration purposes (that is, would not allow one of the spouses to petition for immigration benefits for the other), even if they are legal in the country where a bigamous marriage was celebrated. Any immigrant coming to the United States to practice polygamy will not be admitted.

Many U.S. courts (e.g. Turner v. S., 212 Miss. 590, 55 So.2d 228) treat bigamy as a strict liability crime: in some jurisdictions, a person can be convicted of a felony even if he or she reasonably believed he or she had only one legal spouse. For example, a person who mistakenly believes that their spouse is dead or that their divorce is final can still be convicted of bigamy if they marry a different person.

Polygamy became a significant social and political issue in the United States in 1852, when The Church of Jesus Christ of Latter-day Saints (LDS Church) made it known that a form of the practice, called plural marriage, was part of its doctrine. Opposition to the practice by the United States government resulted in an intense legal conflict, and resulted in it being outlawed federally by the Edmunds Act in 1882. The LDS Church president Wilford Woodruff announced the church's official abandonment of the practice on September 25, 1890. However, breakaway Mormon fundamentalist groups living mostly in the western United States, Canada, and Mexico still practice plural marriage.

Some other Americans practice polygamy including some American Muslims.

Other restrictions

Marriage between first cousins is illegal in most states. However, it is legal in some states, the District of Columbia and some territories. Some states have some restrictions or exceptions for first cousin marriages and/or recognize such marriages performed out-of-state.

Marriage and immigration

According to the U.S. Census Bureau "Every year over 450,000 United States citizens marry foreign-born individuals and petition for them to obtain a permanent residency (Green Card) in the United States." In 2003, 184,741 immigrants were admitted to the U.S. as spouses of U.S. citizens.

There are conditional requirements in order to obtain a green card through the marriage process. The prospect must have a conditional green card. This becomes permanent after approval by the government. The candidate may then apply for United States citizenship.

A conditional residence green card is given to applicants who are being processed for permanent residence in the United States because they are married to a U.S. citizen. It is valid for two years. At the end of this time period if the card holder does not change the status of their residency they will be put on "out of status". Legal action by the government may follow.

There are different procedures based on whether the applicant is already a U.S. citizen or if the applicant is an immigrant. The marriage must also be legal in, if appropriate, the emigrant's country.

Immigration Marriage Fraud Amendments of 1986

Public Law 99-639 (Act of 11/10/86) was passed to deter marriage fraud among immigrants. The United States Citizenship and Immigration Services summarizes the law and its implications: "Its major provision stipulates that aliens deriving their immigrant status based on a marriage of less than two years are conditional immigrants. To remove their conditional status the immigrants must apply at a U.S. Citizenship and Immigration Services office during the 90-day period before their second-year anniversary of receiving conditional status. If the aliens cannot show that the marriage through which the status was obtained was and is a valid one, their conditional immigrant status may be terminated and they may become deportable."

The conditional immigration status can be terminated for several causes, including divorce, invalid marriage, and failure to petition Immigration Services to remove the classification of conditional residency. If Immigration Services suspects that an alien has created a fraudulent marriage the immigrant is subject to removal from the United States. The marriage must be fraudulent at its inception, as can be determined by several factors. The factors include the conduct of parties before and after the marriage, and the bride and groom's intention of establishing a life together. The validity must be proved by the couple by showing insurance policies, property, leases, income tax, bank accounts, etc. Cases are decided by determining whether the sole purpose of the marriage was to gain benefits for the immigrant.

The punishment for fraud is a large monetary penalty and the possibility of never becoming a permanent resident of the United States. According to the statute, "Any individual who knowingly enters into a marriage for the purpose of evading any provision of the immigration laws shall be imprisoned for not more than 5 years, or fined not more than $250,000, or both" (I.N.A. § 275(c); 8 U.S.C. § 1325(c)). The U.S. citizen or resident spouse could also face criminal prosecution, including fines or imprisonment. They could be prosecuted for either criminal conspiracy (see U.S. v. Vickerage, 921 F.2d 143 (8th Cir. 1990)) or for establishing a "commercial enterprise" to fraudulently acquire green cards for immigrants (see I.N.A. § 275(d); 8 U.S.C. § 1325(d)).

These Amendment Acts cover spouses, children of spouses, and K-1 visa fiancés.

Basic immigration law

The Immigration and Nationality Act of 1952 has been amended many times, but still remains the basic and central body of immigration law.

Intersection of immigration law and family law

Immigrants who use the reason of family ties to gain entry into the United States are required to document financial arrangements. The sponsor of a related immigrant must guarantee financial support to the family. These guarantees form a contract between a sponsor and the federal government. It requires the sponsor to support the immigrant relative at a level equivalent to 125% of the poverty line for his or her household size. A beneficiary of the contract, the immigrant, or the Federal Government may sue for the promised support in the event the sponsor does not fulfill the obligations of the contract. The sponsor is also liable for the prevailing party's legal expenses.

Divorce does not end the sponsor's obligation to provide the support deemed by the contract. The only ways to terminate the obligation are the immigrant spouse becomes a U.S. citizen, the immigrant spouse has worked forty Social Security Act eligible quarters (10 years), the immigrant spouse is no longer considered a permanent alien and has left the U.S., the immigrant spouse obtained an ability to adjust their status, or the immigrant spouse dies. A sponsor's death also cuts off the obligation, but not in regards to any support the sponsor already owes which will be paid but the sponsor's estate.

MAIL-ORDER BRIDE AND IMMIGRATION FRAUD

A mail-order bride is a foreign woman who contacts American men and immigrates for the purpose of marriage.

Initially, it was conducted through mailed catalogs, but now, more often, on the internet. Prospective brides are typically from developing nations such as South/ Southeast Asia, the Philippines, Thailand, Sri Lanka, India, Macao, Hong Kong, and China. Brides from Eastern European countries have been in demand. The mail-order bride phenomenon can be traced as far back as the 1700s and 1800s. This was due to the immigration of European colonizers who were in far away areas and wanted brides from their homeland.

First world governments have speculated that some foreign women marry men in their country as an easy immigration route, staying married long enough to secure permanent citizenship, and then divorcing their husbands. Whether the brides choose to remain married or not, they could still sponsor the rest of their families to immigrate. Precautions have been taken by several countries such as the United States, Great Britain, and Australia. They have fought the proliferation of the mail-order bride industry through amending immigration laws. The United States addressed the mail-order bride system by passing the Immigration Marriage Fraud Amendment of 1986. Great Britain and Australia have experienced similar immgiration and are trying to deal with the issue.

Lesbian, gay, bisexual, and transgender immigrants

In 2000, 36,000 same-sex bi-national couples were living in the United States. A majority of these couples were raising young children. Female couples head 58% of bi-national families; 33% are male couples.

History

The revision of American immigration law imposed a ban on homosexual people began in 1952. The language barred "aliens afflicted with psychopathic personality, epilepsy or mental defect." Congress explicitly intended this language to cover "homosexuals and sex perverts." The law was amended in 1965 to more specifically prohibit the entry of persons "afflicted with... sexual deviation." Until 1990, "sexual deviation" was grounds for exclusion from the United States, and anyone who admitted being a homosexual was refused entry. Lesbian and gay individuals are now admitted and US citizens may petition for immigrant visas for their same-sex spouses under the same terms as opposite-sex spouses.

Boutilier v. Immigration Service, 1967

In 1967, the Supreme Court confirmed that, when describing a homosexual person, they were to be referred to as a "psychopathic personality." Twenty-one-year-old Clive Boutilier, a Canadian, had moved to the United States in 1955 to join his mother, stepfather, and 3 siblings who already lived there. In 1963, he applied for US citizenship, admitting that he had been arrested on a sodomy charge in 1959. He was ordered to be deported. He challenged his deportation until it became a federal matter and became a case for the Supreme Court. In a six-three decision, the court ruled that Congress had decided to bar gay people from entering the United States: "Congress was not laying down a clinical test, but an exclusionary standard which it declared to be inclusive of those having homosexual and perverted characteristics..." Congress used the phrase 'psychopathic personality' not in the clinical sense, but to effectuate its purpose to exclude from entry all homosexuals and other sex perverts." Boutilier was torn from his partner of eight years. According to one historian, "Presumably distraught about the Court's Decision... Boutillier attempted suicide before leaving New York, survived a month-long coma that left him brain-damaged with permanent disabilities, and moved to southern Ontario with his parents, who took on the task of caring for him for more than twenty years." He died in Canada on April 12, 2003, only weeks before that country moved to legalize same-sex marriage.

Even with the ban being enforced homosexual people still managed to come to the United States for several reasons, but especially to be with the people they loved. The fight to allow homosexual immigrants into the United States continued in the mid-1970 with an Australian national named Anthony Sullivan. He was living in Boulder, Colorado, with his American partner, Richard Adams. When Sullivan's visitor's visa was about to expire, they managed to persuade the county clerk to issue them a marriage license, with which Sullivan applied for a green card as Adams' spouse.

They received a negative reply from the Immigration and Naturalization Service. Sullivan and Adams sued, and in 1980, the Ninth Circuit Court of Appeals concluded that because Congress intended to restrict the term "spouse" to opposite-sex couples, and because Congress has extensive power to limit access to immigration benefits, the denial was lawful. The ban was finally repealed in 1990, but without making any provision for gays and lesbians to be treated equally with regard to family-based immigration sponsorship. Sponsorship became possible only after the 2013 US Supreme Court decision in US v Windsor that struck down a provision to the contrary in the Defense of Marriage Act.

Common-law marriage in the United States

Common-law marriage, also known as sui juris marriage, informal marriage, marriage by habit and repute, or marriage in fact is a form of irregular marriage that survives only in seven U.S. states and the District of Columbia along with some provisions of military law; plus two other states that recognise domestic common law marriage after the fact for limited purposes. It is arguably the original form of marriage, in which a couple took up residency together, held themselves out to the world as a married couple, and otherwise behaved as a married couple. It has been gradually abolished in Western nation states since the sixteenth century, when the Council of Trent in 1563 ruled that no marriage thenceforth would be valid in the eyes of the Roman Catholic Church unless it were solemnised by a priest.

This ruling was quickly adopted in predominantly Roman Catholic countries, and eventually became the norm in Protestant nations as well. In 1753, the Kingdom of Great Britain enacted Lord Hardwicke's Act, which provided no marriage in England and Wales was legally valid unless performed under the auspices of the Church of England, with exceptions for Jews and Quakers. The Act did not apply to Scotland or to the American colonies, and Ireland was still a separate country in 1753; so common law marriage continued in the future United States until individual states abolished it.

The term common law marriage is often used colloquially or by the media to refer to cohabiting couples, regardless of any legal rights that these couples may or may not have, which can create public confusion both in regard to the term and in regard to the legal rights of unmarried partners.

FEDERAL INCOME TAX AND OTHER PROVISIONS

If the marriage is recognized under the law and customs of the state or jurisdiction in which the marriage takes place (even in a foreign country), the marriage is valid for tax purposes (Rev. Rul. 58-66). Specific state or jurisdiction requirements for a common law marriage to be recognised must be considered by couples contemplating filing joint returns.

In February 2015, the United States Department of Labor issued an amended definition of "spouse" under the Family and Medical Leave Act of 1993 (FMLA) in response to the United States v. Windsor decision recognizing same-sex marriage. The new DOL rule became effective March 27, 2015, and extends FMLA leave rights and job protections to eligible employees in a same-sex marriage or a common law marriage entered into in a state or jurisdiction where those statuses are legally recognized, regardless of the state in which the employee currently works or resides.

Contractibility of domestic common law marriage

A domestic common law marriage is contracted within a particular jurisdiction. If contracted in another jurisdiction, it is a foreign common law marriage, just like any type of regular marriage contracted out-of-state.

In 1855, defending the idea of common law marriage, a New York judge described marriage as "the most sacred" of social relationships and said that society would be threatened "if an open and public cohabitation as man and wife for 10 years...followed by the procreation of children, could be overturned."

Today, domestic common law marriages can be contracted in the following jurisdictions:

1. Colorado
2. The District of Columbia
3. Iowa
4. Kansas
5. Montana
6. Oklahoma; but see the note below regarding Oklahoma law being unclear.
7. Rhode Island
8. Texas
9. Military law; a defective state marriage was still valid under military law due to the length of time the defendant lived as married.

Additionally, these two jurisdictions recognize domestic common law marriage in the limited circumstances indicated:

1. New Hampshire recognizes domestic common law marriage for purposes of probate only.
2. Utah recognizes only common law marriages that have been validated in a judicial proceeding. A common law marriage may be validated by a court of law up to one year after the alleged marriage has been terminated.

Of the remaining 41 states, 13 never permitted and 28 no longer permit common law marriages to be contracted within their jurisdiction. The latter group will only recognize a domestic common law marriage if it was contracted in the state prior to the date of abolition. Nevertheless, all states recognise validly contracted foreign common law marriages, because they recognize all validly contracted foreign marriages. E.g., California abolished the common law contract of marriage in 1895 and, thus, will only continue to recognize a domestic common law marriage contracted in California prior to that date; but any validly contracted out-of-state common law marriage will be recognized by California, because it recognizes all validly contracted foreign marriages under Cal. Family Code 308.

Domestic contract of common law marriage was abolished in the following 28 states on the dates indicated. Note that Massachusetts (which included Maine, 1652 - 1820) abolished common law marriage during the colonial period and before it was abolished in England and Wales.

- Alabama (2016)
- Alaska (1917), as the Territory of Alaska
- Arizona (1913), previously part of New Mexico Territory (which see, below), 1860-1863; then the Territory of Arizona to 1912
- California (1895)
- Florida (1968)
- Georgia (1997)
- Hawaii, as the Territory of Hawaii (1920); previously the independent Kingdom of Hawaii, to 1893; then Republic of Hawaii, 1894-1898.
- Idaho (1996)
- Illinois (1905)
- Indiana (1958)
- Kentucky (1852)
- Maine (1652, when it became part of the Massachusetts Bay Colony; it became a separate state in 1820)
- Massachusetts (1646)
- Michigan (1957)
- Minnesota (1941)
- Mississippi (1956)
- Missouri (1921)
- Nebraska (1923)
- Nevada (1943)
- New Jersey (1939)
- New Mexico (1860), as the Territory of New Mexico, a state from 1912
- New York (1933, also 1902 –1908),
- North Dakota (1890)
- Ohio (1991)
- Pennsylvania (2005)
- South Carolina (2019)
- South Dakota (1959)
- Wisconsin (1917)

These 13 states have never permitted domestic common law marriage; but like all 50 states and the District of Columbia, they recognise all validly contracted out-of-state marriages, including validly contracted common law marriages.

- Arkansas
- Connecticut
- Delaware
- Louisiana
- Maryland
- North Carolina
- Oregon
- Tennessee
- Vermont
- Virginia
- Washington
- West Virginia
- Wyoming

Outside of confederation, the Territory of Guam does not recognise common law marriage. The Commonwealth of the Northern Mariana Islands also does not recognise common law marriage but might recognise customary marriage. In Santos v. Commonwealth, Petitioner argued that common law marriage was sufficiently similar to Carolinian customary marriage that it should be recognised as the same. The Court ruled that, while CNMI statute provides that (English) common law provides the rule of decision in the absence of statutory law or customary law to the contrary, Petitioner did not argue that her marriage was a marriage under customary law but a marriage under common law; thus, whereas a validly contracted marriage under Carolinian or Chamorro customary law might be held a valid marriage, a common law marriage could not be.

Marriage under tribal law is also distinct from state marriage law. Many Aboriginal nations permit common law marriage or its historic tribal equivalent. For example, the Navajo Nation permits common law marriage and also allows its citizens to marry through tribal ceremonial processes and traditional processes. Otherwise, common law marriages can no longer be contracted in any of the other states.

INTERJURISDICTIONAL RECOGNITION

All U.S. jurisdictions recognize all validly contracted out-of-state marriages under their laws of comity and choice of law/conflict of laws rules - including marriages that cannot be legally contracted domestically. Likewise, an invalidly contracted out-of-state marriage will not be valid domestically, even if it could have been validly contracted domestically. E.g., California allows first cousins to marry but Nevada does not. If two first cousins attempt to marry in Nevada, that marriage will not be valid in either Nevada or California, notwithstanding it could be legally contracted in California. But if they attempt to marry in California, their attempt will be successful and the marriage will be valid in both California and Nevada, notwithstanding the marriage could not be legally contracted in Nevada. (The Full Faith and Credit Clause of the United States Constitution does not apply to common law marriages because they are not public acts (i.e. statutes, ordinances, general laws, etc.), not public records, and not judicial proceedings.)

Proof a common law marriage exists or existed

Because there is no marriage certificate or other public record to directly document the marriage, it can be difficult to prove a common law marriage if marital validity is contested in a probate or dissolution proceeding.

Similar problems of proof may arise if the parties to a common law marriage were not actually domiciled in the state where they lived at the time they sought to contract the marriage; or they may have thought they were contracting a marriage but they did not actually conform to the law of the state in which they were living. The essential question is whether the marriage was validly contracted under the laws of the jurisdiction where the parties allege their marriage was contracted.

Dissolution (aka divorce)

Because common law marriage is merely an irregular way to contract a lawful marriage, the same formal judicial proceeding is required to dissolve it. There is no such thing as "common law divorce" because divorce never existed at common law but was created by statutory law. So although it is possible to be married by common law in nine U.S. jurisdictions, divorce must be done by statutory law in all jurisdictions.

Definitive legislation in states that permit domestic common law marriage

The requirements to contract a valid common law marriage differ between jurisdictions as follows:

Colorado

Colorado's Supreme Court revised the elements for common law marriage in three related rulings on January 11, 2021, in light of Obergefell v. Hodges, 576 U.S. 644, 674–75 (2015), and also in light of changing social practices, in the cases of In re Marriage of Hogsett & Neale, 2021 CO 1 (January 11, 2021), In re Estate of Yudkin, 2021 CO 2 (January 11, 2021), and In re Marriage of LaFleur & Pyfer, 2021 CO 3 (January 11, 2021). The Colorado Bar Association summarizes the holding of the cases in a summary of the lead case, Hodges, which states:

The Supreme Court revisited the test for proving a common law marriage that the Court articulated over three decades ago in People v. Lucero, 747 P.2d 660 (Colo. 1987). Because many of the indicia of marriage identified in Lucero have become less reliable, particularly in light of the recognition of same-sex marriage and other social and legal changes, the Court refined the test and held that a common law marriage may be established by the mutual consent or agreement of the couple to enter the legal and social institution of marriage, followed by conduct manifesting that mutual agreement. The core inquiry is whether the parties intended to enter a marital relationship, that is, to share a life together as spouses in a committed, intimate relationship of mutual support and obligation.

Colorado, by statute, no longer recognizes common law marriages entered by minors in Colorado, and also does not recognize foreign common law marriages entered into by minors, even if that marriage would have been valid where entered into under local law. See Section 14-2-109.5, Colorado Revised Statutes. The constitutionality of this limitation as applied to foreign marriages has not been tested in litigation.

Colorado, Montana, and Texas are the only U.S. states to recognize both putative marriage and common law marriage.

DISTRICT OF COLUMBIA

According to the District of Columbia Department of Human Services, a common law marriage is "A marriage that is legally recognized even though there has been no ceremony and there is no certification of marriage. A common law marriage exists if the two persons are legally free to marry, if it is the intent of the two persons to establish a marriage, and if the two are known to the community as husband and wife."

Common law marriages have been recognized in the District of Columbia since 1931. Holding common law marriages legal, District Court of Appeals Justice D. Laurence Groner said,

"We think it cannot now be controverted that an agreement between a man and woman to be husband and wife, consummated by cohabitation as husband and wife, constitutes a valid marriage unless there be in existence in the State in which the agreement is made, a statute declaring the marriage to be invalid unless solemnized in a prescribed manner. We think it equally true that the rule now generally recognized is that statutes requiring a marriage to be preceded by a license or to be solemnized by a religious ceremony without words of nullity as to marriages contracted otherwise are directory merely and failure to procure the license or to go through a religious ceremony does not invalidate the marriage. ... There is nothing in the statute which declares that a marriage shall not be valid unless solemnized in the prescribed manner, nor does it declare any particular thing requisite to the validity of the marriage. The act confines itself wholly with providing the mode of solemnizing the marriage and to the persons authorized to perform the ceremony.

Indeed, the statue itself declares the purpose underlying the requirements to be secure registration and evidence of the marriage rather than to deny validity to marriages not performed according to its terms."

Iowa

The three elements of a common law marriage are: (1) the present intent and agreement to be married; (2) continuous cohabitation; and (3) public declaration that the parties are husband and wife. The public declaration or holding out to the public is considered to be the acid test of a common law marriage.

Adm. Rule 701—73.25 (425) of the Iowa Administrative Code, titled Common Law Marriage, states:

A common law marriage is a social relationship that meets all the necessary requisites of a marriage except that it was not solemnized, performed or witnessed by an official authorized by law to perform marriages. The necessary elements of a common law marriage are: (a) a present intent of both parties freely given to become married, (b) a public declaration by the parties or a holding out to the public that they are husband and wife, (c) continuous cohabitation together as husband and wife (this means consummation of the marriage), and (d) both parties must be capable of entering into the marriage relationship. No special time limit is necessary to establish a common law marriage. Edit: 701—73.26 Rescinded, effective October 2, 1985.

This rule is intended to implement Iowa Code section 425.17.

Kansas

Under Kansas Statute 23-2502, both parties to a common law marriage must be 18 years old. The three requirements that must coexist to establish a common law marriage in Kansas are: (1) capacity to marry; (2) a present marriage agreement; and (3) a holding out of each other as husband and wife to the public.

Montana

A common law marriage is established when a couple: "(1) is competent to enter into a marriage, (2) mutually consents and agrees to a common law marriage, and (3) cohabits and is reputed in the community to be husband and wife."

Oklahoma

The situation in Oklahoma has been unclear since the mid-1990s, with legal scholars reporting 1994, 1998, 2005, and 2010 each as the year common law marriage was abolished in the state. However, as of September 12, 2016, the Oklahoma Tax Commission continues to represent common law marriage as legal there, and the Department of Corrections continues to reference common law marriage, though that could refer to older marriages. No reference to the ban appears in the relevant statutes; the 2010 bill that attempted to abolish common law marriage passed the state Senate, but died in a House committee. and a reputed ban in 2010 cannot be found in its statutes.

RHODE ISLAND

The criteria for a common law marriage are: (1) the parties seriously intended to enter into the husband-wife relationship; (2) the parties' conduct is of such a character as to lead to a belief in the community that they were married.

Texas

The Texas Family Code, Sections 2.401 through 2.405, define how a common law marriage (which is known as both "marriage without formalities" and "informal marriage" in the text) can be established in one of two ways. Both parties must be at least age 18 to enter into a common law marriage.

First, a couple can file a legal "Declaration of Informal Marriage", which is a legally binding document. The form must be completed by both marriage partners and sworn or affirmed in presence of the County Clerk. The Declaration is formally recorded as part of the Official County Records by Volume and Page number, and is then forwarded by the County Clerk to the Texas Bureau of Vital Statistics, where it is again legally recorded as formal evidence of marriage. This is the same procedure that is used when a marriage license is issued and filed; the term "Informal" refers only to the fact that no formal wedding ceremony (whether civil or religious) was conducted.

Second, a couple can meet a three-prong test, showing evidence of all of the following:

1. first, an agreement to be married;
2. after such agreement, cohabitation within the State of Texas; and
3. after such agreement, representation to others (within the State of Texas) that the parties are married.

Regarding the second prong, in the actual text of the Texas Family Code, there is no specification on the length of time that a couple must cohabitate to meet this requirement. As such, an informal marriage can occur under Texas law if the couple lives together for as little as one day, if the other requirements (an agreement to be married and holding out as married to the public) can be shown.

Likewise, a couple can cohabit for 50 years, but if they never have an agreement to be married, or hold themselves out to the public as married, their 50-year cohabitation will not make them informally married under Texas law.

Dissolution of this type marriage requires formal Annulment or Divorce Proceedings, the same as with the other more recognized forms of 'ceremonial' marriages. However, if a couple does not commence a proceeding to prove their relationship was a marriage within two years of the end of their cohabitation and relationship, there is a legal presumption that they never agreed to be married, but this presumption is rebuttable.

New Hampshire

New Hampshire recognizes common law marriage for purposes of probate only.

In New Hampshire "[P]ersons cohabiting and acknowledging each other as husband and wife, and generally reputed to be such, for the period of 3 years, and until the decease of one of them, shall thereafter be deemed to have been legally married." Thus, the state posthumously recognizes common law marriages to ensure that a surviving spouse inherits without any difficulty.

UTAH

The status of common law marriage in Utah is not clear. Government websites claim that common law marriage does not exist in Utah but other legal websites state that "non-matrimonial relationships" may be recognized as marriage within one year after the relationship ends. Whether this amounts to recognition of non-marital relationship contracts (dubbed "palimony agreements" by the media after the famous California case Marvin v. Marvin), or post-factum recognition of common law marriage is a subject for debate.

In any case, Utah will only recognise the relationship if it has been validated by a court or administrative order: "[A] court or administrative order must establish that" the parties: (1) "are of legal age and capable of giving consent"; (2) "are legally capable of entering a solemnized marriage under the provisions of Title 30, Chap. 1 of the Utah Code; (3) "have cohabited"; (4) "mutually assume marital rights, duties, and obligations"; and (5) "hold themselves out as and have acquired a uniform and general reputation as husband and wife" In Utah, the fact that two parties are legally incapable of entering into a common law marriage, because they are already married, does not preclude criminal liability for bigamy or polygamy. Representative legislation in some states that no longer permit domestic common law marriage

Alabama

Alabama abolished common law marriage effective January 1, 2017. Common law marriages contracted before this date are still valid. Such a valid common law marriage exists when there is capacity to enter into a marriage, the parties must be at least 16 with legal parental consent and present agreement or consent to be married, public recognition of the existence of the marriage, and consummation.

Florida

Florida abolished common law marriage effective January 1, 1968. Marriages contracted prior to this date are not affected. Additionally, Florida recognizes valid common law marriages from other states.

California

California Family Code Section 308 provides that a marriage validly contracted in another jurisdiction is valid in California. Thus, a common law marriage validly contracted in another jurisdiction is valid in California notwithstanding it could not be legally contracted within California; and a common law marriage that was not validly contracted in another U.S. jurisdiction is not valid in California. All other states have similar statutory provisions. Exceptions to this rule are marriages deemed by the jurisdiction to be "odious to public policy".

Pennsylvania

Pennsylvania's domestic relations marriage statute now reads: "No common law marriage contracted after January 1, 2005, shall be valid. Nothing in this part shall be deemed or taken to render any common law marriage otherwise lawful and contracted on or before January 1, 2005, invalid." The situation in Pennsylvania became unclear in 2003 when an intermediate appellate court purported to abolish common law marriage even though the state Supreme Court had recognized (albeit somewhat reluctantly) the validity of common law marriages only five years before. The Pennsylvania legislature resolved most of the uncertainty by abolishing common law marriages entered into after January 1, 2005.

However, it is still not certain whether Pennsylvania courts will recognize common law marriages entered into after the date of the Stamos decision and before the effective date of the statute (i.e., after September 17, 2003, and on or before January 1, 2005), because the other intermediate appellate court has suggested that it might not follow the Stamos decision.

Divorce

Divorce is the province of state governments, so divorce law varies from state to state. Prior to the 1970s, divorcing spouses had to prove that the other spouse was at fault, for instance for being guilty of adultery, abandonment, or cruelty; when spouses simply could not get along, lawyers were forced to manufacture "uncontested" divorces. The implementation of no-fault divorce began in 1969 in California and became nationwide with the passage of New York's law in 2010. No-fault divorce (on the grounds of "irreconcilable differences", "irretrievable breakdown of marriage", "incompatibility", or after a separation period etc.) is now available in all states. State law provides for child support where children are involved, and sometimes for alimony.

Relevant types of unions

Domestic partnerships

Domestic partnerships are a version of civil unions. Registration and recognition are functions of states, localities, or employers; such unions may be available to couples of the same sex and, sometimes, opposite sex. Although similar to marriage, a domestic partnership does not confer the 1,138 rights, privileges, and obligations afforded to married couples by the federal government, but the relevant state government may offer parallel benefits. Because domestic partnerships in the United States are determined by each state or local jurisdictions, or employers, there is no nationwide consistency on the rights, responsibilities, and benefits accorded domestic partners. Some couples enter into a private, informal, documented domestic partnership agreement, specifying their mutual obligations because the obligations are otherwise merely implied, and written contracts are much more valid in legal circumstances.

Cohabitation

The term is used in a legal setting often to mean, as applied to spouses, living together. Otherwise, cohabitation means two unmarried people, who are in a loving, most often intimate, relationship, living together. Many couples cohabit as a way to experience married life before marriage. Some cohabit instead of marrying. Others may live together because other arrangements are less desired. In the past few decades, societal standards that discouraged cohabitation have faded; it is now considered more acceptable.

Children of cohabiting, instead of married, parents are prone to a more changing family unit. In 2011, The National Marriage Project found about 2⁄3 of children of cohabitees saw them break up before they were 12 years old, as opposed to 1⁄4 otherwise. Abrahamic religions are among those that traditionally attach a stigma, such as under a rubric of "living in sin"; however such beliefs are today only sternly rebuked, by the parents of short-term heterosexual cohabitees, by their most orthodox, socially conservative, strains.

DIVORCE IN THE UNITED STATES

Divorce in the United States is a legal process in which a judge or other authority dissolves the marriage existing between two persons. Divorce restores the persons to the status of being single and permits them to marry other individuals. In the United States, marriage and divorce fall under the jurisdiction of state governments, not the federal government.

Although such matters are usually ancillary or consequential to the dissolution of the marriage, divorce may also involve issues of spousal support, child custody, child support, distribution of property and division of debt.

History of Divorce in US

19th century

By the mid- to late 19th century, divorce rates in the United States increased rapidly, and Americans obtained more divorces annually than were granted in all of Europe. Previously, divorces in the US were mainly granted to the middle and upper-classes due to their cost, but the legal process became less expensive. Other proposed explanations include the popular acceptance of divorce as an alternative to marital unhappiness, decay of the belief in immortality and future punishment, discontent with the existing constitution of society, the habits of mobility created by better transportation, and the greater independence of women resulting in their enlarged legal rights and greater opportunities of self support. The divorce rate continued to increase in the early 20th century. In 1890, 3 couples per 1,000 were divorced, rising to 8 couples by 1920.

The Married Women's Property Acts in the United States were passed by the various states to give greater property rights to women and, in some cases, allowing them to sue for divorce. The women's rights movement debated the issue of whether to allow divorce, with Jane Swisshelm and Elizabeth Cady Stanton as early supporters, with Horace Greeley and Antoinette Brown Blackwell opposed. Unlike other issues, the movement was unable to achieve agreement. :477 Stanton eventually come to see marriage law reform as more important than women's voting rights. :156 Against Stanton, Lucy Stone sought to remove the advocacy of divorce from the women's platform to prevent the appearance of moral laxity. :72 In government, Robert Dale Owen proposed laws granting greater freedom of divorce, which later came to fruition. The National Woman Suffrage Association, founded in 1869, included advocacy for divorce reform. :488

20th century

Prior to the latter decades of the 20th century, divorce was considered to be against the public interest, and civil courts refused to grant a divorce except if one party to the marriage had betrayed the "innocent spouse." Thus, a spouse suing for divorce in most states had to show a "fault" such as abandonment, cruelty, incurable mental illness, or adultery. If an "innocent" husband and wife wished to separate, or if both were guilty, "neither would be allowed to escape the bonds of marriage." Divorce was barred if evidence revealed any hint of complicity between spouses to manufacture grounds for divorce, such as if the suing party engaged in procurement or connivance (contributing to the fault, such as by arranging for adultery), condonation (forgiving the fault either explicitly or by continuing to cohabit after knowing of it), or recrimination (the suing spouse also being guilty).

Divorce is governed by state rather than federal law, and a number of strategies were devised in several states to make divorce easier. By 1909, Reno, Nevada was "the divorce capital of the world." At that time, only six months in Nevada established state residency, and the Nevada courts, well aware of the contribution of divorce seekers to Nevada's hospitality industry, accepted the resident's uncorroborated assertion of grounds for divorce, usually "extreme cruelty.".

In 1927, the Nevada Legislature, "in response to a perceived threat to Reno's divorce supremacy from France and Mexico and a divorce-trade war that had been going on since the end of World War I between Nevada, Idaho, and Arkansas," lowered the residency period to three months, and in 1931 the Legislature that voted for "wide-open gambling" lowered it to six weeks. Providing accommodations and other amenities for visitors, who could not leave Nevada during the six weeks, became a major Reno industry; greeters met the arriving trains, and there were a variety of divorce ranches. In 1942, the U.S. Supreme Court ruled in Williams v. North Carolina that other states had to recognize these divorces, under the "full faith and credit" clause of the U.S. Constitution.

By 1916, the U.S. led the world in number of divorces. In populous New York State, where adultery was the easiest grounds for divorce, attorneys would provide a divorce package of a prostitute and a photographer. Significant numbers of divorce seekers went to the cities on the Mexican side of the Mexico-U.S. border, or to Haiti, where they found welcoming attorneys, who sometimes advertised in the U.S. A memory of the practice is reflected in the song "Haitian Divorce," by Steely Dan.

By the 1960s, deception to bypass the fault system had become a widespread concern, if not actually a widespread practice, and a consensus grew for change. The National Association of Women Lawyers was instrumental in convincing the American Bar Association to create a Family Law section in many state courts, and pushed strongly for no-fault divorce law around 1960 (cf. Uniform Marriage and Divorce Act). In 1969, California became the first U.S. state to pass a no-fault divorce law.

The introduction of no-fault divorce led to a rise in divorce rates in the United States during the 1970s. The National Center for Health Statistics reports that from 1975 to 1988 in the US, in families with children present, wives file for divorce in approximately two-thirds of cases. In 1975, 71.4% of the cases were filed by women, and in 1988, 65% were filed by women.

Lenore Weitzman's 1985 book The Divorce Revolution, using data from California in 1977-78, reported that one year after divorce, the standard of living for women declined 73%, compared with an increase of 42% for men. Richard Peterson calls Weitzman's methodology into question, using the same data to calculate a 27% decrease for women and a 10% increase for men.

21st century

The median length for a marriage in the US today is 11 years, with 90% of divorces settled out of court. Lower-income couples are currently more likely to get a divorce than higher-income couples. By the seventh wedding anniversary, the divorce rate among highly educated people who married in the early 2000s is 11%, while that for couples without college degrees is 17%.

In 2015, the Manhattan Supreme Court ruled that Ellanora Baidoo could serve her husband divorce papers through a Facebook message, and she became the first to do so.

LAW

Divorce in the U.S. is governed by state rather than federal law. The laws of the state(s) of residence at the time of divorce govern, not those of the location where the couple was married. All states recognize divorces granted by any other state, and all impose a minimum time of residence to file for a divorce, Nevada and Idaho currently being the shortest at six weeks.

All states allow no-fault divorce on grounds such as irreconcilable differences, irremediable breakdown, and loss of affection. Some states mandate a separation period before no-fault divorce. Mississippi, South Dakota and Tennessee are the only states that require mutual consent for no-fault divorce. The rest of the states permit unilateral no-fault divorce.

Since the mid-1990s, three states of the united states have enacted covenant marriage laws which give couples the option to make divorce more difficult, Louisiana, Arkansas, and Arizona. For example, couples who choose covenant marriage may be required to undergo counseling before a divorce can be granted, or to submit their conflicts to mediation. In states lacking such provisions, some couples sign contracts undertaking the same obligations.

A summary (or simple) divorce, available in some jurisdictions, is used when spouses meet certain eligibility requirements, or can agree on key issues beforehand. For example, to qualify for summary divorce in California, a couple must meet all of the following requirements:

- Have been married less than five years,
- Have no children together,
- Do not own any real property,
- Do not rent any real property other than current dwelling,
- Do not owe more than $6,000 for debts since date of marriage,
- Own less than $41,000 in community property (property acquired during marriage), not counting vehicles,
- Do not own more than $41,000 in separate property (property acquired before marriage), not counting vehicles,
- Agree to forgo spousal support,
- Have a signed agreement which divides property (including cars) and debts, and
- Meet residency requirement, if applicable.

Grounds for divorce

Though divorce laws vary between jurisdiction, there are two basic approaches to divorce: fault-based and no-fault. Fault grounds, when available, are sometimes still sought. This may be done where it reduces the waiting period otherwise required, or possibly in hopes of affecting decisions related to a divorce, such as child custody, child support, alimony, and so on. A court may still take into account the behavior of the parties when dividing property, debts, evaluating custody, and support. States vary in the admissibility of such evidence for those decisions.

No-fault divorce

Under a no-fault divorce system the dissolution of a marriage does not require an allegation or proof of fault of either party. Only three states (Mississippi, South Dakota and Tennessee) require mutual consent (in Tennessee it is needed only in certain circumstances) for a no-fault divorce to be granted. No-fault grounds for divorce include incompatibility, irreconcilable differences, and irremediable breakdown of the marriage.

At-fault divorce

Fault divorces used to be the only way to break a marriage, and people who had differences, but did not qualify as "at fault", only had the option to separate (and were prevented from legally remarrying).

However, there are ways (defenses) to prevent a fault divorce:

- Collusion
- Condonation
- Connivance
- Provocation
- Recrimination

A defense is expensive, and not usually practical as eventually most divorces are granted.

Comparative rectitude is a doctrine used to determine which spouse is more at fault when both spouses are guilty of breaches.

Jurisdiction

In the United States, the Federal Government does not have the authority to issue a divorce. The state has the only authority over issuing accepting a marriage, and issuing a divorce. This creates the question of which state can one get divorced in. All states have rules for jurisdiction, which is typically a time frame the person filing the divorce has lived in the state. Most states require the person filing for a divorce to be a physical resident of the state for six months. Some states require twelve months and some states, like Nevada, only require six weeks. Without proper jurisdiction a state cannot issue a divorce.

PROPERTY DIVISION AND SPOUSAL SUPPORT

States vary in their rules for division of assets in a divorce. The major difference is between states that use a community property system and states that do not. In community property states, community property belongs to the spouses equally. The following states use community property regimes: Arizona, California, Idaho, Louisiana, Nevada, New Mexico, Texas, Washington, and Wisconsin. Alaskan law gives couples the option to create community property by written agreement.

Most community property states start with the presumption that community assets will be divided equally, whereas "equitable distribution" states presume fairness may dictate more or less than half of the assets will be awarded to one spouse or the other. Commonly, assets acquired before marriage are considered individual, and assets acquired after, marital. Depending on the state, an equitable or equal division of assets is then sought.

In some states, educational degrees earned during the marriage may be considered marital property. In such states, a resolution of the divorce will often entail payment from the educated spouse to the other spouse a share of their expected future earnings that are due to a degree they earned during the marriage, and may require the expertise of labor economists or other statistical and financial experts.

Alimony, also known as 'maintenance' or 'spousal support' is still being granted in many cases, especially in longer term marriages. Alimony is more likely in cases where a spouse has remedial needs that must be met in order for the spouse to become fully employable, for example that one spouse gave up career opportunities or development in order to devote themselves to the family.

Child support and custody

In cases involving children, governments have a pressing interest in ensuring that disputes between parents do not spill over into the family courts. All states now require parents to file a parenting plan, or to decide on child custody and visitation either by reaching a written agreement or in a court hearing, when they legally separate or divorce.

The spouse given custody (or the spouse with the greater share of residence time in the case of joint custody), may receive assets to compensate their greater child-care expenses.

Alternatives to litigation

Collaborative divorce

Collaborative divorce (uncontested divorce) is becoming a popular method for divorcing couples to come to agreement on divorce issues. In a collaborative divorce, the parties negotiate an agreed resolution with the assistance of attorneys who are trained in the collaborative divorce process and in mediation, and often with the assistance of a neutral financial specialist and/or divorce coach. The parties are empowered to make their own decisions based on their own needs and interests, but with complete information and full professional support. Once the collaborative divorce starts, the lawyers are disqualified from representing the parties in a contested legal proceeding, should the collaborative law process end prematurely. Most attorneys who practice collaborative divorce claim that it can be substantially less expensive than other divorce methods (regular divorce or mediation). However, should the parties not reach any agreements, any documents or information exchanged during the collaborative process cannot later be used in further legal proceedings, as the collaborative process is confidential proceedings. Furthermore, there are no set enforceable time lines for completion of a divorce using collaborative divorce.

Mediated divorce

Divorce mediation is an alternative to traditional divorce litigation that attempts to help opposing spouses find common ground during the divorce process. In a divorce mediation session, a mediator facilitates the discussion between the spouses by assisting with communication and providing information and suggestions to help resolve differences. At the end of the mediation process, the separating parties will have typically developed a tailored divorce agreement that they can submit to the court. Parties to mediation do not need to retain attorneys. However, if the parties choose to retain attorneys their attorneys may be included in the mediation session. The mediator can provide both parties with information but will not offer advice to either. Divorce mediators may be attorneys, mental health professionals, or financial experts who have experience in divorce cases. Divorce mediation can be significantly less expensive than litigation. The adherence rate to mediated agreements is much higher than that of adherence to court orders.

Summary divorce

Many states allow for couples to file for a summary divorce based upon a jointly filed divorce petition. A summary divorce means the spouses have discussed the terms required by state law to issue a divorce and they have reached an mutual agreement. Almost every state allows for this type of "uncontested" divorce. An uncontested joint divorce petition will often save a divorcing couple both time and money.

FEDERAL LAWS RELATING TO DIVORCE

Since the 1980s, federal legislation has been enacted affecting the rights and responsibilities of divorcing spouses. For example, federal welfare reform mandated the creation of child support guidelines in all 50 states in the 1980s. ERISA includes provisions for the division of qualified retirement accounts between divorcing spouses. The IRS established rules on ignoring alimony as a source of taxable income. Federal bankruptcy laws prohibit discharging in bankruptcy of alimony and child support obligations. COBRA allows a divorced spouse to obtain and maintain health insurance.

Qualified Domestic Relations Orders

A "qualified domestic relations order" (QDRO) is an order that creates or recognizes the existence of an alternate payee's right to receive, or assigns to an alternate payee the right to receive, all or a portion of the benefits payable with respect to a participant under a retirement plan, and that includes certain information and meets certain other requirements.

A domestic relations order is a judgment, decree, or order (including the approval of a property settlement) that is made pursuant to state domestic relations law (including community property law) and that relates to the provision of child support, alimony payments, or marital property rights for the benefit of a spouse, former spouse, child, or other dependents of a participant.

A state authority, generally a court, must actually issue a judgment, order, or decree or otherwise formally approve a property settlement agreement before it can be a domestic relations order under ERISA. The mere fact that a property settlement is agreed to and signed by the parties will not, in and of itself, cause the agreement to be a domestic relations order.

Statistics

Initiation

According to a study published in the American Law and Economics Review, women file slightly more than two-thirds of divorce cases in the US. There is some variation among states, and the numbers have also varied over time, with about 60% of filings by women in most of the 20th century, and over 70% by women in some states just after no-fault divorce was introduced, according to the paper.

CUSTODY

In their 1997 study titled "Child Custody Policies and Divorce Rates in the US," Kuhn and Guidubaldi find it reasonable to conclude that women anticipate advantages to being single, rather than remaining married. In their detailed analysis of divorce rates, Kuhn and Guidubaldi conclude that acceptance of joint physical custody may reduce divorce. States whose family law policies, statutes, or judicial practice encourage joint custody have shown a greater decline in their divorce rates than those that favor sole custody.

Rates of divorce

"Rate of divorce" usually refers to the number of divorces that occur in the population during a given period. However it is also used in common parlance to refer to the likelihood of a given marriage ending in divorce (as opposed to the death of a spouse).

In 2002 (latest survey data as of 2012), 29% of first marriages among women aged 15–44 were disrupted (ended in separation, divorce or annulment) within 10 years. Beyond the 10-year window, population survey data is lacking, but forecasts and estimates provide some understanding. It is commonly claimed that half of all marriages in the United States eventually end in divorce, an estimate possibly based on the fact that in any given year, the number of marriages is about twice the number of divorces. Amato outlined in his study on divorce that in the late of 1990s, about 43% to 46% of marriages were predicted to end in dissolution. According to his research, only a small percentage of marriages end in permanent separation rather than divorce. Using 1995 data, National Survey of Family Growth forecast in 2002 a 43% chance that first marriages among women aged 15–44 would be disrupted within 15 years. More recently, having spoken with academics and National Survey of Family Growth representatives, PolitiFact.com estimated in 2012 that the lifelong probability of a marriage ending in divorce is 40%–50%.

Variables that may affect rates of divorce include:

- race/ethnicity
- importance of religion to the couple
- divorce in family of origin
- timing of the first birth of any children (before marriage, within 7 months, after 7 months, or never)
- if one spouse has generalized anxiety disorder

A 2008 study by Jenifer L. Bratter and Rosalind B. King conducted on behalf of the Education Resources Information Center examined whether crossing racial boundaries increased the risk of divorce. Using the 2002 National Survey of Family Growth (Cycle VI), the likelihood of divorce for interracial couples to that of same-race couples was compared. Comparisons across marriage cohorts revealed that, overall, interracial couples have higher rates of divorce, particularly for those that married during the late 1980s. The authors found that gender plays a significant role in interracial divorce dynamics: According to the adjusted models predicting divorce as of the 10th year of marriage, interracial marriages that are the most vulnerable involve White females and non-White males (with the exception of White females/Hispanic White males) relative to White/White couples. White wife/Black husband marriages are twice as likely to divorce by the 10th year of marriage compared to White/White couples. Conversely, White men/non-White women couples show either very little or no differences in divorce rates. Asian wife/White husband marriages show only 4% greater likelihood of divorce by the 10th year of marriage than White/White couples. In the case of Black wife/White husband marriages, divorce by the 10th year of marriage is 44% less likely than among White/White unions. Intermarriages that did not cross a racial barrier, which was the case for

White/Hispanic White couples, showed statistically similar likelihoods of divorcing as White/White marriages.

A 2011 study at the University of Iowa found that a woman's loss of virginity before age 18 was correlated with a greater number of occurrences of divorce within the first 10 years of marriage.

A 2012 study cited by Pew Research Center found that an estimated 78% of women with bachelor's degrees, and 65% of men with bachelor's degrees who married between 2006-2010 can expect their marriages to last at least two decades. Women with a high school degree or less, on the other hand, face a meager 40% probability of their marriages surviving the same period.

Studies have shown that men who "earn high incomes have a decreased probability of getting a divorce". However, higher income makes a woman's chances of marriage less likely and it has no connection to possible divorces. In 1995, divorce rates have gone down due to education rates going up. This is because educated individuals make higher incomes in most cases, which result in less financial stress when couples set down to get married. Lower income couples value and respect marriage just as much as higher income couples, however lower income couples are more likely to get a divorce because of financial strains on their marriage. Having low income is not the only factor that can potentially lead to divorce. Religious beliefs, morals and compatibility all come into play when it comes to long term marital statuses.

4

CHINESE MARRIAGE AND DIVORCE LAWS

Traditional Chinese marriage is a ceremonial ritual within Chinese societies that involves not only a union between spouses, but also a union between the two families of a man and a woman, sometimes established by pre-arrangement between families. Marriage and family are inextricably linked, which involves the interests of both families. Within Chinese culture, romantic love and monogamy was the norm for most citizens. Around the end of primitive society, traditional Chinese marriage rituals were formed, with deer skin betrothal in the Fuxi era, the appearance of the "meeting hall" during the Xia and Shang dynasties, and then in the Zhou dynasty, a complete set of marriage etiquette ("six rituals") gradually formed.

The richness of this series of rituals proves the importance the ancients attached to marriage. In addition to the unique nature of the "three letters and six rituals", monogamy, remarriage and divorce in traditional Chinese marriage culture are also distinctive.

MARRIAGE IN A CONFUCIAN CONTEXT

In Confucian thought, marriage is of grave significance to both families and society, as well as being important for the cultivation of virtue. Traditionally incest has been defined as marriage between people with the same surname. "One of the earliest marriage prohibitions, and one surviving to this day, was that forbidding persons of the same surname to marry. An imperial decree of 484 A.D. states that this rule was promulgated far back in the Chou dynasty, which was from 1122 to 255 B.C.' Any one marrying within his clan received sixty blows, and the marriage was declared null and void. It was feared that such mating would produce weak offspring." From the perspective of a Confucian family, marriage brings together families of different surnames and continues the family line of the paternal clan.

This is generally why giving birth to a boy is preferred over a girl. Therefore, the benefits and demerits of any marriage are important to the entire family, not just the individual couples. Socially, the married couple is thought to be the basic unit of society. In

Chinese history, there have been many times when marriages have affected the country's political stability and international relations. For International Relations,"intermarriage has continued throughout Chinese history as a means of establishing and maintaining relations among families in the private sphere, as well as a factor in political careers. " For example, "Marriage alliances, literally 'harmonious kinship,' was something new in its Han-era application. It was a part of a formal peace treaty arrangement at the interstate level, designed to pacify the powerful Hsiung-nu empire" During the Han Dynasty, the rulers of the powerful Xiongnu tribe demanded women from the imperial family.

Many periods of Chinese history were dominated by the families of the wife or mother of the ruling emperor. For the country's political stability, during the Qing dynasty, although no "evidence of prohibitions against ethnic intermarriage within the Eight Banners", "in elite families of the ruling class, primary wives were almost entirely Manchu, while qie (commonly translated as "concubines") and other partners of lower status could be Han". In the Qing Dynasty, most of the high officials were mainly Manchu, so in order to protect the interests of the family, in the selection of a wife will be very important whether the woman was born in the "eight banners". For example, "the ethnicity apparent in the maiden names of wives in genealogies from elite Manchu descent groups, such as the Imperial Lineage."

China: Marriage Law

Chapter I

Article 1 This Law is the fundamental code governing marriage and family relations.

Article 2 A marriage system based on the free choice of partners, on monogamy and on equality between man and woman shall be applied.

The lawful rights and interests of women, children and old people shall be protected. Family planning shall be practised.

Article 3 Marriage upon arbitrary decision by any third party, mercenary marriage and any other acts of interference in the freedom of marriage shall be prohibited. The exaction of money or gifts in connection with marriage shall be prohibited.

Bigamy shall be prohibited. Maltreatment and desertion of one family member by another shall be prohibited.

Chapter II Marriage Contracts

Article 4 Marriage must be based upon the complete willingness of both man and woman. Neither party may use compulsion on the other party, and no third party may interfere.

Article 5 No marriage shall be contracted before the man has reached 22 years of age and the woman 20 years of age. Late marriage and late childbirth shall be encouraged.

Article 6 No marriage may be contracted under any of the following circumstances:

if the man and the woman are lineal relatives by blood, or collateral relatives by blood up to the third degree of kinship; or

if the man or the woman is suffering from leprosy, a cure not having been effected, or from any other disease which is regarded by medical science as rending a person unfit for marriage.

Article 7 Both the man and the woman desiring to contract a marriage shall register in person with the marriage registration office. If the proposed marriage is found to conform with the provisions of this Law, the couple shall be allowed to register and issued marriage certificates. The husband-and-wife relationship shall be established as soon as they acquire the marriage certificates.

Article 8 After a marriage has been registered, the woman may become a member of the man's family or vice versa, depending on the agreed wishes of the two parties.

Chapter III Family Relations

- Article 9 Husband and wife shall have equal status in the family.
- Article 10 Both husband and wife shall have the right to use his or her own surname and given name.
- Article 11 Both husband and wife shall have the freedom to engage in production and other work, to study and to participate in social activities; neither party may restrict or interfere with the other party.
- Article 12 Both husband and wife shall have the duty to practice family planning.
- Article 13 The property acquired by the husband and the wife during the period in which they are under contract of marriage shall be in their joint possession, unless they have agreed otherwise.
- Husband and wife shall enjoy equal rights in the disposition of their jointly possessed property. Article 14 Husband and wife shall have the duty to maintain each other.
- If one party fails to perform this duty, the party in need of maintenance shall have the right to demand maintenance payments from the other party.
- Article 15 Parents shall have the duty to bring up and educate their children; children shall have the duty to support and assist their parents.
- If parents fail to perform their duty, children who are minors or are not capable of living on their own shall have the right to demand the costs of upbringing from their parents.
- If children fail to perform their duty, parents who are unable to work or have difficulty in providing for themselves shall have the right to demand support payments from their children.

- Infanticide by drowning and any other acts causing serious harm to infants shall be prohibited.
- Article 16 Children may adopt either their father's or their mother's surname.
- Article 17 Parents shall have the right and duty to subject their children who are minors to discipline and to protect them. If children who are minors cause damage to the state, the collective or individuals, their parents shall have the duty to compensate for the losses financially.
- Article 18 Husband and wife shall have the right to inherit each other's property.
- Parents and children shall have the right to inherit each other's property.
- Article 19 Children born out of wedlock shall enjoy the same rights as children born in wedlock. No one may harm or discriminate against them.
- The father of a child born out of wedlock shall bear part or the whole of the child's living and educational expenses until the child can support himself.
- Article 20 The state shall protect lawful adoption. The relevant provisions of this Law governing the relationship between parents and children shall apply to the rights and duties in the relationship between foster-parents and foster-children.
- The rights and duties in the relationship between a foster-child and his natural parents shall terminate with the establishment of his adoption.
- Article 21 Maltreatment and discrimination shall not be allowed between step-parents and step-children.
- The relevant provisions of this Law governing the relationship between parents and children shall apply to the rights and duties in the relationship between step-fathers or step-mothers and their step-children who receive care and education from them.
- Article 22 Grandparents who can afford it shall have the duty to bring up their grandchildren who are minors and whose parents are dead. Grandchildren who can afford it shall have the duty to support their grandparents whose children are dead.
- Article 23 Elder brothers or elder sisters who can afford it shall have the duty to bring up their younger brothers or sisters who are minors, if their parents are dead or have no means to bring them up.

Chapter IV Divorce

Article 24 Divorce shall be granted if husband and wife both desire it. Both parties shall apply to the marriage registration office for divorce. The marriage registration office, after clearly establishing that divorce is desired by both parties and that appropriate arrangements have been made for the care of any children and the disposition of property, shall issue the divorce certificates without delay.

- Article 25 If one party alone desires a divorce, the organization concerned may carry out mediation or the party may appeal directly to a people's court to start divorce proceedings.
- In dealing with a divorce case, the people's court should carry out mediation; divorce shall be granted if mediation fails because mutual affection no longer exists.
- Article 26 If the spouse of a soldier in active service desires a divorce, the soldier's consent must be obtained.
- Article 27 A husband may not apply for a divorce when his wife is pregnant or within one year after the birth of the child. This restriction shall not apply in cases where the wife applies for a divorce, or when the people's court deems it necessary to accept the divorce application made by the husband.
- Article 28 If, after divorce, both parties desire to resume their husband-and-wife relationship, they shall apply for registration of remarriage with the marriage registration office. The marriage registration office shall allow them to register.
- Article 29 The relationship between parents and children shall not come to an end with the parents divorce. After divorce, whether the children are put in the custody of the father or the mother, they shall remain the children of both parents.
- After divorce, both parents shall still have the right and duty to bring up and educate their children.

In principle, the mother shall have the custody of a breast-fed infant after divorce. If a dispute arises between the two parents over the custody of their child who has been weaned and they fail to reach an agreement, the people's court shall make a judgment in accordance with the rights and interests of the child and the actual conditions of both parents.

Article 30 If, after divorce, one parent has been given custody of a child, the other parent shall bear part or the whole of the child's necessary living and educational expenses. The two parents shall seek agreement regarding the amount and duration of such payment. If they fail to reach an agreement, the people's court shall make a judgment.

The agreement or court judgment on the payment of a child's living and educational expenses shall not prevent the child from making a reasonable request, when necessary, to either parent for an amount exceeding what was decided upon in the said agreement or judgment.

Article 31 At the time of divorce, the husband and the wife shall seek agreement regarding the disposition of their jointly possessed property. If they fail to reach an agreement, the people's court shall make a judgment, taking into consideration the actual circumstances of the property and the rights and interests of the wife and the child.

Article 32 At the time of divorce, debts incurred jointly by the husband and the wife during their married life shall be paid out of their jointly possessed property. If such property is insufficient to pay the debts, the two parties shall discuss alternative ways of payment. If they fail to reach an agreement, the people's court shall make a judgment. Debts incurred separately by the husband or the wife shall be paid by the party who incurred them.

Article 33 If, at the time of divorce, one party has difficulty in supporting himself or herself, the other party shall render appropriate financial assistance. Specific arrangements shall be worked out by both parties through consultation. If they fail to reach an agreement, the people's court shall make a judgment.

Chapter V Supplementary Provisions

Article 34 Persons violating this Law shall be subject to administrative or legal sanctions in accordance with the law and on the merits of each case.

Article 35 In cases where a person refuses to abide by the judgments or rulings on costs of upbringing, maintenance or support payments, or on the partitioning or inheritance of property, the people's court shall enforce the execution of the judgments or rulings in accordance with the law. The organizations concerned shall have the duty to assist such executions.

Article 36 The people's congresses of national autonomous areas and their standing committees may formulate certain adaptations or supplementary provisions in keeping with the principles of this Law and in the light of the specific conditions of the local nationalities in regard to marriage and family. Provisions formulated by autonomous prefectures and autonomous counties must be submitted to the standing committee of the people's congress of the relevant province or autonomous region for approval. Provisions formulated by autonomous regions must be submitted to the Standing Committee of the National People's Congress for the record.

Article 37 This Law shall come into force as of January 1, 1981.

JURISDICTION FOR INTERNATIONAL DIVORCE IN CHINA

Under Chinese laws, there is no prohibition for divorcing until you have been married for a certain length of time, as there is in some countries (for example to divorce through the English courts you must be married for 1 year or more). In China, even if you married yesterday, you are entitled to apply for divorce today if you believe your marriage has irretrievably broken-down. However, if a husband and wife do not agree to divorce, the Chinese court may suggest reconciliation. However, the possibility for the Chinese court to accept a divorce application will depend on satisfying the court's jurisdiction. In order for British and other expats to divorce within the Chinese courts, one of the following jurisdiction criteria must be met:

1. Either the husband or wife is Chinese;
2. The marriage is registered in China;
3. Either spouse has been habitually resident in China for at least one year;
4. Both parties mutually agree to divorce in China on the basis that they married outside of China and neither are Chinese, but they are habitually living in China continuously for a year or more.

Grounds for divorce in China

'Irretrievable break-down of marriage' is the principle which the Chinese court must adhere to when making the decision on divorce. Within the Chinese courts, one of the following circumstances should be used to support the assertion of 'irretrievable breakdown of marriage':

- One party to the marriage has committed adultery, or is cohabiting with a third party;
- Domestic violence, or maltreatment and desertion of one party to the marriage by another;
- Bad habits of one spouse for example gambling or drug addiction, which remain persistent despite repeated warnings;
- Separation of the parties for two full years caused by incompatibility;
- Any other circumstances causing alienation of mutual affection between the parties.

In addition, a divorce shall be granted if one party to the marriage is declared to be missing and the other party files an action for divorce because of this.

In a summary, during the course of divorce proceeding, the party who is the applicant for divorce should provide enough evidence to prove that the marriage has broken down irretrievably.

FINANCIAL AND CHILDREN MATTERS

While processing a divorce, the Chinese courts may also make orders concerning marital assets and arrangements for any children.

Correctly drafted prenuptial agreements or marital agreements will be followed by the court. Where the parties do not have a prenuptial or marital agreement, the Chinese court will generally respect a mutual agreement in relation to family assets and maintenance that has been reached between the parties. If an agreement cannot be reached, the Chinese courts will impose orders to divide assets, provide maintenance for any children, and set out arrangements for the children's care.

The main principle followed by the Chinese courts is that the 'children's best interests' must be taken in to account. This applies to domestic and international family cases. Within contested divorce proceeding, parents are required to file evidence in support of their application for child custody, for example. The Chinese court would also ensure that the rights and duties of the non-custodial parent are taken into account.

How long does expat divorce in China take?

Under the Procedural Law of PRC, a domestic case that is settled using the summary procedure takes between 3 and 6 months. In international cases that may involve service of documents overseas, and collection of evidence overseas, the length of the divorce may be more. In addition, for cross-border family cases, the period within which a judgment can be appealed is 30 days, whereas for domestic cases it is 15 days.

Ancient Chinese marriages

Marriages in early societies

In modern Chinese thinking, people in "primitive" societies did not marry, but had sexual relationships with one another indiscriminately. Such people were thought to live like animals, and they did not have the precise concept of motherhood, fatherhood, sibling, husband and wife, and gender, not to mention match-making and marriage ceremony. Part of the Confucian "civilizing mission" was to define what it meant to be a Father or a Husband, and to teach people to respect the proper relationship between family members and regulate sexual behavior.

Mythological origin

The story about the marriage of sister and brother Nüwa and Fu Xi told how they invented proper marriage procedures after marrying. At that time the world was unpopulated, so the siblings wanted to get married but, at the same time, they felt ashamed. So they went up to Kunlun Mountains and prayed to the heavens. They asked for permission for their marriage and said, "if you allow us to marry, please make the mist surround us." The heavens gave permission to the couple, and promptly the peak was covered in mist. It is said that in order to hide her shyness, Nüwa covered her blushing face with a fan. Nowadays in some villages in China, the brides still follow the custom and use a fan to shield their faces.

Historic marriage practices

Endogamy among different classes in China were practiced, the upper class like the Shi class married among themselves, while commoners married among themselves also, avoiding marriage with slaves and other ordinary people. This practice was enforced under the law.

MATERNAL MARRIAGE AND MONOGAMY

In a maternal marriage, the husband moved in the woman's family home after the marriage. This happened in the transformation of antithetic marriage into monogamy, which signified the decline of matriarchy and the growing dominance of patriarchy in ancient China.

Marriage matters in Xinjiang (1880–1949)

Even though Muslim women are forbidden to marry non-Muslims in Islamic law, from 1880 to 1949 it was frequently violated in Xinjiang since Chinese men married Muslim Turki (Uyghur) women, a reason suggested by foreigners that it was due to the women being poor, while the Turki women who married Chinese were labelled as whores by the Turki community, these marriages were illegitimate according to Islamic law but the women obtained benefits from marrying Chinese men since the Chinese defended them from Islamic authorities so the women were not subjected to the tax on prostitution and were able to save their income for themselves.

Chinese men gave their Turki wives privileges which Turki men's wives did not have, since the wives of Chinese did not have to wear a veil and a Chinese man in Kashgar once beat a mullah who tried to force his Turki Kashgari wife to veil. The Turki women also benefited in that they were not subjected to any legal binding to their Chinese husbands so they could make their Chinese husbands provide them with as much their money as she wanted for her relatives and herself since otherwise the women could just leave, and the property of Chinese men was left to their Turki wives after they died.

Turki women considered Turki men to be inferior husbands to Chinese and Hindus. Because they were viewed as "impure", Islamic cemeteries banned the Turki wives of Chinese men from being buried within them, the Turki women got around this problem by giving shrines donations and buying a grave in other towns. Besides Chinese men, other men such as Hindus, Armenians, Jews, Russians, and Badakhshanis intermarried with local Turki women.

The local society accepted the Turki women and Chinese men's mixed offspring as their own people despite the marriages being in violation of Islamic law. Turki women also conducted temporary marriages with Chinese men such as Chinese soldiers temporarily stationed around them as soldiers for tours of duty, after which the Chinese men returned to their own cities, with the Chinese men selling their mixed daughters with the Turki women to his comrades, taking their sons with them if they could afford it but leaving them if they couldn't, and selling their temporary Turki wife to a comrade or leaving her behind.

Marriage during the Han Dynasty (202 BCE – 220 CE)

Marriages during this time included a number of mandatory steps, of which the most important of them was the presentation of betrothal gifts from the groom and his family to the bride and her family. The bride's family then countered with a dowry. Sometimes the bride's family would buy goods with the betrothal money. Using a betrothal gift for family financial needs rather than saving it for the bride was viewed as dishonorable because it appeared as though the bride has been sold. A marriage without a dowry or a betrothal gifts was also seen as dishonorable. The bride was seen as a concubine instead of a wife.

Once all the goods were exchanged the bride was taken to the ancestral home of the groom. There she was expected to obey her husband and his living relatives. Women continued to belong to their husband's families even if they had passed. If the widow's birth family wanted her to marry again, they would often have to ransom her back from her deceased husband's family. If they had any children they stayed with his family.

Marriage brokers during the Ming Dynasty

In the Ming period, marriage was considered solemn and according to the law written in The Ming Code (Da Ming Lü), all commoners' marriages must follow the rules written in Duke Wen's Family Rules (Wen Gong Jia Li). The rules stated that "in order to arrange a marriage, an agent must come and deliver messages between the two families." A marriage broker had the license to play important roles by arranging marriages between two families. Sometimes both families were influential and wealthy and the matchmaker bonded the two families into powerful households. Studies have shown that, "In the Ming and Qing dynasties, a number of noble families emerged in Jiaxing of Zhejiang, where marriage is the most important way to expand their clan strength." Hence, marriage brokers were crucial during the Ming era, which offered us an insight of the lives of the Ming commoners.

Instead of using the more gender general term "mei ren" texts more frequently referred to marriage brokers as "mei po". Since "po" translates to "grannies" in English, it suggests that elderly female characters dominated the "marriage market". Indeed, in the novel The Golden Lotus (Jing Ping Mei), the four matchmakers Wang, Xue, Wen, Feng were all elderly female characters. In ancient China, people believed that marriages belong to the "Yin" side (the opposite is "Yang"), which corresponds to females.

In order to maintain the balance between Yin and Yang, women should not interfere with the Yang side and men should not interfere with the Yin side. Since breaking the balance may lead to disorder and misfortune, men were rarely seen in marriage arrangements. Furthermore, unmarried girls were not in the occupation because they themselves knew little about marriage and were not credible in arranging marriages. As a result, almost all marriage brokers in the literary work were presented as elderly females.

Being a successful marriage broker required various special skills. Firstly, the broker must be very persuasive. The broker must persuade both sides of the marriage that the arrangement was impeccable, even though many times the arrangement was actually not perfect. In Feng Menglong's "Old Man Zhang Grows Melons and Marries Wennü" in the collection Stories Old and New (Gu Jin Xiao Shuo), he wrote about an eighty-year-old man who married an eighteen-year young girl. The marriage was arranged by two matchmakers, Zhang and Li. Given the age difference, the marriage seemed impossible, but the two brokers still managed to persuade the father of the girl to marry her to the old man. Feng Menglong described them as "Once they start to speak the match is successfully arranged, and when they open their mouths they only spoke about harmony."

The brokers gave powerful persuasions by avoiding about mentioning the differences between the couples they arranged. Which, only speak about the positive side. In addition to persuasion techniques, the brokers must possess great social skills. They needed to know a network of people so that when the time comes for marriage, they were able to seek the services of the brokers. Finally, when someone came to the broker, she must be able to pick out a matching suitors according to her knowledge of the local residents.

Normally a perfect couple must have similar social status, economic status, and age. Wealthy families would look for a bride of similar social status who could manage the family finances and, most importantly, produce sons to inherit the family's wealth. Poor families, on the other hand, will not be as demanding and will only look for a bride who is willing to work hard in the fields. Sometimes they even need to travel to neighboring towns for a match, hence the verse "Traveling to the east household, traveling to the west household, their feet are always busy and their voices are always loud." Furthermore, mediators are required to know some mathematics and simple characters in order to write the matrimonial contract. The contract included "the sum of the bride price, the identity and age of both partners, and the identity of the person who presided over the wedding ceremony, usually the parents or grandparents." Without the knowledge of math and simple written characters, composing such a detailed contract would be impossible.

The matchmakers made a living not only by facilitating successful marriage arrangements, but also by delivering messages between the two families. When they visited the households to deliver messages, the hosts usually provided them food and drinks to enjoy, hence the verse "Asking for a cup of tea, asking for a cup of alcohol, their faces are 3.3 inches thick (they are really cheeky)."

However, these "visiting payments" were tiny compared to the payment they receive for a successful marriage. The visiting payment was always measured by "wen" or cash. Whereas the final payment was measured by "liang" or taels, and one tael was equivalent to a thousand wen. Therefore, the brokers would spend most of their time travelling back and forth between the two households to persuade them of the marriage. In addition, the matchmakers receive payments for introducing young girls to wealthy men. In Zhang Dai's diary The Dream Collection of Tao'an (Tao'an Meng Yi), he described a scene in which matchmakers brought young beautiful girls to the houses of wealthy customers to choose. Even if the customer was not satisfied he would reward the matchmaker several hundreds wen.

As marriage brokers, these grannies also possessed the "guilty knowledge" of secret affairs. In The Golden Lotus (Jing Ping Mei), the matchmaker Wang speculated that Ximen Qing was fond of the married woman Pan Jinlian, so she introduced Pan to Ximen, helped them to have an affair and hide the secret for them. According to the law married woman must be loyal to her husband, and anyone who discovered an affair of the woman should report her immediately. Although, the matchmakers were licensed to keep secrets about affairs because keeping privacy of their clients was their obligation. Even so, they were usually criticized for doing so. In The Golden Lotus Wang was blamed for egging ladies on having improper affairs.

TRADITIONAL MARRIAGE RITUALS

Chinese marriage became a custom between 402 and 221 BC. Despite China's long history and many different geographical areas, there are essentially six rituals, generally known as the three letters and six etiquettes. Unfortunately for some traditional families, the wife's mother cannot go to her son-in-law's family until one year (according to the Chinese lunar calendar or Chinese Lunar New Year) after the wedding has elapsed. However, during this one year the daughter can go back at any time.

Six etiquettes

The wedding ceremony consisted of six basic procedures: making a proposal of marriage (nacai), requesting the bride's name and date of birth(wenming), sending news of divination results and betrothal gifts (naji), sending wedding presents to the bride's house (nazheng), requesting the date of the wedding (qingqi), and fetching in the bride in person (qinying). The details of each ritual could vary.

1. **Proposal:** After an unmarried boy's parents found a potential daughter-in-law, they located a matchmaker whose job was to assuage the conflict of interests and general embarrassments when discussing the possibility of marriage on the part of two families largely unknown to each other. Marriages were chosen based upon the needs of reproduction and honor, as well as the need of the father and husband.
2. **Birthdates:** If the selected girl and the boy and her parents did not object to the proposal, the matchmaker would match the birthdates; lit. 'the 8 cyclic characters for year, month, day and hour of birth of a man, which determine his fate') in which suan ming (Chinese fortune telling) is used to predict the future of that couple-to-be. If the result of suan ming was good, they then would go to the next step, submitting bride price.
3. **Bridewealth (betrothal gifts):** At this point the bridegroom's family arranged for the matchmaker to present a bride price (betrothal gifts), including the betrothal letter, to the bride's family.
4. **Wedding gifts:** The groom's family would then send an elaborate array of food, cakes, and religious items to the bride's family.
5. **Arranging the wedding:** Before the wedding ceremony, two families would arrange a wedding day according to Chinese tung shing. Selecting an auspicious day to assure a good future for the couple is as important as avoiding what is believed to be an unlucky day. In some cases there may be no auspicious dates and the couple will have to review their potential date range.
6. **Wedding ceremony:** The final ritual would be the actual wedding ceremony where bride and groom become a married couple, which consists of many elaborate parts (see below):

- **Wedding procession:** Before the meeting party's arrival, the bride would be helped by a respectable old woman to tie up her hair with colorful cotton threads. She would wear a red skirt, as red traditionally symbolizes happiness. When the party arrived, the bride must cry with her mother to symbolize her reluctance to leave home. She would then be led or carried by her elder brother to the sedan. From here, the wedding procession from the bride's home to the groom's home consists of a traditional band, the bride's sedan, the maid of honors sedans (if there are maids of honor), and bride's dowry in the forms other than money. The most common dowries included scissors like two butterflies never separating, rulers indicating acres of fields, and vases for peace and wealth.

- **Welcoming the bride:** The wedding procession of the bride's family stops at the door of the groom's home. In the meeting party the groom would meet a series of difficulties intentionally set in his path. Only after coping with these could he pass to see his wife-to-be.
- **Actual wedding ceremonies:** On the arrival of the sedan at the wedding place, there would be music and firecrackers. The bride would be led along the red carpet in a festive atmosphere. The groom, also in a red gown, would kowtow three times to worship the heaven, parents and spouse. Equivalent to exchanging vows in the west, the couple would pay respect to the Jade Emperor, the patron family deities (or patron buddhas and bodhisattvas), paying respect to deceased ancestors, the bride and groom's parents and other elders, and paying respect to each other. Then, the new couple would go to their bridal chamber and guests would be treated to a feast.
- **Wedding** banquets In Chinese society, the wedding banquet is known as x-ju, and is sometimes far more important than the actual wedding itself. There are ceremonies such as the bride presenting wines or tea to parents, spouse, and guests. In modern weddings, the bride generally picks red (following Chinese tradition) or white (more Western) for the wedding, but most will wear the red traditional garment for their formal wedding banquet. Traditionally, the groom is not responsible for the cost of the wedding invitation sweet treats (often pastries), the banquet invitations, and the wedding itself. Wedding banquets are elaborate and consist usually of 5–10 courses, with ingredients such as shark fin, abalone, lobster, squab, sea cucumber, swift nests or fish roe in soup or as decoration on top of a dish to symbolize fertility, and local delicacies. Traditionally, the father of the bride is responsible for the wedding banquet hosted on the bride's side and the alcohol consumed during both banquets. The wedding banquets are two separate banquets: the primary banquet is hosted once at the bride's side, the second banquet (smaller banquet) at the groom's side. While the wedding itself is often based on the couple's choices, the wedding banquets are a gesture of thanks and appreciation, to those that have raised the bride and groom (such as grandparents and uncles). It is also to ensure the relatives on each side meet the relatives on the other side. Thus out of respect for the elders, wedding banquets are usually done formally and traditionally, which the older generation is thought to be more comfortable with. On the night of the wedding day, there was a custom in some places for relatives or friends to banter the newlyweds. Though this seemed a little noisy, both of them dropped shyness and got familiar with each other. On

the third day of the marriage, the new couple would go back to the bride's parents' home. They would be received with also a dinner party including relatives.

Modern practices

Since the late 1990s, it has become popular to create an elaborate wedding album, often taken at a photography studio. The album usually consists of many pictures of the bride and groom taken at various locations with many different outfits. In Singapore, these outfits often include wedding outfits belonging to different cultures, including Arab and Japanese wedding outfits. In contrast to Western wedding pictures, the Chinese wedding album will not contain pictures of the actual ceremony and wedding itself.

In Mandarin Chinese, a mang nian, or 'blind year', when there are no first days of spring, such as in year 2010, a Year of the Tiger, is considered an ominous time to marry or start a business. In the preceding year, there were two first days of spring.

In recent years, Confucian wedding rituals have become popular among Chinese couples. In such ceremonies, which are a recent innovation with no historic antecedent, the bride and groom bow and pay respects to a large portrait of Confucius hanging in the banquet hall while wedding attendants and the couple themselves are dressed in traditional Chinese robes.

Before the bride and groom enter the nuptial chambers, they exchange nuptial cups and perform ceremonial bows as follows:

1. first bow – Heaven and Earth
2. second bow – ancestors
3. third bow – parents
4. fourth bow – spouse

Traditional divorce process

In traditional Chinese society, there are three major ways to dissolve a marriage.

The first one is no-fault divorce. According to the Tang Code, the legal code of the Tang Dynasty (618–907), a marriage may be dissolved due to personal incompatibility, provided that the husband writes a divorce note.

The second way is through state-mandated annulment of marriage. This applies when one spouse commits a serious crime (variously defined, usually more broadly for the wife) against the other or his/her clan. If the couple does not take the initiative to divorce when arose the situation of, the state will intervene to force them to divorce. If one side refused to divorce, the law must investigate the criminal liability of the party with a one-year prison sentence. Once a divorce is adjudged, they must not be reunited.

The third way of Chinese divorce process is mutual divorce. It is a way that both husband and wife can have the power to divorce. However, It requires both of their agreement. In Chinese Marriage, this way of divorce is to ensure both husband and wife have the equal power to protect themselves, such as their property. It also enhanced the concept of responsibility in Chinese marriage. Divorce is a responsibility to each other. So, the country or the government won't intervene the divorce most of the time.

Finally, the husband may unilaterally declare a divorce. To be legally recognized, it must be based on one of the following seven reasons:

- The wife lacks filial piety towards her parents-in-law. This makes the parents-in-law potentially capable of breaking a marriage against both partners' wills.
- She fails to bear a son.
- She is vulgar or lewd/adulterous.
- She is jealous. This includes objecting to her husband taking an additional wife or concubine.
- She has a vile disease.
- She is gossipy.
- She commits theft.

There are, however, three clearly defined exceptions, under which unilateral divorce is forbidden despite the presence of any of the seven aforementioned grounds:

- She has no family to return to.
- She had observed a full, three-year mourning for a parent-in-law.
- Her husband was poor when they married, and is now rich.

The above law about unilateral divorce was in force from Tang Dynasty up to its final abolition in the Republic of China's Civil Code (Part IV) Section 5, passed in 1930.

Divorce in contemporary China

After the establishment of the People's Republic in 1949, the country's new Marriage Law also explicitly provided for lawful divorces. Women were permitted to divorce their husbands and many did, sparking resistance from rural males especially. Kay Ann Johnson reported that tens of thousands of women in north central China were killed for seeking divorces or committed suicide when blocked from doing so.

Divorce was rare during the Mao era (1949–1976), but it has become easier and more commonplace in the post-reform era. A USC U.S.-China Institute article reports that the divorce rate in 2006 was about 1.4/1000 people, about twice what it was in 1990 and more than three times what it was in 1982. Still, the divorce rate in China is less than half what it is in the United States. One of the most important breakthroughs in the marriage institution were amendments added to the Marriage Law in 2001, which shortened the divorce-application procedure and added legitimate reasons for divorce, such as emphasizing the importance of faithfulness within a married couple, a response to rising failure of marriages due to unfaithful affairs during marriages that have come into public knowledge.

With the rising divorce rates nowadays, public discussions and governmental organs often criticize the lack of effort in marriage maintenance which many couples express. This is evident, for example in the new 'divorce buffer zones' established in the marriage registration offices in certain provinces, which is a room where the couples wait, as a stage within the divorce application procedure, and are encouraged to talk things over and consider giving their marriage another chance. However, such phenomena don't contradict the increasing permissiveness of the systems and of married couples which lead to the constant growth in divorce rates in China.

Amendments have also been made to Article 32 of the revised 2001 Marriage Law. Parties to a marriage can apply for Divorce under, and by showing, the following grounds:

- Bigamy or a married person cohabiting with a third party;
- Domestic violence or maltreatment and desertion of one family member by another;
- Bad habits of gambling or drug addiction that remain incorrigible despite repeated admonition;
- Separation caused by incompatibility, which lasts two full years;
- Any other circumstances causing alienation of mutual affection.

Monogamy

In ancient China, women's social status was not as good as men. A woman could only obey and rely on her husband. She shared her husband's class, whether he was a peasant, merchant, or official; accordingly, the clothes she could wear and the etiquette she was expected to display depended on her husband's background and achievements. If her husband was dead, she could remarry but would be seen as not decent. The neo-Confucian opposition to widow remarriage was expressed in an oft-quoted aphorism of Zhu Xi: "It is a small matter to starve to death, but a large matter to lose one's virtue." Moreover, the government has also issued measures against widow remarriage. For example"The state reinforced the neo-Confucian attitude against widow remarriage by erecting commemorative arches to honour women who refused to remarry. In 1304, the Yuan government issued a proclamation declaring that all women widowed before they were thirty who remained chaste widows until they were fifty were to be so honoured. The Ming and Qing continued the practice."

The virtues of chaste widowhood were extolled by instructions for women, such as the Nu Lun Yu (Analects for Women). While a man could have though only one wife but many concubines and marry someone else as new wife if the wife died before him. The general dignitaries also had only one wife but many concubines.

Sororate marriage

Sororate marriage is a custom in which a man marries his wife's sister(s). Later it is expanded to include her cousins or females from the same clan. It can happen at the same time as he marries the first wife, at a later time while the wife is still alive, or after she dies. This practice occurred frequently among the nobility of the Zhou Dynasty (1045 BC – 256 BC), with cases occurring at later times.

Multiple wives with equal status

- Emperors of some relatively minor dynasties are known to have multiple empresses.
- Created by special circumstances. For example, during wartime a man may be separated from his wife and mistakenly believe that she had died. He remarries, and later the first wife is found to be alive. After they are reunited, both wives may be recognized.
- Qianlong Emperor of Qing dynasty began to allow polygamy for the specific purpose of siring heirs for another branch of the family (see Levirate marriage). Called "multiple inheritance", if a man is the only son of his father, and his uncle has no son, then with mutual agreement he may marry an additional wife. A male child from this union becomes the uncle's grandson and heir. The process can be repeated for additional uncles.

Beside the traditional desire for male children to carry on the family name, this allowance partially resolves a dilemma created by the emperor himself. He had recently banned all non-patrilineal forms of inheritance, while wanting to preserve the proper order in the Chinese kinship. Therefore, a couple without son cannot adopt one from within the extended family. They either have to adopt from outside (which was regarded by many as passing the family wealth to unrelated "outsiders"), or become heirless. The multiple inheritance marriages provided a way out when the husband's brother has a son.

Ruzhui marriage

The custom of ruzhui applied when a relatively wealthy family had no male heirs, while a poorer family had multiple male children. Under these circumstances, a male from the poorer family, generally a younger sibling, will marry into the wealthier family in order to continue their family line. In a ruzhui (lit., 'the [man] becoming superfluous') marriage, the children will take on the surname of the wife.

CONCUBINAGE

In ancient China, concubinage was very common, and men who could afford it usually bought concubines and took them into their homes in addition to their wives. The standard Chinese term translated as "concubine" means "concubine: my and your servant. In the family hierarchy, the principal wife (diqi) ranked second only to her husband, while a concubine was always inferior to the wife, even if her relations with the husband were more intimate. Women in concubinage were treated as inferior, and expected to be subservient to the wife (if there was one). The women were not wedded in a whole formal ceremony, had less right in the relationship, and could be divorced arbitrarily. They generally came from lower social status or were bought as slaves.

Women who had eloped may have also become concubines since a formal wedding requires her parents' participation.

The number of concubines was sometime regulated, which differs according to the men's rank. In ancient China, men of higher social status often supported several concubines, and Chinese emperors almost always had dozens of, even hundreds of royal concubines.

Polyandry

Polyandry, the practice of a woman having multiple husbands, is traditionally considered by Han as immoral, prohibited by law, and uncommon in practice. However, historically there have been instances in which a husband in poverty rents or pawns his wife temporarily. However amongst other Chinese ethnicities polyandry existed and exists, especially in mountainous areas.

In a subsistence economy, when available land could not support more than one family, dividing it between surviving sons would eventually lead to a situation in which none would have the resources to survive; in such a situation the sons of a family would wed a woman together. Polyandry in certain Tibetan autonomous areas in modern China remains legal. This however only applies to the ethnic minority Tibetans of the region and not to other ethnic groups.

5

MARRIAGE AND DIVORCE LAWS OF INDIA

There are four marriage laws in India; Hindu Marriage Law, Christian Marriage Law, Muslim Marriage Law, and Special Marriage Law. A marriage certificate appears to be the only legal declaration that confirms two adult Indian citizens are married. Marriage registration abides by the provisions of the Marriage Act enforced since 1955. A marriage certificate is accepted as legitimate evidence in all government establishments, banks, and other private organisations.

The Supreme Court of India compulsorily stipulated marriage certificates for all married couples in 2006. This was a revolutionary step taken toward protecting women's rights in India. Marriage registration comes with a set of benefits and features. The groom must be above 21 years old to apply for a marriage certificate, while the bride should not be below 18. A marriage registration certificate is needed when someone applies for a passport or VISA. It is also required for the woman to open bank accounts after her marriage if she changes her surname after marriage.

Thus, the government tried to emphasize the necessity of issuing a marriage certificate to all the citizens by every possible means. However, the norms of marriage registration vary from one religion to another, but the underlying idea remains the same. A marriage certificate can now be downloaded online too.

This reduces the hassle that would have been involved otherwise in the traditional method where a couple needed to visit the Registrar's office and be physically available for all the tedious procedures, starting from submitting documents to collecting the marriage certificate. Divorce is a big life disruptor that may cause a great deal of stress—financial, emotional, and even spiritual and thus is one of the most traumatic events that can happen to any marriage. Divorce gets associated with religion in India since it is a personal affair.

The Divorce Process in India is governed by the Hindu Marriage Act of 1955 for Jains, Sikhs, Hindus, and Buddhists. The Dissolution of Muslim Marriage Act, 1939, rules divorce laws for Muslims, the Parsi Marriage and Divorce Act,1936 governs divorce laws for Parsis, and the Indian Divorce Act,1869 governs divorce laws for Christians. The Special Marriages Act of 1954 governs all inter-community marriages.

MATRIMONIAL LAWS IN INDIA

Marriage is the blissfully state of the two parties which conveys not only the act or formalities should be performed by them but also the status as husband and wife in the society. Marriage is a foundation of stable family, two soul united as a spouse, a permanent union of hearts. Earlier times marriage was recognized as religious as well as social institution and not legal one but as times changes, now it is considered as ones personal choice and marriage between two individual and not between two families.

Thus, it moved to become a contract and requires fulfilling legal requirements. Marriage as per law means a contract between man and woman united together to support each other in a shared household. Right to marry is recognized under article 21 of the Indian Constitution well as article 16 of Universal Declaration of Human Rights, 1948.

Meaning of marriage differ from person to person some will say union of lives, some will say bond of love, some will say life imprisonment and some will say something else. Matrimonial laws in India were based on English matrimonial law at the time they were drafted as they were drafted by warren hasting in 1772.

However there is no single uniform code of law for marriage rather we have different laws for different religions. For Hindu we have The Hindu marriage act, 1955 , for Muslim the Muslim Personal Law (Shariat) Application Act 1937 , for Christian and Parsi: The Indian Christian Marriage Act, 1872 and The Parsi Marriage and Divorce Act, 1936 respectively. For the one who don't profess any religion we have The Special Marriage Act, 1954 to govern their marriage.

Hindu Marriage Law

Marriage under Hindu is considered to be sacrament bond and is union for upcoming seven lives and is not subject to dissolution because it is not a mere contract between man and woman. Vedas teaches that marriage is also considered as duty of a person.

- The Hindu marriage act, 1955 amends and codifies the matrimonial law among Hindus. This act applies to Hindu, Buddhist, Jain or Sikh.
- Act states capacity to marry and these conditions are mentioned in the section 5 which says there should be no spouse living at the time of marriage which means Hindu culture does not entertains bigamy, bride and groom at the time of wedding must be sound mind, give their free consent and are not insane .Both must have completed the age of 21 , don't relate to each other within the degrees of prohibited relationships and are not sapindas to each other.
- Section 7 defines the ceremonies to be performed in the Hindu marriage in order to solemnize which are sagai , kanyadan and saptapadi.
- Sagai is a ring exchange ceremony performed by bride and groom.
- kanyadan is a emotional and sentimental ceremony where a dad donates their daughter to groom and transfers his responsibility to groom of her daughter.
- Saptapadi is the ceremony where bride and groom take seven rounds of the god of fire in Hindu religion where sacred fire act as invocation and meanwhile priest chants sacred texts(mantras). When the seventh step is taken the marriage is solemnised in Hindu religion.
- In Samit Subhash Agarwal v. Kamlesh Lataprasad Gupta , husband challenged the validity of marriage and court held that taking seven pheras around agarbatii doesn't mean they have not took seven around the scared fire and makes their marriage invalid.
- Forms of marriage

The ancient Hindu law recognized three kinds of marriage which are valid and regular. These were Brahma (arrange marriage), Gandharva (love marriage) and Asura (bride sold by father for money).

- o Brahma marriage is known to be the arranged marriage where a father and family members of the girl finds groom for her. This kind of marriage is mostly practised in past times and marriage of bride and groom will be done according to the shastric rites and ceremonies.
- o Gandharva marriage is also known as love marriage where bride and groom voluntary unite and marry according to their choice irrespective of their father's choice. This kind of marriage is practised in the modern time and according to shastric rites and ceremonies are being performed.
- o Asura marriage is forced marriage where a bride is sold by his father to groom and his family.

- However, the current Hindu Marriage Act does not include such forms of marriage in it. As the people in today's worlds do things according to their choice not as per their parents choice. And also time is changing and parents also give importance to their child's choice and understands that they have to live together so let them decide themselves.

- Registration of marriage

Section 8 has given power to make rules for proof of marriage to state government. Hindu marriage registrar has given all the power to direct time for the parties to show their evidence and to get their certificate after payment of a prescribed fee.

Muslim Marriage Law

- Muslim law is largely uncodified in India as Quran is silent or incomplete.
- Muslim marriage is a civil contract where two persons enter into contract with the view of sexual pleasure and legalisation of children. The Islamic concept of marriage is different from Hindu marriage as in Hindu it is sacrament bond but in Islam, it is a contract.

Essentials of a valid Muslim marriage:

1. **Proposal and acceptance**- proposal in urdu is stated as ijab and acceptance of the proposal is 'qubul' in urdu. Both ijab as well as qubul has to be done in same meeting and in the presence of proper and competent witnesses otherwise it will be not be a valid marriage

2. **Competency of parties**-both partied must attained their puberty, which means they must be major. Bride and groom must be of sound mind while performing nikah and should be Muslim.

3. **Free consent of parties**- while reading nikah free consent of both the parties is required that means consent must be free from coercion, fraud, mistake of fact in order to term as free consent.

4. **Dower or mahr** is defined as the sum of money or property given by husband to his wife in consideration of marriage contract as a mark of respect to the wife.

5. **Free from Legal Disability**-Under Muslim law, marriage is not permitted under certain circumstances and this restrictions/prohibition can be divided into three parts: Absolute Prohibition, Relative Prohibition, and Miscellaneous Prohibition.

Muslim marriages are classified into four:

- Sahih marriage or valid marriage:

It is the marriage where each and every kind of conditions are fulfilled in order to known as valid marriage

- Fasid is irregular marriage where irregularity if removed then this type of marriage could be convert to Sahih marriage. Grounds for Fasid marriage are marrying to a fifth wife, marrying to the women who is undergoing Iddat, marrying without proper witnesses, marrying to a woman who is idol worshipper.

- Batil is void from the beginning and cannot be converted to valid marriage after removing irregularities like fasid marriage. Grounds for batil marriage are woman practicing polyandry or marrying to man who worships fire, couples sharing common ancestors, man marrying his sister in law during the lifetime of his wife.
- Muta marriage is a temporary marriage and the object of contract is enjoyment and time period of it must be fixed with proposal and acceptance in the same meeting, dower should be fixed. Muta marriage with Hindu women is considered to be void.

Christian Marriage Law

- The Indian Christian Marriage Act, 1872 codifies the matrimonial law among Christians.
- Indian Christians takes place in church in the presence of witnesses as well as clergymen.they exchange their ring take vows while reading of the Bible take place.

Conditions for certified Christian marriage:

Section 60 of the Act states the Christian marriage condition which is as follows:

- The age of man and women must be 21 and 18 respectively.
- Neither of the party shall have living partner.
- In front of licensed person as stated under section 9 , and two credible witnesses other than such person, each of the marrying party must say to each other that they accept each other as their better half.

Solemnization of Marriage

According to section 4 marriages done between Christian or non-Christian will be solemnized according to the sections in the act and any marriage without provision stated in the act shall be void.

- Persons authorized to solemnize Christian marriage

Section 5 states the Christian marriage to to be solemnized by whom.

- Time specified for solemnizing marriage

Section 10 states the time for solemnizing the marriage which is from six in the morning to seven in the evening.

- Place of solemnization

Section 11 permits the clergyman of the Church of England to solemnize a marriage in the church unless there is no church within the 5 miles from the shortest distance from such please.

- Notice of marriage as per schedule I

Section 12 states any of the party is suppose to give the notice as mentioned in the I schedule of the act to the concerned minister by whom the marriage is going to be solemnized. The notice must contain the important information such as name along with surname as well as profession, residence, dwelling place of both parties along with time they lived there, church chosen by them for solemnization of the marriage.

- Publication of such notice

Section 13 , when the notice reached to the minister of religion, he shall affix the notice in the church.

- Procedure of receipt of notice

Section 16 once the notice is fixed in the church by minister of religion he must send that notice to each of the other marriage registrars in the same district or as given in the act.

- Issue of certificate

Section 17 states when minister sends the notice to the either party to the marriage then he must make the declarations as per Section 18 .Issue of certificate should be done only after expiry of 4 days from the notice delivered and parties fulfilled the lawful impediment in order to get certificate.

- Solemnization of marriage

Section 25 of the Act states that after the certificate issued as per section 17 in front of 2 credible witness ,the minister is supposed to solemnize the marriage in any of the form of ceremony he adopts.

- Section 26 states that if the marriage is not solemnized within the 2 months from the date of issue of certificate issued to the parties then the marriage will be void and new certificate should be issued to the parties.

- Granting Certificate of marriage

Section 61 states once the marriage is solemnized as per provision stated in the section 60 authorized person shall issue the certificate of marriage of solemnization after paying of the prescribed fee (25 paise) and when declaration has been made. The certificate must be signed by the authority as well as parties to the marriage. Section 61 makes the marriage certificate important as it is the proof of marriage and it will act as evidence of a valid marriage in the court.

Parsi Marriage Law

- The Parsi Marriage and Divorce Act, 1936 codifies the matrimonial law among Parsis.
- There are various ceremonies performed in the parsi wedding some of them are bride and groom have to face each other and a curtain is to placed between them and rice is thrown by bride and groom on each other while priest chants the prayers .Priest will be asking the certain questions to the bride groom and witnesses which will include whether the consent of the couple is free or not, after answering of the question priest will recite blessings.

Essentials of valid Parsi marriage

Under Section 3 given:

1. Party to the marriage should not be related to each other in any of the degrees of consanguinity or affinity as stated in schedule in I.
2. Parsi marriage ceremony of "Ashirvad" to be performed by priest in the presence of two witnesses other than the priest.
3. Male should be of 21 years and female should be of 18.
4. If the above conditions are fulfilled then the child born out of this union will be consider as legitimate.

Section 4 explains remarriage is unlawful if the party to marriage has not divorced their earlier partner.

Section 6 says about the

Certificate and registry of marriage both parties to the marriage under this act after solemnization of marriage must be certified by the priest which should be sign by priest contracting parties as well as two witnesses after paying of the fee of 2 rupees by husband to registrar. Registrar must enter the certificate in his records.

The Special Marriage Act, 1954

The Special Marriage Act, 1954 is an Act of the Parliament of India with provision for civil marriage (or "registered marriage") for people of India and all Indian nationals in foreign countries, irrelevant of the religion or faith followed by either party. The Act originated from a piece of legislation proposed during the late 19th century. Marriages solemnized under Special Marriage Act are not governed by personal laws.

Henry Sumner Maine first introduced Act III of 1872, which would permit any dissenters to marry whomever they chose under a new civil marriage law. In the final wording, the law sought to legitimize marriages for those willing to renounce their profession of faith altogether ("I do not profess the Hindu, Christian, Jewish, etc. religion").

It can apply in inter-caste and inter-religion marriages. The Bill faced opposition from local governments and administrators, who believed that it would encourage marriages based on lust, which would inevitably lead to immorality.

The Special Marriage Act, 1954 replaced the old Act III, 1872. The new enactment had three major objectives:

1. To provide a special form of marriage in certain cases,
2. to provide for registration of certain marriages and,
3. to provide for divorce.

Applicability

1. Any person, irrespective of religion.
2. Hindus, Muslims, Buddhists, , Sikhs, Christians, Parsis, or Jews can also perform marriage under the Special Marriage Act, 1954.
3. Inter-religion marriages are performed under this Act.
4. This Act is applicable to the entire territory of India and extends to intending spouses who are both Indian nationals living abroad.
5. Indian national living abroad.

Requirements

1. The marriage performed under the Special Marriage Act, 1954 is a civil contract and accordingly, there need be no rites or ceremonial requirements.
2. The parties have to file a Notice of Intended Marriage in the specified form to the Marriage Registrar of the district in which at least one of the parties to the marriage has resided for a period of not less than thirty days immediately preceding the date on which such notice is given.
3. After the expiration of thirty days from the date on which notice of an intended marriage has been published, the marriage may be solemnised, unless it has been objected to by any person.
4. The marriage may be solemnised at the specified Marriage Office.
5. Marriage is not binding on the parties unless each party states "I, (A), take thee (B), to be my lawful wife (or husband)," in the presence of the Marriage Officer and three witnesses.

Conditions for marriage

1. Each party involved should have no other subsisting valid marriage. In other words, the resulting marriage should be monogamous for both parties.

2. The groom must be at least 21 years old; the bride must be at least 18 years old.
3. The parties should be competent in regard to their mental capacity to the extent that they are able to give valid consent for the marriage.
4. The parties should not fall within the degree of prohibited relationship.

Court Marriage is a union of two soul where oath ceremony is performed according to Special Marriage Act-1954 before the Registrar of Marriage in the presence of three witnesses thereafter a court marriage certificate is issued directly by the Registrar of Marriage appointed by the Govt. of India.

SUCCESSION TO THE PROPERTY

Succession to the property of person married under this Act or customary marriage registered under this Act and that of their children, are governed by Indian Succession Act. However, if the parties to the marriage are Hindu, Buddhist, Sikh or Jain religion, the succession to their property will be governed by Hindu succession Act.

The Supreme Court of India, in 2006, made it required to enroll all relational unions. In India, a marriage can either be enlisted under the Hindu Marriage Act, 1955 or under the Special Marriage Act, 1954. The Hindu Marriage Act is pertinent to Hindus, though the Special Marriage Act is appropriate to all residents of India regardless of their religion applicable at Court marriage.

- This act allows inter religion marriage registration in order to known as valid marriage.
- This act is secular litigation.
- Section 4 of the act explains the conditions for a valid marriage under this act:
  - Section 4(a) -Both of the parties must be single at the time of marriage which means they must be divorced or there should not be spouse living of the parties
  - Section 4(b)i -Both the parties must be sound mind in order to give their free consent.
  - Section 4(b)ii -Both the parties must not subjected to mental disorders.
  - Section 4(b)iii -Both the parties must not subjected to attacks of insanity.
  - Section 4(c) -Male must complete the age of 21 and female of 18
  - Section 4(d) -The parties to the marriage should not relate to each other within the degrees of prohibited degrees unless any custom governing each of them permits between the two.
  - Section 4(e) -When the marriage is solemnized in state of Jammu and Kashmir then both of the parties are Indian citizen and domicile in the territories

- Section 5 - Notice of intended marriage.- parties of the marriage whose marriage is solemnized under this act shall have to give notice to the Marriage Officer as mentioned in the II schedule of the act and at least one of the party should reside for a month immediately after the date on which notice is delivered to them.

Same Sex Marriage:

- In India same sex marriage is still not legalized. In the 21st century when we talk about the concept of freedom as well as human rights ,it's the need of the hour to legalized same sex marriage.
- In the Lata Singh v state of Uttar Pradesh ,the Supreme court held that right to marriage is a component of the right to life under article 21 which means each and every citizen of the India have right to marriage as per their choice and personal liberty.
- Sexual orientation of the person should not be the reason to take away the right to marry to them.
- In Navtej Singh Johar v. Union of India abolished section 377 of the Indian penal code, sexual orientation freedom was granted.
- But still same sex union is not recognize in India.

DIVORCE LAWS IN INDIA

Types of a Divorce Petition

According to the Divorce Process in India, there are different kinds of Divorce Petitions:

Divorce with mutual consent

The married pair can seek a divorce from the courts if they voluntarily agree to dissolve their marriage. The marriage will not. However, get immediately dissolved by the court. It is essential to demonstrate that the couple has been living separately for at least a year or two for the grant of the divorce petition.

A divorce petition may be filed not because of a disagreement between the husband and wife but because of financial difficulties that prevent the pair from earning a living. The couple might seek divorce with mutual consent in such instances.

When a husband and wife seek a divorce, they must consider three factors:

- The first consideration is the quantity of time that the pair need at a minimum and a maximum.
- The issue of child custody is the second facet. When a couple divorces by mutual consent, it is up to them to decide who will have custody of their kid. Custody can be shared or exclusive, depending on the parties' agreement.

- The third factor is property, specifically how much of the husband's property and the property the woman will receive.

Various laws specify varying time frames for the completion of the divorce procedure. To commence divorce procedures, both the husband and wife must have lived apart for a minimum of one year, according to Section 13B of the Hindu Marriage Act, 1955.

Christians, on the other hand, live in a different era. The Divorce Act of 1869 section 10A, the spouse must live apart for a minimum of two years before the divorce filing. Living apart does not imply that the couple must reside in two distinct places. It is sufficient to show that they were not living as husband and wife even though they lived together.

Divorce without mutual consent

The following grounds can get used to getting a divorce without mutual consent:

Cruelty

Cruelty may be both physical and mental; if one of the parties believes that the other party's behaviour towards him/her is likely to inflict some mental or bodily damage, this is a valid reason to seek divorce.

Adultery

Adultery was once a criminal offence in India, but adultery got decriminalised in a recent Supreme Court decision. However, it can still get used to seeking a divorce from a spouse who has been committing adultery. In most situations, the husbands are the ones who perpetrate it rather than the women.

Desertion

If one of the parties abandons the other without a valid reason, it is reasonable to divorce the other. The individual who abandons the other spouse, on the other hand, must have the purpose to desert and the proof to back it up. The dissertation must have lasted at least two years in Hindu law, while there is no such time bar under Christian law, and a divorce petition can be filed simply by claiming that the other spouse has committed desertion.

Conversion

A spouse's conversion to another faith is another basis for seeking a divorce from the other. It's not required to wait a certain amount of time before filing for divorce.

Mental Illness

If the spouse cannot execute the regular tasks that he/she gets expected to undertake owing to a mental problem or disease, divorce may get requested. However, if the person's mental condition does not impair his or her ability to execute his or her obligations, the divorce cannot be granted.

Death Presumption

If a spouse has not been heard of for at least seven years, the spouse who has not heard any news about his/her spouse's whereabouts can file divorce since the courts believe the other spouse is dead.

The Abandonment of the World

The offended spouse might seek divorce if the partner intends to abandon the world and obtain a holy order. This resignation, however, must be absolute and irreversible when it comes to the divorce process in India.

Divorce Notice

The divorce process in India takes a lot of time, and hence before you do anything else, you should be aware that you must provide your spouse with a divorce notice. It is to clear your emotions and provide a platform to begin thinking about ending the relationship. A formal divorce notice will inform the other spouse of your intentions for the future relationship.

A spouse can send the other spouse a formal notice of divorce to convey his or her decision to pursue legal action to discontinue the marriage connection. It is a formal communication, and it is the first step in breaking the husband and wife bond.

Alimony

When two individuals marry, they owe each other to support one another. As per the Code of Criminal Procedure, 1973, the right to maintenance applies to every individual economically dependent on the marriage. As a result, any spouse, dependent children, or even poor parents will get included.

Alimony is a monetary allowance or payment that a court requires one spouse to make to the other for support.

When a couple divorces by mutual consent, according to the Divorce law in India, whether either side should pay alimony/maintenance is a matter of mutual agreement. In such circumstances, alimony/maintenance might get paid by either the husband to the wife or the wife to the husband, which is dependent on the couple's mutual agreement.

The court issues the divorce decree based on the conditions agreed upon by the couple. The decree is legally binding on the couple and can get enforced by the court.

How to file a divorce in India

If a couple wishes to divorce, according to the Divorce Process in India, they must take the following steps:

- The couple must first employ a lawyer to give them all the facts.
- The lawyer will submit a petition to the court.

- The spouse will then receive a copy of the petition.
- The spouse might either consent to divorce or file a divorce suit.
- The case's facts will determine the procedure's conclusion.
- In the mutual consent divorce case, the parties must demonstrate that they have lived separately for more than a year.
- The parties are granted six months to contemplate their divorce.
- If, after the six-month term, the parties are still of the view that they desire a divorce, the court can issue a divorce judgement.

Documents required to file a petition for a contested divorce

The following papers are necessary for the filing of a divorce petition for a disputed divorce:

- Proof of husband's address
- Proof of wife's address
- Marriage certificate.
- Both husband and wife must have four passport-size pictures.
- There should be evidence that both the husband and wife have lived apart.
- Evidence demonstrating that attempts to reconcile were made but were unsuccessful.
- Income tax returns in the past two to three years
- Details about the petitioner's occupation and current income
- Both parties' family backgrounds should get disclosed.
- Specifics about the petitioner's property

Contents of a Divorce Petition

The Code of Civil Procedure, 1908 governs filing a divorce lawsuit in India. Starting a divorce process in India begins with either the husband or wife submitting a divorce petition, followed by an affidavit from both parties. The following information must get included in the divorce petition:

- The names of the parties
- The wedding date and location.
- The parties' status and place of residence
- A permanent location where the parties lived together.
- The last place the parties lived together.

- Name of the kid (if any), as well as a copy of their birth certificate
- The cause for filing for divorce or separation
- The parties must provide a written declaration guaranteeing that they are not misrepresenting the court.
- If the court is pleased with the petition and facts are given, the court can issue a judgement granting the couple a mutual divorce.

Grounds for dissolution of marriage

The Indian court system's secular attitude has promulgated several personal laws based on diverse religious religions. Separate marriage legislation and reasons for divorce govern Hindus, Christians, and Muslims in India.

1. Grounds for Divorce under the Hindu Marriage Act of 1955

Divorce is a method by which the marriage or marital union between two adults terminated or comes to an end, so it is also known as dissolution of marriage. It is the way to dissolve the bonds of matrimony under the rule of law of any particular country. In India divorce has different procedure in different religion as till date India has not adopted Uniform Civil Code. So the Hindu marriage Act, 1955 governs the divorce for the Hindus, Jain, Sikhs, and Buddhists.

The dissolution of Muslim marriage Act, 1939 for Muslims, the parsis marriage and divorce Act, 1936 for parsis, and Indian divorce Act, 1869 for Christians. There is one more act for inter-community marriages and it is governed by The special marriage Act, 1954. Divorce also provide both individual to normalise their status as if they both are not married. Divorce erases all the rights and obligations from both side of parties or spouses.

The Hindu Marriage Act of 1955 specifies the following reasons for divorce in India.

- **Adultery:** It gets defined as the act of engaging in any type of sexual connection, including intercourse outside of marriage. Adultery is a criminal felony that requires extensive proof to establish. According to a 1976 modification to the law, a single act of adultery is sufficient for the petitioner to get a divorce.
- **Cruelty** – When a spouse gets exposed to any type of mental or physical damage that puts his or her life, limb, or health in jeopardy, he or she has the right to petition for divorce. Intangible acts of cruelty such as mental torture get evaluated on a sequence of episodes rather than a single action. Cruelty includes food deprivation, continual ill-treatment and abuse to get a dowry, bizarre sexual acts, and so on.
- **Desertion** – If one of the spouses willingly abandons his or her partner for at least two years, the abandoned spouse has the right to petition for divorce on the grounds of desertion.

- **Conversion** – If one of the spouses changes to a different faith, the other spouse may seek divorce on this basis.
- **Mental Illness** – If the petitioner's spouse suffers from incurable mental disorder and insanity and cannot get expected to continue together, the mental disorder might cause divorce.
- **Leprosy** – In the instance of a 'virulent and incurable type of leprosy, the other spouse may submit a petition on this basis.
- **Venereal Condition** – If one of the spouses is suffering from a severe disease that is easily contagious, the other spouse may petition for divorce. Sexually transmitted illnesses, such as AIDS, are classified as venereal diseases.
- **Renunciation** – A spouse has the right to divorce if the other spouse renounces all worldly activities by joining a religious organisation.
- **Not Heard Alive** – If a person is not heard alive or seen for seven years by people anticipated to be 'naturally heard of the individual, the person is believed to be dead. If the other spouse wishes to remarry, he or she should petition for divorce.
- **No Resumption of Cohabitation** — If the couple fails to resume their cohabitation after the court has issued a separation judgement, it becomes grounds for divorce.

The following are the reasons for divorce in India on which only the woman can submit a petition.

- If the husband has a history of rape, bestiality, or sodomy
- If the marriage gets solemnised before the Hindu Marriage Act and the husband marries again while the first wife is still living, the first wife may seek divorce.
- A girl has the right to divorce if she was married before the age of fifteen and renounces the marriage before eighteen.
- After a year of no cohabitation and the husband failing to pay the court-ordered support, the wife may file for divorce.

2. Grounds for Divorce under the Dissolution of Muslim Marriage act, 1939

A Muslim woman in India can seek divorce for the following reasons, according to the Dissolution of Muslim Marriage Act, 1939.

- For the past four years, the husband's whereabouts have remained unclear.
- For at least two years, the husband has neglected to maintain his wife.
- The spouse got imprisoned for seven years or more.
- The spouse is unable to fulfil his marital responsibilities.
- If the girl marries before the fifteen years of age and decides to divorce before the age of eighteen
- The husband engages in nasty behaviour.

3. The Indian Divorce Act of 1869 specifies the following reasons for divorce.

- Infidelity
- Conversion to a different faith
- For at least two years before the divorce, one of the couples suffered from insanity, leprosy, or a contagious venereal illness.
- Not seen or heard from in seven years or more.
- Failure to comply with the return of conjugal rights for at least two years
- Inflicting cruelty and causing mental anguish, both of which can be harmful to one's health and life.
- A divorce can be sought based on rape, sodomy, or bestiality by the wife.

4. Grounds for Divorce under the Parsi Marriage and Divorce Act, 1936 (Amendment 1988)

- Seven years of continuous absence
- Failure to consummate a marriage within a year
- Insanity, if the other spouse was unconscious of the fact at the time of the marriage and the divorce was filed within three years of the marriage.
- Pregnancy by a man other than the husband provided the husband was uninformed of the incidence at the time of marriage and did not engage in sexual activity after learning of the condition. The divorce must get filed within two years after the marriage's conclusion.
- Adultery, bigamy, fornication, rape, or any other heinous sexual crime
- Cruel behaviour
- Inflicting venereal illness on the wife or driving her into prostitution.
- Imprisoned for seven years or more
- Two or more years of desertion
- Inability to resume cohabitation following the issuance of a maintenance order or a judicial separation judgement.

Factors influencing the duration and amount of alimony

The length of the marriage typically determines alimony amounts and duration when it comes to the divorce process in India.

- Lifetime alimony is available to couples who have been married for more than ten years.
- When determining alimony, the age of the husband also gets considered. Typically, alimony is granted to a young recipient for a limited time if the court believes that

he or she will soon be able to become financially secure through anticipated job brilliance.

- Alimony is also popular to bring both couples' economic situations into balance. The higher-earning spouse is entitled to a sizable alimony payment.
- The spouse who gets expected to have a successful job is obligated to pay a large amount of alimony.
- If one of the couples is in bad health, the other gets forced to make a large alimony payment to ensure the other spouse's adequate medicine and well-being.
- In India, the rules and conditions of alimony payment differ from one personal law to the next. Because of legislation establishing precise procedures for giving alimony, none of the Indian personal laws is immune from criticism.

Judicial separation

Judicial Separation is a legal separation of a husband and wife initiated by a petition filed in court by either the husband or the wife. In the event of judicial separation, the pair is still officially married, but they live apart, and neither couple is permitted to remarry.

Section 10 of the Hindu marriage act of 1955 governs judicial separation under the Hindu religion. If a decree for judicial separation is passed, it is no longer obligatory for the parties to cohabit with each other. On being satisfied by the facts presented by one of the parties, the court can rescind the decree.

Difference between judicial separation and divorce

Although many people believe that Judicial Separation and Divorce are the same, there is a very fine line between the two. However, there are some distinctions between these notions, such as:

- The first distinction is that a petition for judicial separation can get submitted at any time before marriage. Still, a divorce petition can only get filed one year after the marriage's completion.
- The judicial separation procedure is significantly speedier and less time-consuming since only one stage is passing a decree for separation. However, in the event of divorce, there are two stages before the court issues its ruling: the stage of reconciliation and, if the parties still desire to split, the stage of divorce.
- Judicial Separation may also get defined as a temporary suspension of marriage, in which both parties continue to get referred to as husband and wife. On the other hand, Divorce is a full stop to the marriage, which they no longer refer to as husband and wife.
- Although the pair get separated following the decree of judicial separation, they cannot remarry; nevertheless, when the decree of divorce is issued, both parties

cease to be husband and wife and, as a result, are separated and can choose to remarry.

- When a couple is judicially separated, it is possible that they will remarry because the separation is only temporary. However, once a divorce order is issued, there is no turning back and no chance of reconciliation.

In the last decade, the Indian society has seen significant changes in the divorce process in India. However, attitudes about divorce differ across India. Even though divorce has become a more common term than it was previously, our society has not embraced it in the manner that it should be.

As a result, rather than making the difficult decision to divorce and be happy, couples remain silent and strive to improve their married lives. Divorce is still viewed as a war between right and wrong, rather than as a choice made by two people to live a better life in a better way.

When this stage of life arrives, no one can avoid it. As a result, it is essential to understand our rights and responsibilities, what happens when a divorce petition gets filed, etc. The accompanying article looks at the many ways spouses might pursue divorce.

Marriages in India are regulated by personal as well as generalised marriage Acts. Court marriage registration demands a notice that must be delivered to the marriage registrar within one month of marriage. Supporting documents are also produced during this time as age proof, identity proof, address proof, and for fulfilling other sorts of legal purposes.

If the bride stays in a separate district, then a copy of the notice is sent to that district's magistrate for a thorough investigation. The scrutiny status remains active for one month, within which any party involved in the marriage can object. The Registrar is entitled to declare any marriage as void if he feels the necessity to do so.

6

MARRIAGE AND DIVORCE LAWS OF GERMANY

In Germany, marriage may only be contracted before a registrar. A religious ceremony is optional. This instructional pamphlet conveys general information only. Please contact the appropriate registrar's office ("Standesamt") for detailed information. Applications should be filed with the registrar's office in Germany where either party has his or her residence. If neither party has a residence in the Federal Republic of Germany, the registrar's office has to be contacted, where the marriage should take place.

Marriage in Germany is governed by the Bürgerliches Gesetzbuch in sections 1297 to 1588 of the fourth book of the code as a branch of family law. Marriage may only be conducted by a civil registrar, although couples may also participate in religious ceremonies. People who are not citizens or residents may marry in Germany. Since 1 October 2017, same-sex couples may marry.

Marriages are considered legal unions or "legally binding contracts" between the persons involved. Marriage has traditionally been protected from the outset under the Constitution. Everybody getting married in Germany must first appear physically at a Standesamt for a civil ceremony. This is actually all that is needed, and the great majority of couples go no further. Witnesses are not required at the civil ceremony. The cost of the Standesamt wedding (and document processing) can range from €65 to €200 and the ceremony usually is conducted in German so it may be advisable (and in certain circumstances mandatory) to have an interpreter present. This is particularly important if both partners and any witnesses do not speak fluent German.

Couples planning to get married in Germany should get started with the legal formalities as soon as possible. Several months out is not too soon. Things can usually be disposed of in far less time than that, but a number of legal issues, particularly previous marriages, can create a hassle.

The first places to check when you decide to get married are your local embassy or consulate and the local magistrate's office (Standesamt). Ask at these places what documentation is needed. Requirements may vary from region to region and there may be some extra requirements depending on the nationality, previous marital status and other circumstances of one or both partners.

Recent research suggests that marriage is becoming more popular in Germany. Figures from the Federal Statistical Office of Germany (Statistisches Bundesamt Destatis), show that the total number of marriages has steadily increased over the past few years; from 373,655 in 2013 to 416,615 in 2018, an increase of 11.5%.

According to deutschland.de, couples in Germany are also marrying later in life. A total of 407,000 couples tied the knot in Germany in 2017, and they were roughly five years older than wedding couples 25 years ago. On average, women now marry at 31.5 years of age, and men at 34. These figures are the eighth highest in Europe; Sweden ranks number one with 33.3 years for women and 35 for men.

The legal requirements for getting married in Germany

To marry in Germany, you have to be at least 18 years old. If you or your partner is not German, there are a few extra things to bear in mind. You must have been living in the locality for at least 21 days before visiting the town hall to give your intention to marry.

Foreigners who are not from the EU cannot usually get married in Germany on a visitor visa. Instead, they will need a visa that is valid for three to six months. If they are marrying a German citizen, they can normally obtain a residence permit.

Planning a wedding in Germany

To begin the marriage process you need to submit an application at the local registry office (standesamt) located in the town hall (rathaus), and give notice of the impending marriage (Antrag auf Eheschlielung).

You then need to make an appointment at the town hall and attend a meeting; here they will explain the process and documentation you need to submit. You should aim to arrange this meeting several months before you intend to marry, to give you both ample time to gather and submit all the required documents.

Ideally, both partners should attend the meeting in person. However, if one partner is unable to attend, the other may go on their own; as long as the absent partner has given them power of attorney to act on their behalf. Make sure to check the opening hours before you visit, as offices are often only open for a couple of hours during the week. After approval, you must marry within six months; otherwise, you will have to start the process all over again.

Documents to submit

The appropriate civil registrar's office in Germany provides information on the required documents. It is advisable to contact the registrar's office well in advance to make sure that you can be married on the intended date. The registrar's office will answer any further questions which may arise. Only the information provided by the registrar's office is binding in the individual case.

Typically both fiancés are required to submit the following documents to the registrar:

- Certified true copy of identification document with photograph (e.g. passport, identity Card)
- Birth certificate (not older than 6 months) in original or as certified true copy showing parents' names. A translation might be required. A baptismal certificate is not acceptable. Certificate of Naturalization must also be exhibited if applicant has been naturalized.
- If widowed, original death certificate or certified copy of deceased spouse. A translation might be required.
- If divorced, a certified copy of the divorce decree accompanied by a translation into German made by a certified translator.
- If the previous marriage was dissolved by a court other than a German court, the divorce decree might have to be approved by the appropriate German federal-state administration of justice department.
- If one of the fiancés is a minor, a statement executed by a legal representative, i.e. father and mother or guardian, before a notary public, giving consent in accordance with the laws of the individual's country. Since some German States require a special form of consent, the appropriate registrar should be contacted for detailed Information.
- All persons not registered in Germany but marrying there require an "Ehefähigkeitszeugnis", which is a Certificate of no impediment to marriage, stating that they are legally free to marry. Under certain conditions, US citizens may obtain such a certificate from US missions in Germany, please see the US Embassy's website.
- In case the civil registrar's office requires an affidavit ("eidesstattliche Versicherung") stating that the applicant is unmarried, it can be taken at the competent German Mission in the US. Please contact your German mission in advance. Consulate Finder

If one or both partners is a foreigner

If either one of the partners is a foreigner documents may be sent to a higher regional court in order to verify the legal status of that person.

Though it is no bar to a marriage, those planning to return to their homeland one day may wish to consider the legal status of their partner. There may be some bar, such as nationality, criminal record or medical condition, that would keep the partner from accompanying you. Your embassy or consulate can advise you on all emigration formalities. It is also a good idea to check if a marriage in Germany will be recognized in your home country.

CIVIL/RELIGIOUS/TRADITIONAL CEREMONIES

They take steps at the Standesämter to avoid any trappings (organ music, for example, or stained-glass windows) that might rightly or wrongly be deemed "too Christian." This is in deference to the Muslims, Jews, atheists and secular people who marry at the registrar's office, and who may be sensitive about such things.

Nevertheless, the wedding rooms are usually nice, exclusively for weddings and located in one of the community's finer buildings. Frankfurt, for example, has two magistrate's offices: one in the baroque city hall, or Römer, the other in the equally handsome Bolongaro Palace in the heart of the picturesque old Höchst district. The right atmosphere is created with flowers, subdued lighting, oil paintings and deep carpeting.

If there is to be a more traditional wedding it must take place after the civil ceremony. Germany has many magnificent cathedrals, palaces and castles that offer wedding arrangements. There are agencies in most larger cities that will rent out the clothing necessary for the wedding; not only for the groom and ushers, but also, what was once but rarely seen in America, for the bride and bridesmaids. Wedding coaches, drawn by four white horses, are also available as well as antique cars, limousines and the like.

Same-Sex Marriage

Civil Partnerships in Germany were recognized legally in 2001. The law was passed essentially to pave the way for same-sex marriages. While the process was the same when getting married or entering into a civil partnership, there were some legal differences between the two unions. The German legislature voted to remove those legal differences in July 2017. On October 1, 2017 same-sex marriage became legal with all the benefits and obligations of marriage as prescribed by the Constitution. The passage of the law has obviated the need for any future "civil partnerships." Couples already entered into a civil partnership can convert that to an official marriage or can continue with the civil partnership and enjoy the full legal protections and obligation of a marriage.

It should be noted that same-sex marriages that are officially recognized in other countries, are also recognized as legal marriages in Germany.

Declining divorce rates

In addition to the rising number of marriages in recent years, data from Destatis also shows that divorce rates are steadily declining. A total of 187,640 marriages ended in 2011, in comparison to 148,066 in 2018; a decrease of around 21%. Marriages also appear to last longer now than in previous decades. Those who split up these days have been together on average nearly 15 years, while couples who separated 20 years ago stayed together on average 12 years.

Gay marriage in Germany

As previously mentioned, same-sex marriage became legal in Germany in October 2017. Since then, more than 10,000 same-sex couples have tied the knot.

According to a survey by German press agency DPA, more than 10,000 same-sex couples got married in the first year after the law changed. Of these couples, 1,056 held their wedding in Cologne, which had proven to be particularly popular for same-sex weddings. The survey also found that more male gay marriages take place in German cities, while female couples tend to get married in smaller towns or villages.

German wedding traditions and customs

German weddings have many customs that expats should probably be aware of. The night before the wedding, for example, guests attend a raucous party called a polterabend. Everyone takes turns breaking porcelain plates to wish the new couple luck.

The bride and groom may also have to take part in the baumstamm sägen, a ritualistic sawing of logs. The act of sawing at the same time shows that the couple can work together and give their marriage endurance.

And the fun doesn't stop there, either. On the wedding day, the groomsmen traditionally kidnap the bride after the ceremony and take her to a bar. It is then up to the groom to track her down. But there's a price to pay when he finds her; he must pay the entire bill his groomsmen racked up while they were waiting for him to arrive.

Friends of the bride and groom often play pranks on the couple, too. This can include stunts like filling the room with balloons or hiding alarm clocks to wake them the next morning.

When it comes to wedding rings, it's tradition to wear the engagement ring on the left-hand ring finger, and the wedding ring on the right hand. Find out more in our guide to wedding ring traditions from around the world.

Many German wedding traditions are familiar to expats. For instance, it's still common for the bride to wear white (although it's increasingly popular to wear colors). The bride's father also walks her down the aisle, and the newlyweds kick off the celebrations with the first dance. Couples also cut the wedding cake at midnight, and the bride throws her bouquet; the person who catches it marries next – so, expect some competition!

NEW GERMAN MARRIAGE LAW CAUSES CONTROVERSY

In Germany, marriage has been controlled by the state for over a century, with religious ceremonies optional. A new law should change all that, but it's raising some questions -- especially among immigrants.

German couples will soon be able to get married in church without first going through a civil ceremony in the registry office for the first time in 130 years. The new rules were recently announced with several other changes to the Personenstandsrecht, or law of civil status, and take effect starting in January 2009.

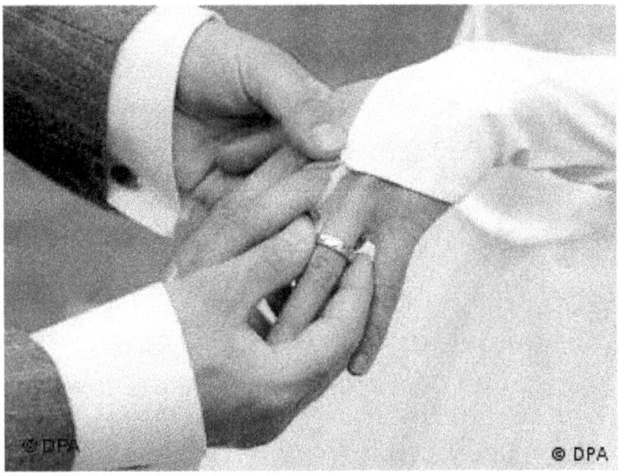

Civil marriages were introduced in Germany in 1875, when purely religious unions were made illegal. Couples are still allowed to marry in churches, synagogues and other religious institutions, but only after first having a civil ceremony. Priests had faced the possibility of jail or being fined for marrying couples who had not concluded a civil marriage before going to the altar, although in recent years the offence has been treated as a minor misdemeanor.

Going backwards

Many are unhappy with the changes, including Seyran Ates, a lawyer and women's rights activist. She has criticized the new laws, telling the German daily Westdeutsche Allgemeine Zeitung that they will open the floodgates for multiple and forced marriages among Muslims. Under Islamic law, a man is allowed to be married to four separate women at any one time. However, women and children have very few rights in purely religious unions.

"From now on, a practice that is forbidden in Turkey can take place freely here," Ates said.

The head of Central Council of Ex-Muslims, Mina Ahadi, has characterized the planned changes as a step backwards. Women are often forced into marriages conducted by imams and have no rights. Ahadi added that in addition to Muslim men possibly engaging in multiple unions, this change will also open the door for minors to be taken as brides. Ahadi is calling on the German parliament to reverse the decision.

Politicians speak out

Members of the German parliament, or Bundestag, say that it won't just be Muslim men who abuse the system. Max Stadler, a representative from the opposition free-market liberal Free Democratic Party said that the state does much more than hand out marriage certificates. Under German law, proof that a former marriage is completely dissolved must be shown prior to a civil union.

Left party member Wolfgang Neskovic warned that the new law may lead to "bizarre discrepancies," especially if a couple chooses to have both a civil and religious wedding.

"In the event of both a civil and religious double marriage then one is, for all intents and purposes, married to two partners," he added.

NEW LAW NOT FINALIZED

Thousands of couples get married in Germany every year

There does seem to be some hope for the critics. Social Democrat Dieter Wiefelspuetz, a member of the Bundestag, has called for a review of the new legislation after the summer break.

Wiefelspuetz warned that if even just a fraction of the apprehensions that have been expressed becomes a reality, then the social structure of the nation will experience a massive backslide.

Despite the new rules, all couples choosing to tie the knot in church only should beware. Their marriage has little legal force: rights of inheritance, tax advantages, support in case of divorce and other standard rights of next-of-kin cannot be legally enforced.

DIVORCE & SEPARATION IN GERMANY

Research suggests that divorce is becoming less common in Germany. Figures from the Federal Statistical Office of Germany (Statistisches Bundesamt Destatis), show that a total of 187,640 marriages were dissolved in 2011, compared with 148,066 in 2018; a decrease of around 21%.

According to Eurostat, the EU statistics agency, divorce rates in Germany have historically been slightly higher than the EU average. This looks to be changing, however. For instance, in 2010 the divorce rate in Germany was 2.3 per 1,000 inhabitants, above the EU average of 2.0. In 2017, however, the divorce rate had fallen to 1.9 per 1,000 inhabitants, below the EU average of 2.0.

Statistics from Destatis also show that marriages now appear to last longer than in previous decades. Those who split up these days have been together on average nearly 15 years, while couples who separated 20 years ago stayed together on average 12 years.

Legal consequences of a divorce as regards

The personal relations between the spouses (e.g. the surname)

The divorced spouse retains the married name as determined by the spouses. Spouses may, by declaration to the registry of births, deaths and marriages, reassume their birth name or the name that they had until the determination of the married name, or attach their birth name or the name they had at the time of the determination of the married name before or after the married name (Section 1355(5) of the Civil Code).

The division of property of the spouses

Allocation of the home and the household effects:

In principle, the following applies pursuant to Sections 1568a and 1568b of the Civil Code concerning the joint home and the division of the household effects after the divorce: the spouse more dependent on the use of the home or the household effects can demand the assignment of the home or the household effects from the other spouse. In this respect, the circumstances of both spouses and the best interests of their children must be taken into account.

In the case of rented accommodation, the spouse who is permitted to remain in the home takes over the tenancy arrangement – irrespective of whether previously both or only one of the spouses was the tenant.

In the case of home ownership, the following applies:

- If only one of the spouses is the owner of the former home, the other has a right of use only in exceptional cases, in particular if this is necessary to avoid unfair hardship, see Section 1568a(2) of the Civil Code.
- If the home is jointly owned by the spouses, the principle referred to in the first paragraph applies.

In both cases, both the spouse to whom the home has been assigned and the spouse who may no longer use his or her property have a claim for a tenancy agreement to be concluded between them and for a typical local rent to be agreed.

Concerning household effects, a distinction is to be made between those jointly owned by the spouses and those belonging to just one of them:

- In the case of household effects belonging to them jointly, the principles referred to in the first paragraph relating to this question apply. The spouse who has to relinquish the household effects can demand appropriate compensation for this.
- The other spouse has no claim to household effects belonging to only one spouse.

Equalisation of accrued gains:

If the spouses live under the statutory matrimonial property regime and they do not reach agreement on the settlement of their assets on divorce, the accrued gains can be equalised on the application of one of the spouses in a separate judicial procedure (Sections 1372 et seq. of the Civil Code). This takes place as follows:

The starting point for the calculation is the value of the assets of each spouse on marriage (initial assets, Section 1374 of the Civil Code) and at the end of the property regime (final assets, Section 1375). Assets inherited or donated to one spouse during the marriage are to be added to that spouse's initial assets. The relevant reference date for the calculation of the final assets is the day on which the divorce petition was served on the other spouse. Accrued gains are the amount by which the final assets of a spouse exceed the initial assets (Section 1373). The person with the lower accrued gains is entitled to half the difference in value compared to the accrued gains of the other person (equalisation claim) (Section 1378(1)). The claim to equalisation of the accrued gains involves payment of a sum of money. The person entitled to equalisation as a rule cannot demand the transfer in their favour of specific assets belonging to the person required to pay the equalisation claim. However, in exceptional cases, the family court (Familiengericht) may also transfer individual assets (Section 1383). However this is possible only if

- this is reasonable for the person required to pay the equalisation claim and
- this enables gross inequity to be avoided for the person entitled to equalisation, which would other arise through the equalisation of accrued gains in cash.

The value of these transferred assets is offset against the equalisation claim.

Instead of the statutory property regime, the spouses may, under German law, also opt for the property regime of the separation of property in notarial form (Section 1414), the community of property (Sections 1415 to 1518) or the optional regime of the community of accrued gains (Section 1519).

Implications for the spouses' pensions

Pension rights accrued by the spouses during the marriage (e.g. entitlement to benefits from the statutory pension scheme, the civil service pension scheme, the occupational pension scheme or from private retirement and disability pension schemes) are in each case divided in half on divorce by means of the equalisation of pension rights. This ensures that both spouses share equally the rights acquired by them during their marriage and that each spouse receives independent pension rights.

THE MINOR CHILDREN OF THE SPOUSES

Parental responsibility

If parents have joint parental responsibility, it continues after the divorce. Except in cases where the child is at risk, the question of parental responsibility will not be examined or decided on by the court unless one of the parents applies to the family court for transfer of parental responsibility or part of parental responsibility to that parent alone. Such an application must be granted if the other parent agrees and the child of at least 14 years of age does not object or if cancellation of joint parental responsibility and transfer to the applicant is likely to be in the child's best interest (Section 1671(1) of the Civil Code). German law generally assumes that it is in child's best interest to have contact with both parents, and therefore grants the child a right to contact with both parents and provides that both parents have a right and a duty of contact (Section 1684(1)). This applies irrespective of the allocation of parental responsibility.

Maintenance claims

Parents have a duty to maintain their children (Section 1601 of the Civil Code). Children are entitled to be maintained if they are incapable of maintaining themselves (Section 1602). The parents' duty of maintenance is subject to their ability to pay (Section 1603). However, parents' duty of maintenance in respect of their children is understood broadly, i.e. as regards the ability to pay, it is the achievable income, not merely the available income that matters (Section 1603(2)). Fundamentally, parents must pay maintenance for their children in proportion to their earning power and financial circumstances. However, a parent looking after a child fulfils their maintenance obligation as a rule in the care and upbringing of the child (Section 1606(3)). After the divorce of the parents, it is therefore as a rule only the parent in whose household the child does not live who is liable to pay cash maintenance.

Maintenance of the child covers all the child's living requirements, including the cost of an appropriate education (Section 1610).

The obligation to pay maintenance to the other spouse?

The spouses must each provide for themselves after the divorce (Section 1569 of the Civil Code). They are accordingly required to engage in appropriate gainful employment (Section 1574(1)). Where this is necessary to obtain appropriate gainful employment, they must undergo education, further training or retraining if it is likely that that education will be successfully concluded (Section 1574(3) of the Code).

However, divorced spouses are entitled to maintenance in the following circumstances:

- as long as, and to the extent that, they cannot be expected to engage in gainful employment because they are looking after a child for whom they have joint responsibility (Section 1570 of the Civil Code) or by reason of illness or other infirmities or weakness of their physical or mental capacity (Section 1572),
- as long as, and to the extent that, they can no longer be expected to engage in gainful employment because of their age at a certain point in time, in particular at the time of the divorce or the end of the care or upbringing of a child of the spouses (Section 1571),
- as long as, and to the extent that, the divorced spouse is undergoing education, further training or retraining in order to make up for gaps in his or her education

or disadvantages caused by marriage; they must commence the education, further training or retraining as soon as possible in order to achieve appropriate gainful employment which will provide a long-term living, and the education must be expected to be successfully concluded (Section 1575 BGB),

- as long as, and to the extent that, they are unable to find appropriate gainful employment after the divorce (Section 1573(1)),
- as long as, and to the extent that, they cannot be expected to engage in gainful employment for other serious reasons and it would be grossly unreasonable to refuse maintenance, taking account of the interests of both spouses (Section 1576),
- to the extent that the income from appropriate gainful employment is insufficient to cover the full cost of maintenance (Section 1573(2)).

The level of the maintenance is determined by the matrimonial living conditions and also covers the costs of appropriate insurance against sickness and the need for care as well as, under certain circumstances, old age and reduced earning capacity too (Section 1578). If the spouse who is obliged to provide maintenance is incapable, on the basis of their earnings and financial circumstances and having regard to their other obligations, of providing maintenance to the party entitled to it without endangering their own proper maintenance, they need provide maintenance only to the extent that this is reasonable, having regard to the needs and to the earning power and financial circumstances of the divorced spouses (Section 1581, first sentence).

The maintenance may be reduced and/or limited in time where continued payment of a maintenance claim without restriction would be inequitable (Section 1578b). The possibility for a reduction/time limit under Section 1578b of the Civil Code extends in particular to Sections 1570-1573, whereby, according to Section 1570, the considerations of equity necessary for the prolongation of the maintenance for care after the child's 3rd birthday, for reasons relating to the child or parents, represent a special time limit arrangement.

The interests of a child of the spouses entrusted to the spouse entitled to maintenance for care or upbringing must be taken into account in the evaluation under Section 1578b of the Civil Code. In addition, consideration must be given to the extent to which disadvantages caused by marriage have arisen with regard to the possibility for the spouse to take care of their own maintenance. Disadvantages exist if the income earned by the spouse entitled to maintenance is lower than it would have been without the marriage. According to Section 1578b(1), third sentence, of the Civil Code, such a disadvantage may arise from childcare and from the organisation of household management and gainful employment. When assessing the disadvantages caused by marriage, all circumstances of the specific individual case must be taken into account in the comprehensive assessment, including the duration of a marriage.

7

MARRIAGE AND DIVORCE LAWS IN JAPAN

Marriage in Japan is a legal and social institution at the center of the household (ie). Couples are legally married once they have made the change in status on their family registration sheets, without the need for a ceremony. Most weddings are held either according to Shinto traditions or in chapels according to Christian marriage traditions.

Traditionally, marriages in Japan were categorized into two types according to the method of finding a partner—omiai, meaning arranged or resulting from an arranged introduction, and ren'ai, in which the husband and wife met and decided to marry on their own—although the distinction has grown less meaningful over postwar decades as Western ideas of love have altered Japanese perceptions of marriage.

According to the 2010 census, 58.9% of Japan's adult population is married, 13.9% of women and 3.1% of men are widowed, and 5.9% of women and 3.8% of men are divorced. The annual number of marriages has dropped since the early 1970s, while divorces have shown a general upward trend.

MARRIAGE AND FERTILITY

The decline of marriage in Japan, as fewer people marry and do so later in life, is a widely cited explanation for the plummeting birth rate. Although the total fertility rate has dropped since the 1970s (to 1.43 in 2013), birth statistics for married women have remained fairly constant (at around 2.1) and most married couples have two or more children. Economic factors, such as the cost of raising a child, work–family conflicts, and insufficient housing, are the most common reasons for young mothers (under 34) to have fewer children than desired.

The number of single-child or childless couples has increased since 2002 (to 23.3 percent in 2010) even as the desire for larger families remains the same. Only 2% of births occurred outside of marriage, compared to 30-60% of births in Europe and North America. This is due to social taboos, legal pressure, and financial hurdles.

Half of Japan's single mothers live below the poverty line, among the highest for OECD countries. In addition, an estimated 3.5 million Japanese children, one in six of those below the age of 18, are from households classed as experiencing "relative poverty" by the OECD.

Fewer marriages

Almost 90% of unmarried Japanese intend to marry, and yet the percentage of people who do not continues to rise. Between 1990 and 2010, the percentage of 50 year-old people who had never married roughly quadrupled for men to 20.1%, and doubled for women to 10.6%. The Ministry of Health, Labour and Welfare predicts these numbers to rise to 29% of men and 19.2% of women by 2035. The government's population institute estimated in 2014 that women in their early 20s had a one-in-four chance of never marrying, and a two-in-five chance of remaining childless.

Recent media coverage has sensationalized surveys from the Japan Family Planning Association and the Cabinet Office that show a declining interest in dating and sexual relationships among young people, especially among men. However, changes in sexuality and fertility are more likely an outcome of the decline in family formation than its cause. Since the usual purpose of dating in Japan is marriage, the reluctance to marry often translates to a reluctance to engage in more casual relationships.

The majority of Japanese people remain committed to traditional ideas of family, with a husband who provides financial support, a wife who works in the home, and two children. Labor practices, such as long working hours, health insurance, and the national pension system, are premised on a traditional breadwinner model. As a result, Japan has largely maintained a gender-based division of labor with one of the largest gender pay gaps in the developed world, even as other countries began moving towards more equal arrangements in the 1970s.

However, economic stagnation, anemic wage growth, and job insecurity have made it more and more difficult for young Japanese couples to secure the income necessary to create a conventional family, despite their desire to do so. Japan was once well known for lifetime employment, but after the burst of the Japanese asset price bubble and the 1997 Asian financial crisis, regular employment for unmarried men age 25-34 dropped from 78% in 1982 to 55% in 2010 as companies began employing more people on temporary or part-time contracts. These non-regular employees earn about 53% less than regular ones on a comparable monthly basis, according to the Labor Ministry, and as primary earners are seven times more likely to fall below the poverty line. Men in this group are more than twice as reluctant to consider marriage, and in their 30s they are about 40% less likely to be married than those with regular employment.

According to the sociologist Masahiro Yamada, the failure of conventions to adapt to the economic and social realities of Japanese society has caused a "gap in family formation" between those who succeed in creating a conventional family and those who remain single and childless.

Later marriages

The average age at first marriage in Japan has climbed steadily from the middle of the 20th century to around 31 for men and 29 for women in 2013, among the highest in Asia. Women postpone marriage for a variety of reasons, including high personal and financial expectations, increasing independence afforded by education and employment, and the difficulty of balancing work and family. Masahiro Yamada coined the term "parasite singles" for unmarried adults in their late 20s and 30s who live with their parents, though it usually refers to women. Men who do not aggressively pursue marriage are known as "herbivore men".

International marriages

Of the 599,007 marriages registered in 2019, 21,919 (or about 1 in 30) were between a Japanese and a foreign national, according to the Ministry of Health, Labour, and Welfare. The number of international unions rose rapidly in the 1980s and 90s, peaked in 2006 at 44,701 (about 1 in 16), and has declined since then. Changes in the Immigration Control Act in 2005, which made it more difficult for Philippine nationals to work in Japan, are one cause of the decline. Filipino women saw the largest drop, from 12,150 in 2006 to 3,118 or 20.1% of foreign brides in 2013. Many Filipino women come to Japan as entertainers, and some have been victims of domestic violence.

Of the 14,911 non-Japanese brides in 2019, most came from China (about 31.6%), followed by the Philippines (about 24.5%), Korea (about 11.2%), Thailand (about 6.6%), Brazil (about 2.1%), United States (about 1.9%). The 7,008 grooms came from Korea (about 25.1%), United States (about 14.1%), China (about 13%), and Brazil (about 4.7%).

Of the 1 million children born in Japan in 2013, 2.2% had one or more non-Japanese parent. The rise in international households has sometimes led to conflicts over custody. Biracial Japanese children are often called "hāfu", although the term is considered offensive by some.

For an international marriage to take place in Japan, the following documentation is required:

- A sworn Affidavit of Competency to Marry
- An original birth certificate
- Passport, Japanese Drivers License, or Residents Card (Zairyo Card)
- Certificate of Marriage Notification

In certain cases additional documentation is required, notably for those from China.

Domestic violence

According to a summary of surveys by Japan's Gender Equality Bureau in 2006, 33.2% of wives and 17.4% of husbands have experienced either threats, physical violence, or rape, more than 10% of women repeatedly. This violence almost always occurred after marriage. Dating abuse has also been reported by 13.5% of women and 5.2% of men.[8

Marriage law

A marriage is legally recognized once a couple has successfully submitted the required documents to the city hall registrar to change their status in their koseki (family registration sheet) family registration sheet. No ceremony is required under Japanese law. The family registration sheet serves as birth certificate, proof of citizenship, marriage license, and death certificate. A register is kept for each nuclear family, under the name of the head of the household, with the spouse and unmarried children who are registered as dependents.

A couple who marries must file a marriage registration form (kon'in todoke) to create a new registration sheet (shinkoseki) under a common surname. Since 1947, couples have been permitted to choose either the surname of the husband or wife, consistent with a ban on separate surnames first imposed in 1898. Married couples are estimated to choose the man's surname 96% of the time, although some women continue to use their maiden name informally. The ban has survived several legal challenges on the basis of gender inequality, most recently in 2015. When marriage is used to adopt a male heir, the husband takes his wife's family name.

International marriages are subject to separate rules within Japan. Foreigners in Japan do not have their own family registration sheet, and therefore those who marry a Japanese national are listed on his or her family's sheet. Foreign spouses in Japan are eligible for a long-term dependent visa.

Children born out of wedlock are recorded as illegitimate on their mother's family register, although they can be legitimized by a later acknowledgment of paternity. Illegitimate children were eligible for half the inheritance of legitimate ones until a court ruling in 2013.

Marriage of Japan's formality takes the form of civil marriage. A marriage is effected by filing notification of it. A wedding ceremony performed by a religious or fraternal body is not a necessary element for a legal marriage.

According to Articles 731–737 of the Civil Code,

- A man before attaining 18 years of age, a woman before attaining 16 years of age, may not marry. (Article 731)
- A minor shall obtain the consent of at least one parent to marry. (Article 737)
- Bigamy is prohibited. (Article 732)

- [declared unconstitutional in 2016 by the Supreme Court : A woman may not remarry within 6 months of the day of dissolution or cancellation of the previous marriage, except the case in which she both gets pregnant before the day and gives birth to the child. #1 (Article 733)]
- Lineal relatives by blood, collateral relatives within the third degree of kinship by blood #2, may not marry, except between an adopted child and their collateral relatives by blood through adoption. #3 (Article 734)
- Lineal relatives by affinity may not marry. #3 (Article 735)
- An adoptive parent or a lineal ascendant of an adoptive parent may not marry with an adopted child, their spouse, their lineal descendant, or a spouse of their lineal descendant. #3 (Article 736)

1. It is considered that this remarriage prohibition is to avoid confusion as to the identification of the child's father.
2. between one and one's sibling, uncle, aunt, nephew, niece by blood.
3. It may be a case in which this prohibition shall apply after the termination of a family relationship between the two parties.

If one or both in the couple is a Japanese national, the marriage is recorded in a family register with one concerned Japanese at its head.

It's a rule in principle that the two shall have the family name in common following their marriage. However, if one of them is a non-Japanese, this rule does not apply. They can use one of the spouse's names as their family name or keep their names after marriage. If a Japanese spouse changes their family name to their spouse's, the name change must be filed within 6 months of the marriage. In a family register, a foreigner doesn't have their own entry, while he / she can be recorded in it as a spouse, for example.

INTERNATIONAL MARRIAGE

Paternity

A child born to a married woman is assumed to be the child of her husband, although her husband may file in family court to disavow paternity if the paternity of the child is questioned. If a child is born to an unmarried woman, or if paternity is disavowed by the mother's husband, the father may later claim paternity through family court proceedings, or the child may file in family court to force his or her father to be recognized as the father.

Children are given the family name of their parents at the time of birth. If the father is unknown at the time of the child's birth, the child is given the family name of the mother, but may have his or her name changed to the father's family name after the father recognizes paternity.

Adoption

Child adoption in Japan is relatively uncommon, mainly due to lack of government support and legal trouble encountered from the child's birth parents. In Japan, even if a parent is legally unfit to see their child, the parent is still the child's legal guardian and their consent is required for everyday decisions, such as the child's education or field trips that may pose safety concerns. This is an issue even for parents looking to adopt because a child adopted over the age of 6 will still be registered in their birth parent's koseki, as written in Article 817-2 of the Japanese Civil Code. As a result, if parents want a special adoption, where the child is registered under the new parent's koseki, the child has to be under the age of 6.

There are two main places to apply to for adoption. The first is a religious adoption agency. These private agencies are allowed to charge a fee for the adoption process, as opposed to the process being free through the government.

The other is the local Child Guidance Center, which is a government agency. In 2010, United Nations Convention on the Rights of the Child noted that the CGC staff did not seem to be properly trained to work in child services and did not seem to be promoting adoption. In 2016, the Child Welfare Act was revised to explicitly state that the CGCs were responsible for the adoption process. Furthermore, when adopting through government agencies, prospective parents must be Japanese married couples.

Surrogacy and Reproductive Technology

Surrogacy

Although there is no law banning birth by surrogacy in Japan, there is a strong stigma against it. "Japan's first surrogate birth was announced in 2001 and led to the Health Ministry calling for an immediate ban. Although this was blocked, the Society of Obstetrics and Gynecology successfully managed to prohibit [its members from conducting] surrogate births in 2003, citing the mental and physical burden to the surrogate mother and the fear that surrogacy could confuse familial relationships."

As a result, Japanese couples tend to seek surrogate mothers abroad. However, "current law in Japan states that the mother of a child is the one who gives birth to the baby," and that children must be registered in the koseki (family registry) to be a Japanese citizen. Since the surrogate is not Japanese and the father is not the surrogate's legal husband, the legal status of children born via surrogates may end up in question. A famous case of this issue is that of the Japanese actress, Aki Mukai, who had twin sons through an American surrogate mother in 2003. The boys only had American citizenship, which resulted in a series of court cases that ultimately culminated in the Supreme Court concluding that surrogacy was ethically wrong and Mukai had to adopt her sons to be considered their mother.

In 2005, a Tokyo-based sperm bank called Excellence began offering surrogate mothers and assisted conception services in South Korea to Japanese couples. At the time, it was the only Japanese company known to provide such a service, according to Excellence's head Yuji Sasaki.

In 2006, a doctor enabled a 61-year-old woman to carry the child of her daughter who was unable to give birth herself after cancer treatment. "The procedure was performed at the Suwa Maternity Clinic by Yahiro Netsu, a long standing supporter of surrogacy procedures. In a statement issued to the press, it said: 'The clinic hopes that Japan will hold forward-looking discussions on surrogate births and that it will take place in Japan without abuses.'" In light of this procedure, "then-Prime Minister Shinzo Abe told reporters that the issue of surrogacy is 'very difficult' and Sanae Takaichi, state minister for gender, equality and population has said that 'the discussion is highly welcome, but it is extremely difficult to judge whether surrogate birth can be encouraged.'"

In 2008, Manyi Yamada was born using donated eggs, the sperm of a Japanese man Ikufumi Yamada, and an Indian surrogate mother. Yamada and his Japanese wife divorced before Manyi's birth and the latter withdrew her consent to adopt Manyi, which left Yamada's application as a single father unlikely to be accepted. An Indian child welfare charity Satya petitioned unsuccessfully to gain custody of Manyi, claiming that "'they have violated Indian laws by not signing a surrogacy agreement and taking custody of a child abandoned by its mother.' The Japanese Justice Minister, Okiharu Yasuoka, indicated to reporters that he would consider granting Manyi a visa but that the legality of the birth was something that would need to be addressed in the near future. 'Whether to permit surrogate pregnancy is a matter to be discussed by respective institutions...The ministry will study the possibilities under the law out of consideration for the child's future.'" Ultimately, the Indian Supreme Court granted custody of Manyi to her grandmother Emiko Yamada.

"The son of a wealthy IT entrepreneur, Mitsutoki Shigeta attracted controversy in 2014 after Thai officials raided his flat in Bangkok on the of suspicion of human trafficking and found at least nine babies, nannies and a pregnant woman." He was quoted as saying 'The best thing I can do for the world is to leave many children,' and as hoping to father between 100 and 1,000 babies. "The case, which became known as the 'baby factory' scandal in the press, cast a spotlight on Thailand's surrogacy industry and the Thai government shortly afterwards introduced a ban on foreigners from paying for surrogacy in the country." A year later, the Thai "Women and Child Welfare Protection Bureau, which is currently taking care of the children, has confirmed that six of the surrogate mothers, three of whom gave birth to twins, are seeking custody," their lawsuit alleging that the bureau is failing to adequately care for the children. By 2018, however, the women had forfeited their rights to the children and the Thai court had awarded paternity rights to "the Japanese businessman"—mostly likely Shigeta—who had fathered them. An additional six babies had also by that point been identified as having been fathered by Shigeta, bringing the total identified so far to 17. A 2018 CNN report revealed that Shigeta has two additional children born to surrogates in India.

Who Can Get Married in Japan?

Article 731 to 737 of the Japanese Civil Code stipulates the following requirements:

- The male partner must be 18 years of age or older and the female partner must be 18 years of age or older.
- A person who is under 18 years of age cannot get married in Japan without a parent's approval.
- Most people related by blood, by adoption or through other marriages cannot get married in Japan.

In addition, for Americans, you must be able to legally marry in your home state; if the legal age of marriage at home is 18, you cannot marry earlier than that in Japan.

For detailed information, please contact a Japanese municipal government office.

For the American Partner ...

Japanese law requires all foreigners who marry in Japan to first prepare a sworn Affidavit of Competency to Marry, affirming they are legally free to marry, from their own country's embassy or consulate in Japan.

- This is a notarial service. You will need to make an appointment.
- Do not use erasable pens to fill out the Affidavit.
- You do not need to bring your non-U.S. citizen fiance/fiancee.

You can download the blank affidavit form here (PDF 158KB). You should use this form if you are planning to marry someone who is not a U.S. citizen. The form has two pages, one to be completed in English and the other to be used to translate the English page into Japanese. The consular officer will notarize only the English language document.

- If your partner is also an American, s/he must also complete a sworn Affidavit of Competency to Marry at the Embassy or consulate. Use this form (PDF 77 KB) in the case of two Americans marrying one another. The form has two pages, one to be completed in English and the other to be used to translate the English page into Japanese. The consular officer will notarize only the English language document.
- These forms are required by Japanese law and are not a requirement of the U.S. Government. No registration of your legal marriage abroad is required by the U.S. Government, and your foreign (i.e. Japanese) partner need not come to our offices.
- You will need to bring your U.S. passport and the $50 notarial fee.

- Once this is signed and sealed at the Embassy or one of our Consulates, this Affidavit is valid for three months.

Member of the Armed Forces should contact their on-base legal office and/or chain of command for proper procedures.

Kon-in Todoke

You will need to fill out a Kon-in Todoke (request of registration of marriage) with 2 signatures from witnesses of any nationality who are over 18 years old. Our staff cannot help you to prepare the documents or be witnesses.

The Japanese Government and/or the local municipal office may also have other requirements for your partner. Please check with the appropriate municipal office.

If your partner is neither Japanese nor American, s/he should also contact his/her Embassy for the marriage procedures needed in their own country.

Get Married

This is the part of this whole procedure that actually makes you and your partner married.

Once all the paperwork above is completed, proceed to the appropriate Japanese municipal government office to submit your Kon-in Todoke. Be sure to confirm local marriage procedures and rules directly with municipal government officials. (For example, depending on the jurisdiction, you may be required to submit a certified copy of your birth certificate and its Japanese translation.)

KEEP RECORDS

Once the marriage procedures are completed, you may ask the municipal government office to issue a Japanese-language "Certificate of Acceptance of Notification of Marriage" (Kon-in Todoke Juri Shomeisho). This is your only proof of marriage. The U.S. Embassy/Consulate does not maintain any record of your marriage in Japan, and under Japanese law we cannot later retrieve marriage records for you from a municipal government office.

There are two versions of the "Certificate of Acceptance of Notification of Marriage." Both versions are legal proof of your marriage. The large fancy version costs around 1,400 yen. The regular A4 size version costs around 350 yen.

You should write down the name and address of the municipal government office that registered your marriage as you'll need to contact them directly in the future to obtain a record of your marriage.

Getting a "Marriage Certificate issued by the U.S. government"

The U.S. Government does not issue marriage certificates for marriages performed overseas. Your Japanese marriage document will be the only proof of your marriage. If anyone (i.e. Japanese Immigration) asks for your "marriage certificate issued by your own government," there will be none.

Translating Your Proof of Marriage

While proof of your marriage is shown by the Japanese-language marriage document you get at the ward or city office, sometimes a notarized translation of the Japanese marriage document can be handy for use in the U.S.

If you would like to have the translation notarized, you can use our fill-in-the-blanks translation templates:

- For the large fancy marriage document, use this form (PDF 13 KB) for the translation.
- For the smaller A4-size marriage document, use this form (PDF 16 KB) for the translation.

This is a notary service. Please see our notary page for more information.

Please note that we will be attaching the translation to the original marriage document at the time of notary. Also, whoever translated the document needs to come in for the notary.

Remember, this is not a marriage certificate issued by the U.S. government.

Validity of Marriages Abroad

In general, marriages which are legally performed and valid abroad are also legally valid in the United States. You do not have to report your marriage to the U.S. Embassy/ Consulate. For more information please read the Department of State website.

Wedding ceremonies

A common description of Japan's religious syncretism says: "Born Shinto, married Christian, die Buddhist." In practice, however, elements of all three major traditions tend to be practiced side-by-side. Japanese weddings usually begin with a Shinto or Western Christian-style ceremony for family members and very close friends before a reception dinner and after-party at a restaurant or hotel banquet hall. There the couple's extended families and friends make speeches and offer "gift money" in a special envelope. Close family pay about twice as much as friends.

JAPANESE SHINTO CEREMONIES

Traditional Shinto ceremonies ('shinzen shiki'), which account for around one in six of Japanese weddings, are held in the main building of a shrine. A priest performs a ritual purification for the couple, then announces their marriage to the kami ("gods" or "spirits") of the shrine and asks for their blessing. The bride and groom take three sips each from three cups of sake, a ritual called sansankudo (literally "three cups thrice").

Japanese brides wear a kimono, which is either a shiromuku ("pure white dress"), iro uchikake ("colorful outer robe"), or kurobiki furisode, the black and patterned kimono once worn at weddings of the nobility during the Edo period (1603–1868), with either an open white watabōshi or a tsunokakushi. Grooms wear a black crested haori jacket and loose, skirt-like hakama with a vertical stripe.

Christian chapel ceremonies

Christian wedding ceremonies have since the mid-1990s displaced the Shinto rite and continue to remain Japan's wedding ceremony of choice. Christian wedding ceremonies have in the last thirty years moved from the sideline to the mainstream of Japanese society. The popularity of Christian wedding ceremonies represents new widespread acceptance, commercialization, and popularity of a religious ceremony. The postwar history of Christian wedding ceremonies is best understood in light of the efforts made by traditional Christian churches and the bridal industry to meet the religious needs and demands of Japan's largely "nonreligious" (mushūkyō) constituency.

Although the Japanese have unprecedented access to the Catholic Church, the majority of weddings in Japan follow the Protestant liturgy. As such the ceremony includes elements typical to a traditional Protestant wedding including hymns, benedictions, prayers, bible readings, an exchange of rings, wedding kiss, and vows before God. It is typical for a bride to enter with her father and then be "given away" to her husband—an exchange that usually involves bowing and shaking hands. In recent years, the custom of lowering the veil has also become popular. During the veil lowering the mother of the bride lowers the veil for her daughter before she continues down the "virgin road" with her father toward her husband. In the case of a non-Japanese wedding minister, the ceremony is commonly performed in a mix of Japanese and a western language (typically, English).

Non-religious or civil ceremonies

Non-religious or civil ceremonies often take place in a banquet hall, before or during the reception party, with a Master of Ceremonies officiating and guests seated around tables. Although these ceremonies often adopt Western elements, especially a wedding dress for the bride and a tuxedo for the groom, they forego any religious connotations.

Some younger couples choose to abandon formality entirely for a "no host party" wedding, which emphasizes celebration rather than ceremony. The guests consist primarily of the couple's friends, who pay an attendance fee.

GETTING DIVORCED IN JAPAN

As complicated as divorces can be, the actual procedure of finalizing your divorce in Japan can be quite simple. That is, given the condition that the divorce is amicable, mutually agreed on, and the couple does not have children. If this is the case, a divorce can be finalized within an hour or two at the city hall where the two individuals are officially registered in.

There are four types of divorce in Japan:

- Divorce by agreement (Kyōgi Rikon), based on mutual agreement.
- Divorce by mediation in a family court (Chōtei Rikon), completed by applying for mediation by the family court (for cases in which divorce by mutual agreement cannot be reached).
- Divorce by decision of the family court (Shinpan Rikon), which is divorce completed by family court decision when divorce cannot be established by mediation.
- Divorce by judgment of a district court (Saiban Rikon). If divorce cannot be established by the family court, then application is made to the district court for a decision (application for arbitration is a prerequisite). Once the case is decided, the court will issue a certified copy and certificate of settlement, to be attached to the Divorce Registration.

"Neither marriage registration nor divorce have to occur in person. One person can submit the documentation with a seal bearing the other's name resulting in a certain number of fraudulent registrations every year."

Foreign citizens must show evidence that they are able to be divorced in their country of nationality and that the procedures used in Japan are compatible with those of their home country.

Divorce by agreement = kyogi rikon

If this is the case, all you need to have is a rikon todoke, a certificate of divorce, which you can obtain at any city hall in Japan, but submit only at the one you are registered in. This document needs to be filled in by both parties in the marriage, as well as two different individuals above the age of 20. These individuals do not have to be your relatives. You will also need to present your legal ID, such as a passport or your residence card. Ideally, you should both be present when submitting the divorce papers, but one of the two can submit the document on behalf of both parties as well. In this case, indicate on the certificate whether you would like to be informed by the city hall when the divorce is finalized.

Divorce through arbitration = chotei rikon

This typically occurs when one of the parties wants to get divorced and the other doesn't, or when the couple does not want to communicate directly to each other. In this case, the family court will mediate the divorce. To apply for this, consult a legal representative as each case and documents that need to be submitted differ.

Divorce by judgment of a district court = saiban rikon

This is when a divorce cannot be completed by family court. Instead, an application is sent to the district court for a decision. After a decision, the court issues a copy (which is certified) and a certificate of settlement, which is then attached to divorce registration. To go through this option you will need to hire a lawyer to represent you in court. Typically, this will cost you somewhere from ¥300,000 to ¥500,000, though these fees largely depend on the actual case and the lawyer.

Know your rights

According to the Japanese law, everything you have acquired after your marriage should be split into two in case of a divorce regardless of who was directly responsible for the divorce. This includes your savings and property. You are also entitled to ask for alimony, called isharyo, in case your partner had an extramarital relationship, was abusing you physically or emotionally or there had been a clear reason for the divorce that your partner can be held liable to. To obtain such kind of compensation, remember that more often than not you will have to go through the family court or the district court, which in other words means that you will have to hire a legal representative.

Regarding children, joint custody is not common in Japan. In most cases, the mother will be given custody, but the father will still have to pay child support.

DISPUTES OVER CHILD CUSTODY AND NATIONALITY

Joint custody of children ends upon divorce. In a divorce by agreement, the husband and wife must determine which parent will have custody of each child. In other types of divorce, custody is determined by the mediator or judge, with a strong preference toward custody by the mother (especially with regard to children born after the divorce).

In the case of international divorce (one spouse is a Japanese national and the other spouse is a non-Japanese national) in Japan, the issues such as whether it is possible to divorce, property distribution, monetary compensation (damages for mental suffering, solatium or consolation money), child support to bring it up, parent-child visitation and contacts etc. may be arisen.

When you wish to divorce, we think that basically you need to consider issues from the standpoint of (1) whether it is possible to divorce, (2) monetary matter and (3) child matter.

Whether it is possible to divorce legally in Japan

Under the Japanese laws, a spouse cannot divorce at his/her sole discretion. Basically a mutual agreement between spouses are needed to divorce in Japan. Divorce based on the spouses' mutual agreement without a Japanese court is called "Kyogi-Rikon" in Japanese. In this case, the spouses both fill a Divorce Paper (it is called "Rikon-Todoke" in Japanese. Witnesses are also needed.) based on their mutual agreement and they submit the Divorce Paper to the local government in Japan, then they can divorce under Japanese laws.

However in the event that a mutual agreement is not obtained, firstly it is necessary to file a petition for mediation (conciliation) with a court for divorce in Japan (it is called "Chotei- Rikon" in Japanese). The mediation (conciliation) is a discussion between the parties in the court with the court as mediators (conciliation commissioners) and if a mutual agreement for divorce is not obtained from the other party, then it is necessary to file a lawsuit for divorce with the court (it is called "Saiban-Rikon" in Japanese).

In a divorce lawsuit in Japan, it is examined whether there is a reason for divorce stipulated in Japanese Civil Code. Infidelity (illicit love affair, or adultery), no bearing/ payment of living expenses and no return home for long time, domestic violence/abusive expression, critical psychiatric disorder are examples of reasons. In addition there is a case that living apart for a long time may be a reason for divorce.

In order to win a divorce lawsuit, certain evidence is necessary. It is important to secure evidences of adultery, violence etc. Our office is in a position to give an advice for such evidences.

Monetary matter regarding the consolation money (compensation), distribution of property, etc.

Under the Japanese laws the spouse who caused a reason for divorce should pay the consolation money. A typical example of such cause is infidelity. The amount of the consolation money varies depending upon the cases. There were cases in the past that the money in the neighborhood of one million yen was ordered by the Japanese court and that the one close to ten million yen was ordered by the Japanese court. Our law office is in a position to provide a client with a rough idea of such amount of money after studying the situations of the client's case.

The distribution of property between spouses under the Japanese laws, means to distribute the common property accumulated during marriage. Basically it is distributed equally between the spouses with some exceptions. The property includes real estate (such as house and land), financial property (such as cash, deposits, shares, bonds, etc.). Accordingly the property distribution may become a large amount.

Child matter (Parental Right, Custody, Child support, etc.)

Under the Japanese laws there are such matters as parental authority (parental rights), parent-child visitation or contacts and child support money pertaining to a child matter.

Parental authority (parental rights or custody) can be simply summarized to decide who of the spouses has the right to live with the child daily after the divorce. If there is no conflict between the spouses, they can decide the matter based on their mutual agreement. However, if no agreement is reached, a decision is made by a court. In such a case, who is the child's caretaker, the age and will of the child and other matters are considered. In addition, Japanese Civil Code does not accept Joint Parental Rights (or Joint Custody) yet, but currently only accepts Sole Parental Rights (or Sole Custody).

It is possible for the spouse who has no parental authority to visit and contact the child periodically. There is a case to agree to make such visitation and contact a few times a month at the time of divorce in view of each life of the divorced couple.

Child support money is the sum paid to the ex-wife or ex-husband who lives with the child by the ex-father or ex-wife who does not live with the child and basically it is decided by their mutual agreement. If a mutual agreement is not reached, a court decides the amount of child support money. Our law office is ready to provide our client with a rough idea of amount of child support money.

Incidentally expenses of married life are usually larger than child support money since they include the living expenses of the spouse.

Laws of which country are applicable to divorce (Governing law)

Japanese laws are not necessarily applicable to the proposed divorce and there is a case where laws of a foreign country are applied. It is difficult to mention generally which laws of a country are applicable, and the applicable laws are decided depending upon the situations of the divorce.

However if either spouse is a Japanese national and has " Habitual Residence" (which is simply defined as the place where he or she lives for a reasonably long period) in Japan, a Japanese court will apply Japanese laws to this divorce case.

With which country's court to file a divorce lawsuit (International jurisdiction)

If an agreement for divorce is not reached through mutual discussion or if either spouse is a national of a country where it is not possible to divorce by mutual agreement or conciliation (mediation), we think that it is necessary to file a divorce lawsuit with a court and in case that both of the spouses live in Japan, they may file a divorce lawsuit with a Japanese court.

However, if either spouse lives in a foreign country, it is necessary to study whether it is possible to file a divorce lawsuit in Japan (International jurisdiction). Generally it is a usual practice to file a divorce lawsuit with a court of the country where the defendant lives under Japanese laws. Accordingly as a principle in the event that the defendant lives in Japan, the divorce lawsuit can be filed in Japan.

Validity of judgment given by a foreign country's court in Japan or validity of judgment given by a Japanese court in a foreign country

There may be a case, for example, where spouses of international marriage live in Japan but they do not get along with each other and that one of the spouses who is a non-Japanese national goes back to his/her mother country and further he/she wins the lawsuit which it files as the plaintiff in his/her mother country. In such a case there is a question whether the judgment of the lawsuit is valid in Japan.

Whether a foreign judgement is valid (enforceable) in Japan or not, this issue shall be decided in accordance wiht Japanese Civil Execution Act. This act stipulates some conditions to make a foreign judgement valid (enforceable) in Japan.

In order to make the divorce procedures in Japan valid in a foreign country, it is necessary to confirm the laws of the foreign country. With regard to such problem our law office is able to resolve the matter since we have working relationships with law offices in foreign countries.

How to divorce as an Expat in Japan

If you are a British national who is resident in Japan, it is possible for you to divorce there, provided that you are able to satisfy the grounds for divorce.

Grounds for divorce

If you are an expatriate living in Japan, you may be able to divorce through the courts in Japan if you meet one of the criteria under Article 770 (1) of the Japanese Civil Code, as follows:

1. Your spouse has committed an act of adultery
2. Your spouse has abandoned you in bad faith;
3. If it has been unclear for three years or more whether your spouse is alive or dead;
4. If your spouse is suffering from severe mental illness and there is no prospect of recovery; or
5. There is any other grave cause making it difficult for you to continue the marriage.

Even if one of the grounds above is proved, the court may dismiss a suit for divorce if it finds that continuing the marriage is reasonable in all the circumstances. The law does not provide for any length of separation as a ground for divorce but the court would consider a separation as a possible grave cause under (5) above.

For those considering a divorce through the courts in Japan, it is important to note that court based conciliation is required prior to filing for divorce.

FINANCES

When considering how assets should be divided on divorce, it is usual for property that is acquired by the couple during their marriage to be divided equally. Property which has been inherited or received as a gift may be disregarded.

Children

When parents divorce in Japan, only one parent will have sole parental authority over the children. This means that the parent with custody is allowed to make all the decisions relating to the children. This extends to deciding to move to another country with the children away from the other parent.

As a British Expatriate considering divorce in Japan, it is essential to also obtain advice from a Japanese family lawyer as well as an English lawyer. Please contact us for details of Japanese specialists or to obtain assistance with divorce through the English Courts.

8

LAWS OF MARRIAGE AND DIVORCE IN CANADA

The Parliament of Canada has exclusive legislative authority over marriage and divorce in Canada under section 91(26) of the Constitution Act, 1867. However section 92(12) of the Constitution Act, 1867 gives the provincial legislatures the power to pass laws regulating the solemnization of marriage. In 2001 there were 146,618 marriages in Canada, down 6.8% from 157,395 in 2000. Prince Edward Island had the highest crude marriage rate (6.5 per 1,000 people) and Quebec had the lowest (3.0).

Marriage ceremonies in Canada can be either civil or religious. Marriages may be performed by members of the clergy, marriage commissioners, judges, justices of the peace or clerks of the court, depending on the laws of each province and territory regulating marriage solemnization. In 2001, the majority of Canadian marriages (76.4%) were religious, with the remainder (23.6%) being performed by non-clergy.

Same-sex marriage has been legal in Canada nationally since 2005. Court decisions, starting in 2003, had already legalized same-sex marriage in eight out of ten provinces and one of three territories.

It's against the law to be married to more than 1 person at a time. You can't come to Canada with more than 1 spouse, even if you were married to more than 1 person in the past.

It's also against the law to marry someone in Canada if 1 of you is already married (it doesn't matter where or when that marriage took place). You can only remarry if you're legally divorced or your spouse has died.

It's a crime in Canada to

- celebrate, aid or take part in the marriage of a child under 16 years old, even if the child agrees to be married

- force anyone into marriage against their will
- take part in or preside over a marriage ceremony knowing that one of the parties doesn't consent to marry
- take a person under 18, who normally lives in Canada, to another country to force them to marry

If you're pressured into marriage, you should contact the police. They will protect you.

In Canada, only a court can give you a civil divorce. Either spouse may apply for a divorce, but you must prove to the court that your marriage has broken down and that you've arranged for the support of any children.

It is a crime to marry a Canadian citizen or permanent resident only to gain entry into Canada. Find out more information about marriage fraud.

MARRIAGE RESTRICTIONS

Consanguinity

The federal Marriage (Prohibited Degrees) Act, Section 2 prevents the following persons from getting married:

1. Subject to subsection (2), persons related by consanguinity, affinity or adoption are not prohibited from marrying each other by reason only of their relationship.
2. No person shall marry another person if they are related lineally, or as brother or sister or half-brother or half-sister, including by adoption.

Consent of the spouses

Both parties must freely consent. Forcing somebody to get married is a criminal offence under s. 293.1 of the Criminal Code. In addition, s. 2.1 of the Civil Marriage Act stipulates, "Marriage requires the free and enlightened consent of two persons to be the spouse of each other."

Age of the spouses

Since 2015, federal law has set the absolute minimum marriageable age at 16. Provinces and territories may set a minimum age higher than that. In Canada the age of majority is set by province/territory at 18 or 19, so minors under this age have additional restrictions (i.e. parental and court consent). Section 293.2 of the Criminal Code also addresses marriages of individuals under the age of 16, reading: Everyone who celebrates, aids or participates in a marriage rite or ceremony knowing that one of the persons being married is under the age of 16 years is guilty of an indictable offence and liable to imprisonment for a term not exceeding five years. Section 2.2 of the Civil Marriage Act also states: No person who is under the age of 16 years may contract marriage. These provisions were enacted in 2015. Before 2015, it was possible for children less than 16 years old to get married in some jurisdictions of Canada, with parental consent or a court order. (The legal marriage age with parental consent was possibly as low as 7 in some Canadian jurisdictions.)

MINIMUM AGE BY PROVINCE AND TERRITORY

- British Columbia: 19, or 16 with parental consent.
- Alberta: 18, or 16 with consent of all parents and legal guardians.
- Saskatchewan: 18, or 16 with a "Consent to Marriage of a Minor" form signed and completed by the parent(s) or guardian(s) in the presence of a Saskatchewan marriage licence issuer, clergy or any person authorized to take affidavits. "If the parent(s) or guardian(s) refuse to consent to the marriage, the minor can apply to a judge of either the provincial or Queen's Bench court for an order dispensing with their consent. The minor may obtain the judge's order by applying to a court house in Saskatchewan."
- Manitoba: 18.
- Ontario: 18, or 16 with written consent from both sets of parents.
- Quebec: 18, or 16 with authorization from the courts.
- New Brunswick: 18, or 16 with an affidavit of consent signed by parents or guardians.
- Nova Scotia: 19, or 17 with a signed consent form.
- Prince Edward Island: 18, or younger with a consent form signed by parent(s).
- Newfoundland and Labrador: 19, or younger wherein "special consents may be required."
- Yukon: 19, or younger with consent of parent(s) or legal guardian(s).
- Northwest Territories: 19, or younger with parental consent.
- Nunavut: 19, or 16 with parental consent.

How does a valid marriage take place?

Marriage Licence

The couple must first get a marriage licence, unless they both regularly attend a place of worship and banns declaring their intention to marry have been proclaimed during a religious service. Marriage licences may be obtained from authorized businesses throughout the province. In Winnipeg, licences can also be obtained at Vital Statistics at 254 Portage Avenue.

The couple must apply together for the marriage licence. It must be obtained at least 24 hours before their wedding, unless the person performing the ceremony is persuaded that the time period should be waived because of exceptional circumstances. The wedding must take place within three months after the licence is issued.

CIVIL MARRIAGE ACT

An Act respecting certain aspects of legal capacity for marriage for civil purposes

Preamble

WHEREAS the Parliament of Canada is committed to upholding the Constitution of Canada, and section 15 of the Canadian Charter of Rights and Freedoms guarantees that every individual is equal before and under the law and has the right to equal protection and equal benefit of the law without discrimination;

WHEREAS the courts in a majority of the provinces and in one territory have recognized that the right to equality without discrimination requires that couples of the same sex and couples of the opposite sex have equal access to marriage for civil purposes;

WHEREAS the Supreme Court of Canada has recognized that many Canadian couples of the same sex have married in reliance on those court decisions;

WHEREAS only equal access to marriage for civil purposes would respect the right of couples of the same sex to equality without discrimination, and civil union, as an institution other than marriage, would not offer them that equal access and would violate their human dignity, in breach of the Canadian Charter of Rights and Freedoms;

WHEREAS the Supreme Court of Canada has determined that the Parliament of Canada has legislative jurisdiction over marriage but does not have the jurisdiction to establish an institution other than marriage for couples of the same sex;

WHEREAS everyone has the freedom of conscience and religion under section 2 of the Canadian Charter of Rights and Freedoms;

WHEREAS nothing in this Act affects the guarantee of freedom of conscience and religion and, in particular, the freedom of members of religious groups to hold and declare their religious beliefs and the freedom of officials of religious groups to refuse to perform marriages that are not in accordance with their religious beliefs;

WHEREAS it is not against the public interest to hold and publicly express diverse views on marriage;

WHEREAS, in light of those considerations, the Parliament of Canada's commitment to uphold the right to equality without discrimination precludes the use of section 33 of the Canadian Charter of Rights and Freedoms to deny the right of couples of the same sex to equal access to marriage for civil purposes;

WHEREAS marriage is a fundamental institution in Canadian society and the Parliament of Canada has a responsibility to support that institution because it strengthens commitment in relationships and represents the foundation of family life for many Canadians;

AND WHEREAS, in order to reflect values of tolerance, respect and equality consistent with the Canadian Charter of Rights and Freedoms, access to marriage for civil purposes should be extended by legislation to couples of the same sex;

NOW, THEREFORE, Her Majesty, by and with the advice and consent of the Senate and House of Commons of Canada, enacts as follows:

PART 1Marriage

Marginal note:Marriage — certain aspects of capacity

2 Marriage, for civil purposes, is the lawful union of two persons to the exclusion of all others.

Marginal note:Consent required

2.1 Marriage requires the free and enlightened consent of two persons to be the spouse of each other.

◉ 2015, c. 29, s. 4

Marginal note:Minimum age

2.2 No person who is under the age of 16 years may contract marriage.

◉ 2015, c. 29, s. 4

Marginal note:Previous marriage

2.3 No person may contract a new marriage until every previous marriage has been dissolved by death or by divorce or declared null by a court order.

◉ 2015, c. 29, s. 4

Marginal note:Religious officials

3 It is recognized that officials of religious groups are free to refuse to perform marriages that are not in accordance with their religious beliefs.

Marginal note:Freedom of conscience and religion and expression of beliefs

3.1 For greater certainty, no person or organization shall be deprived of any benefit, or be subject to any obligation or sanction, under any law of the Parliament of Canada solely by reason of their exercise, in respect of marriage between persons of the same sex, of the freedom of conscience and religion guaranteed under the Canadian Charter of Rights and Freedoms or the expression of their beliefs in respect of marriage as the union of a man and woman to the exclusion of all others based on that guaranteed freedom.

Marginal note:Marriage not void or voidable

4 For greater certainty, a marriage is not void or voidable by reason only that the spouses are of the same sex.

Marginal note:Marriage of non-resident persons

- 5 (1) A marriage that is performed in Canada and that would be valid in Canada if the spouses were domiciled in Canada is valid for the purposes of Canadian law even though either or both of the spouses do not, at the time of the marriage, have the capacity to enter into it under the law of their respective state of domicile.
- Marginal note:Retroactivity

(2) Subsection (1) applies retroactively to a marriage that would have been valid under the law that was applicable in the province where the marriage was performed but for the lack of capacity of either or both of the spouses to enter into it under the law of their respective state of domicile.

- Marginal note:Order dissolving marriage

(3) Any court order, made in Canada or elsewhere before the coming into force of this subsection, that declares the marriage to be null or that grants a divorce to the spouses dissolves the marriage, for the purposes of Canadian law, as of the day on which the order takes effect.

- 2005, c. 33, s. 5
- 2013, c. 30, s. 3
- 2015, c. 29, s. 5(E)

PART 2Dissolution of Marriage For Non-Resident Spouses

Definition of court

6 In this Part, court, in respect of a province, means

(a) for Ontario, the Superior Court of Justice;

(b) for Quebec, the Superior Court;

(c) for Nova Scotia and British Columbia, the Supreme Court of the province;

(d) for New Brunswick, Manitoba, Saskatchewan and Alberta, the Court of Queen's Bench for the province;

(e) for Prince Edward Island and Newfoundland and Labrador, the trial division of the Supreme Court of the province; and

(f) for Yukon and the Northwest Territories, the Supreme Court, and in Nunavut, the Nunavut Court of Justice.

It also means any other court in the province whose judges are appointed by the Governor General and that is designated by the Lieutenant Governor in Council of the province as a court for the purposes of this Part.

- 2005, c. 33, s. 6
- 2013, c. 30, s. 4

Marginal note:Divorce — non-resident spouses

- 7 (1) The court of the province where the marriage was performed may, on application, grant the spouses a divorce if

(a) there has been a breakdown of the marriage as established by the spouses having lived separate and apart for at least one year before the making of the application;

(b) neither spouse resides in Canada at the time the application is made; and

(c) each of the spouses is residing — and for at least one year immediately before the application is made, has resided — in a state where a divorce cannot be granted because that state does not recognize the validity of the marriage.

- Marginal note:Application

(2) The application may be made by both spouses jointly or by one of the spouses with the other spouse's consent or, in the absence of that consent, on presentation of an order from the court or a court located in the state where one of the spouses resides that declares that the other spouse

(a) is incapable of making decisions about his or her civil status because of a mental disability;

(b) is unreasonably withholding consent; or

(c) cannot be found.

- Marginal note:Exception if spouse is found

(3) Despite paragraph (2)(c), the other spouse's consent is required if that spouse is found in connection with the service of the application.

- 2005, c. 33, s. 7
- 2013, c. 30, s. 4

Marginal note: No corollary relief

8 For greater certainty, the Divorce Act does not apply to a divorce granted under this Act.

- 2005, c. 33, s. 8
- 2013, c. 30, s. 4

Marginal note: Effective date generally

- 9 (1) A divorce takes effect on the day on which the judgment granting the divorce is rendered.
- Marginal note: Certificate of divorce

(2) After a divorce takes effect, the court must, on request, issue to any person a certificate that a divorce granted under this Act dissolved the marriage of the specified persons effective as of a specified date.

- Marginal note: Conclusive proof

(3) The certificate, or a certified copy of it, is conclusive proof of the facts so certified without proof of the signature or authority of the person appearing to have signed the certificate.

- 2005, c. 33, s. 9
- 2013, c. 30, s. 4

Marginal note: Legal effect throughout Canada

10 On taking effect, a divorce granted under this Act has legal effect throughout Canada.

- 2005, c. 33, s. 10
- 2013, c. 30, s. 4

Marginal note: Marriage dissolved

11 On taking effect, a divorce granted under this Act dissolves the marriage of the spouses.

- 2005, c. 33, s. 11
- 2013, c. 30, s. 4

11.1 [Repealed, 2013, c. 30, s. 4]

Definition of competent authority

- 12 (1) In this section, competent authority, in respect of a court in a province, means the body, person or group of persons ordinarily competent under the laws of that province to make rules regulating the practice and procedure in that court.
- Marginal note: Rules

(2) Subject to subsection (3), the competent authority may make rules applicable to any applications made under this Part in a court in a province, including rules

(a) regulating the practice and procedure in the court;

(b) respecting the conduct and disposition of any applications that are made under this Part without an oral hearing;

(c) prescribing and regulating the duties of the officers of the court; and

(d) prescribing and regulating any other matter considered expedient to attain the ends of justice and carry into effect the purposes and provisions of this Part.

- Marginal note: Exercise of power

(3) The power of a competent authority to make rules for a court must be exercised in the like manner and subject to the like terms and conditions, if any, as the power to make rules for that court that are conferred on that authority by the laws of the province.

- Marginal note: Not statutory instruments

(4) Rules that are made under this section by a competent authority that is not a judicial or quasi-judicial body are deemed not to be statutory instruments within the meaning and for the purposes of the Statutory Instruments Act.

- 2005, c. 33, s. 12
- 2013, c. 30, s. 4

Marginal note: Regulations

- 13 (1) The Governor in Council may make regulations for carrying out the purposes and provisions of this Part, including regulations providing for uniformity in the rules made under section 12.
- Marginal note: Regulations prevail

(2) Any regulations that are made to provide for uniformity in the rules prevail over those rules.

- 2005, c. 33, s. 13
- 2013, c. 30, s. 4

DIVORCE

The Divorce Act (French: Loi sur le divorce) is the federal Act that governs divorce in Canada. The Constitution of Canada gives the federal Parliament exclusive jurisdiction to regulate the law of marriage and divorce.

Termination of marriage in Canada is covered by the federal Divorce Act.

A divorce may be granted for one of the following reasons:

- the marriage has irretrievably broken down, and the two parties have been living apart for a year (s.8(2)(a) of the Act)
- one party has committed adultery (s.8(2)(b)(i) of the Act)
- one party has treated the other party "with physical or mental cruelty of such a kind as to render intolerable the continued cohabitation of the spouses" (s.8(2)(b)(ii) of the Act)

Key headings of the Divorce Act:

- Interpretation
- Jurisdiction
- Divorce
- Child support orders
- Spousal support orders

- Priority
- Custody orders
- Variation, rescission or suspension of orders
- Provisional orders
- Appeals
- General

History of divorce law in Canada

Pre-Confederation divorce laws

There was no uniform federal divorce law in Canada until 1968. Instead, there was a patch-work of divorce laws in the different provinces, depending on the laws in force in each province at the time it joined Confederation:

- In the three Maritime provinces, divorce was governed by laws enacted by the colonial governments prior to Confederation in 1867 (in Nova Scotia from 1758, in New Brunswick from 1791, and in Prince Edward Island from 1833);
- In the three prairie provinces and the northern territories, divorce was available under the English Matrimonial Causes Act 1857, which was incorporated into their local law in 1870 under the terms of the Rupert's Land Act 1868;
- In 1867, the Colony of British Columbia had declared that the laws of England, as they stood at November 19, 1858, were to apply "so far as they are not from local circumstances inapplicable". This declaration was later held to have included the English Matrimonial Causes Act 1857 as it stood at that time. Until 1937, there was no right of appeal from a divorce proceeding in British Columbia.
- In Quebec, the Civil Code of Lower Canada declared that "Marriage can only be dissolved by the natural death of one of the parties; while both live it is indissoluble."
- In Ontario, divorce was not available until 1930. There was no pre-Confederation divorce law, although several efforts had been made prior to Confederation to bring it about. It was not until 1930, when Parliament passed the Divorce Act (Ontario), that the courts of Ontario were given jurisdiction to grant divorces and annulments. The law granting divorce under this law was according to the law of England as it stood at July 15, 1870 (and thus on the same footing as the prairie provinces and the territories).
- Newfoundland never enacted a divorce law prior to entering Confederation in 1949, and the local courts did not grant judicial separations until 1948. There was therefore no divorce law in Newfoundland after it joined Confederation.

The English Matrimonial Causes Act 1857 provided that a husband could sue on grounds of adultery alone, but a wife would have to allege adultery together with other grounds. That rule applied in those provinces that had adopted the English Act. In 1925, Parliament provided that in those provinces, a wife could sue on grounds of adultery alone.

In 1930, Parliament extended relief to deserted wives, by providing that, in the provinces where divorce was available, they could pursue proceedings on the grounds of desertion, so long as there had been separation from the husband for at least two years.

Parliamentary divorces

The only way for an individual to get divorced in the provinces where there was no divorce law—as well as in cases where the domicile of the parties was unclear—was to apply to the federal Parliament for a private bill of divorce. These bills were primarily handled by the Senate of Canada where a special committee would undertake an investigation of a request for a divorce. If the committee found that the request had merit, the marriage would be dissolved by an Act of Parliament.

In 1963, provision was made for the Senate of Canada to be able to dispose of parliamentary divorce petitions by way of resolution instead of by a private Act.

Foreign divorces

Residents of Ontario, Quebec and Newfoundland could attempt to obtain a divorce in the United States, but the validity of such decrees could be subject to review in the Canadian courts on the issue of domicile. In 1885, the Supreme Court of Canada ruled that a New York divorce was valid, even though the husband was living in Montreal, as "the burden was on the husband of showing that he had actually changed his domicile animo et de facto". The consequences where a divorce was not recognized (e.g., it was obtained in a divorce mill, such as Reno, Nevada once was) and where one of the parties had already remarried proved to be awkward in certain cases.

Reform of the law

1968 Act

In 1968, Parliament passed its first Divorce Act, which established a uniform divorce law across Canada. In addition to bringing about uniformity, the 1968 Act:

- placed both spouses on an equal footing in pursuing a divorce and specified that the grounds included:
  - adultery,
  - conviction of a sexual offence,
  - bigamy,
  - mental or physical cruelty, or

- o a permanent breakdown of the marriage, arising from a separation of three years' duration because of imprisonment of the other spouse,[a] addiction, disappearing in circumstances where it is not known where the spouse may have gone, inability or refusal to consummate a marriage, or living separate and apart during that time.[b] and

- declared that "the domicile of a married woman shall be determined as if she were unmarried, and, if she is a minor, as if she had attained her majority", with one year's residence in the province where the divorce order was sought, and provided that foreign divorces would be recognized as long as the foreign jurisdiction had similar rules with respect to the wife's domicile.

- provided that, where proceedings were initiated in separate provinces by each of the spouses, the one that commenced first would normally be the one that would be allowed to proceed. If both such proceedings were initiated on the same day, they would both be removed to the Divorce Division of the Exchequer Court.

- provided that judgment would be in the form of a decree nisi, which would only become absolute three months later, after the court was satisfied that all rights of appeal had been exhausted.

1986 Act

In 1986, Parliament replaced the Act, which simplified the law of divorce further. It brought forth several significant changes:

- An application for divorce could be initiated by either spouse or both of them jointly.

- Breakdown of the marriage was specified as the sole ground for divorce, as evidenced by the spouses living separate and apart for the one year prior to the divorce proceedings (and being so at the date of their commencement), or by having committed adultery, or physical or mental cruelty, at any time since the celebration of the marriage.

- Domicile was no longer required, and a court had jurisdiction where one of the spouses had been resident in the province for at least one year prior to the commencement of the proceedings.

- The Divorce Division of the Exchequer Court became part of the Federal Court of Canada – Trial Division.

- The divorce became effective 31 days after the judgment granting it was rendered, provided that it is not under appeal.

- Foreign divorces are recognized for all purposes of determining the marital status of any person in Canada, provided that:

- for those granted after July 1, 1968, they were granted in circumstances that conformed to the Canadian rules relating to domicile that existed at the time;
- for those granted on or after the new Act came into force, they were granted in circumstances that conformed to the Canadian rules relating to residence immediately before the commencement of such proceedings; but
- the rules of law relating to the recognition of divorces (otherwise than under the Act) remain in effect.

Later amendments

Religious divorce (1990)

While divorce is a civil matter in Canadian law, lobbying from Jewish women's groups such as the Canadian Coalition of Jewish Women for the Gett served to highlight the problem of agunah in Canada, and the connected problem of obtaining a get in the Jewish rabbinical courts. The Act was amended in 1990 to provide that:

- a spouse (called the "deponent") may file an affidavit upon the other spouse identifying the particulars of the marriage, the nature of any barriers to remarriage in the deponent's religion that are within the other spouse's control, whether such barriers have been removed, or, where a request has been made to have such barriers removed, whether the other spouse has failed to remove them;
- the spouse served with the affidavit has 15 days to respond that such barriers have been removed to the court's satisfaction; and
- the court may dismiss an application by the other spouse, and strike out the other spouse's pleadings, where no response to the deponent's affidavit is received.

There are still certain complications arising from the application of this provision. In one Quebec case, the Supreme Court of Canada ruled that an agreement by divorcing parties, providing that the ex-husband would proceed forthwith to obtain a get, provided grounds for the ex-wife being able to obtain damages as a result of him reneging on it.

Same-sex marriage and divorce (2005)

During the period 2001–2005, same-sex marriage began to be available as a result a series of court cases in almost all provincial and territorial courts, which held that same-sex marriage was required by Section 15 of the Canadian Charter of Rights and Freedoms. In 2004, the Supreme Court of Canada held in the Reference re Same-Sex Marriage that such marriages were within the exclusive legislative authority of the Parliament of Canada, but declined to address the s.15 argument.

In 2005, Parliament passed the Civil Marriage Act, which made same-sex marriage the law throughout Canada, and also amended the Divorce Act to change its corresponding meaning of "spouse" to mean "either of two persons who are married to each other."

Later Canadian and foreign court proceedings revealed complications arising from the application of private international law, so that, while same-sex marriages solemnized in Canada may be legal when its jurisdiction, they must also be valid according to the rules of domicile that apply to the celebrants. As well, the Divorce Act's one-year residence requirement resulted in Canadian divorces not being able to be granted to spouses who are both non-resident. The CMA was amended in 2013 to provide for a separate divorce process to be available, outside the Divorce Act, to nonresident spouses in the province where the marriage took place, and such divorces have immediate effect.

9

MARRIAGE AND DIVORCE LAWS IN ENGLAND

Marriage is available in England and Wales to both opposite-sex and same-sex couples and is legally recognised in the forms of both civil and religious marriage. Marriage laws have historically evolved separately from marriage laws in other jurisdictions in the United Kingdom. There is a distinction between religious marriages, conducted by an authorised religious celebrant and civil marriages conducted by a state registrar.

The legal minimum age to enter into a marriage in England and Wales is eighteen years. Certain relatives are not allowed to marry. For foreign nationals, there are also residency conditions that have to be met before people can be married. Same-sex marriage was introduced under the Marriage (Same Sex Couples) Act in March 2014.

For a marriage to be legally recognised in England and Wales it must comply with certain legal requirements. Even if your marriage is recognised by your community or religion, it may not be a lawful marriage according to English law.

Whether a marriage is legally recognised or not is very important because this can have significant consequences particularly in relation to finances and property rights. Not having a marriage which is recognised in law can leave you in a financially vulnerable position, for example you may have no claim to stay in the marital home, or no access to financial support from your spouse. It is therefore very important to be clear whether a marriage is legally recognised in England and Wales, and to understand the legal consequences of being married.

This guide sets out the criteria that must be complied with for a marriage to be legally recognised. In this guide we will sometimes refer to your spouse, which means your husband or your wife.

If you are not legally married but live with your partner it is important to be aware that the law does not give you any special legal status. There is no legal recognition of a 'common law' husband or wife.

MARRIAGE PROCEDURES

Wedding ceremonies can either be conducted by "authorised celebrants" (usually, but not always, a minister of religion) or by an "authorised registrar". To be legally binding, they must take place with at least two other competent people present as witnesses. The marriage register is signed by the couple, the celebrant and two witnesses. Civil marriages may not take place in religious venues, but since the Marriage Act 1994 may take place in other licensed venues.

Priests of the Church of England and the Church in Wales are legally required to marry people, providing one of them is from the local parish, regardless of whether the couple are practising. Special permission may be granted for out-of-parish weddings. Since the Church of England Marriage Measure 2008 and Marriage (Wales) Act 2010, the right to marry in a church was extended to churches that their parents or grandparents were married in or if they were baptised or confirmed in it.

For civil marriages notices must be posted for 28 clear days, at the appropriate register office. Church of England marriages require the banns to be read out three times at the appropriate church or churches unless a Special Licence has been obtained. In most cases, the appropriate churches will be the parish churches where the parties reside and the one where the ceremony is to take place.

A marriage solemnized between persons either of whom is under the age of sixteen is void. This disability may be referred to as "nonage".

The law of marriage

Until the middle of the 18th century marriages could take place anywhere provided they were conducted before an ordained clergyman of the Church of England. This encouraged the practice of secret marriages which did not have parental consent and which were often bigamous.

Irregular marriages

It also allowed couples, particularly those of wealthy background, to marry while at least one of the partners was under age. The trade in these irregular marriages had grown enormously in London by the 1740s.

In 1753, however, the Marriage Act, promoted by the Lord Chancellor, Lord Hardwicke, declared that all marriage ceremonies must be conducted by a minister in a parish church or chapel of the Church of England to be legally binding.

Parental consent

No marriage of a person under the age of 21 was valid without the consent of parents or guardians. Clergymen who disobeyed the law were liable for 14 years transportation.

Although Jews and Quakers were exempted from the 1753 Act, it required religious non-conformists and Catholics to be married in Anglican churches.

Restrictions removed

This restriction was eventually removed by Parliament in the Marriage Act of 1836 which allowed non-conformists and Catholics to be married in their own places of worship.

It was also made possible for non-religious civil marriages to be held in register offices which were set up in towns and cities.

Minimum age

In 1929, in response to a campaign by the National Union of Societies for Equal Citizenship, Parliament raised the age limit to 16 for both sexes in the Ages of Marriage Act. This is still the minimum age.

Civil partnerships

The Civil Partnership Act 2004, for example, granted civil partnerships to same-sex couples in the United Kingdom with rights and responsibilities identical to civil marriage.

Although the Act was intended to apply only to England and Wales, the devolved Scottish Parliament passed a Legislative Consent Motion which allowed Westminster to legislate on behalf of Scotland.

MARRIAGE (SAME SEX COUPLES) ACT 2013

In 2013, Parliament passed the Marriage (Same Sex Couples) Act which introduced civil marriage for same-sex couples in England and Wales. The legislation allowed religious organisations to opt in to marry same-sex couples should they wish to do so and protected religious organisations and their representatives from successful legal challenge if they did not wish to marry same-sex couples. The legislation also enabled civil partners to convert their civil partnership into marriage and transsexual people to change their legal gender without necessarily having to end their existing marriage.

In Scotland, the Scottish Parliament has legislated to allow same-sex marriages. The Northern Ireland Assembly has not legislated to allow the marriage of same-sex couples in Northern Ireland.

Who can marry?

In order to enter a legally recognised marriage the couple intending to marry must be:

- Not closely related. For example, you cannot marry your brother or sister.

- Over 16 years old. If you are under 18 years old you will need consent from your parents.
- Not already married or in a civil partnership.

If any of these criteria are not met the couple will not be able to get married. If, for some reason a marriage ceremony has occurred and one of the above factors apply, then the marriage is considered void. This means that the marriage is treated in law as never existing.

From 29 March 2014, same sex couples can get married in England and Wales.

The civil preliminaries – what do I have to do before I get married?

For most marriages, both parties must provide at least 16 days' notice of the marriage. You do this at your local register office. A registrar will take information from you and place a notice on a public board in the register office for 15 days. The person you are marrying should do the same.

If any member of the public has reason to believe that you should not be married then they can object to the marriage. If there are no objections then the registrar will provide you with a notice of marriage certificate, which you will need in order to get married.

Where can I get married?

To be legally recognised, a marriage ceremony must take place at one of the following places:

- a register office
- an approved premises
- an Anglican Church (i.e. a Church belonging to the Church of England and Wales)
- a registered building.

A register office is contained usually in an official building of the Local Authority for your area, very often a Town Hall. If you choose to get married here the ceremony must be a civil ceremony, which means that it must not contain any religious content or music (see below).

Approved premises are special places that have been approved by the local authority. They include many castles, stately homes and hotels. If you choose to get married in approved premises you must have a civil ceremony.

An Anglican Church is a church belonging to the Church of England and Wales. Couples will very often have to fulfil certain requirements, religious or otherwise, before the clergy will agree to them getting married in church. If you get married in church the ceremony will be a religious ceremony. This means it will have religious content and music.

A registered building is a building that is registered as a place of worship for religious purpose that is not a church belonging to the Church of England and Wales. Some, but not all, mosques, Hindu temples and Sikh gurdwaras are registered buildings. Synagogues do not have to be registered because different rules apply to Jewish marriages (see below). Local authorities keep lists of registered buildings in their areas and should be able to tell you whether your local place of worship is registered or not.).

Same sex couples cannot get married in an Anglican Church. Same sex couples can get married in other religious buildings if:

1. the religious organisation allows same sex weddings to take place and
2. the building has been registered for the marriage of same sex couples.

The marriage ceremony

Strict rules govern the ceremony itself. These rules depend on whether the ceremony is a civil ceremony, a Jewish or Quaker ceremony, a Church of England ceremony or some other kind of religious ceremony.

It is essential that the rules are complied with otherwise the marriage will not be legally recognised.

Civil marriages

A civil ceremony can take place at a register office or at approved premises. At the civil ceremony the parties getting married are required to state that there is no reason why they cannot marry, and then exchange vows (say formal words) which can take various forms. The ceremony can include music or readings but these cannot be religious. The ceremony should be conducted by the superintendent registrar and/or the registrar of the registration district in which the ceremony takes place. There must also be a minimum of two witnesses present.

Sometimes a civil ceremony is followed by a religious ceremony. However, it is only the civil ceremony which is legally binding on the couple.

RELIGIOUS MARRIAGES

For legal purposes, there are three different types of religious marriage ceremonies. If the correct procedure is not followed the marriage will not be valid.

Church of England marriages must be conducted by a member of the clergy, for example an Anglican Priest, who will register the marriage. The marriage must take place in the presence of two witnesses and in accordance with the rules of the Church of England.

Quaker and Jewish marriages are recognised differently to other religious ceremonies. For example, there is no need for the marriage ceremony to take place in a registered building, nor to be in public. The marriage ceremony can be conducted according to

Jewish or Quaker religious rules. The official preforming the Jewish or Quaker ceremony will register the marriage.

Other religious marriages, such as Muslim, Hindu and Sikh marriages are required to satisfy additional requirements. The marriage must take place in a registered building. Not all buildings are registered, so it is important to check first with your local authority. If the building is not registered then the marriage will not be legally recognised.

The ceremony itself can take any form, provided that:

- it is in public
- there are at least two witnesses present
- either a registrar of the district in which the ceremony is taking place or an authorised person is present
- both parties make the necessary declarations, for example, declaring that there are no lawful objections to the marriage

An authorised person is someone who has been certified by the Registrar General, for example, the Imam of the mosque where the ceremony takes place could be certified as an authorised person to conduct or be present at marriages. If there is someone that you wish to conduct, or be present at, your ceremony you should confirm with them whether they are certified as an authorised person. If you have any concerns it is also advisable to check with your local authority or register office.

Religious marriage ceremonies are not recognised in English law unless the civil content and requirements are complied with as well.

If you want to have a religious marriage or other type of marriage ceremony and, for example, the place you want to get married is not a registered building, or the person you want to conduct or be present during the ceremony is not an authorised person, then you will need to have a civil ceremony beforehand to ensure your marriage is legally recognised.

For all legally recognised ceremonies the married couple must be given a marriage certificate.

SECOND MARRIAGES

Under the law of England and Wales a person commits the criminal offence of bigamy if they marry one person whilst they are married to someone else. If a person marries more than one person and lives with all of their wives or husbands this is called a polygamous marriage, and a person who does this in England and Wales is likely to be committing the offence of bigamy.

This means that if you are married in a legally recognised ceremony in England and Wales, and if your husband or wife is already legally married, then your marriage will not be legally recognised and your husband or wife may be committing a criminal offence.

Alternatively, if you have a religious marriage which is not legally recognised and your spouse is already married to someone else, for example your marriage is a second Islamic marriage recognised in Islamic law, your spouse will not be committing a criminal offence, but your marriage will not be legally recognised and you may be vulnerable to the difficulties mentioned above with regards to finances and property.

If your marriage took place overseas and your spouse is already married then your marriage may be recognised as legal in England and Wales providing that your marriage was legally recognised in the country in which you got married and neither you nor your spouse's domicile (see above) is England and Wales. If you are not sure about your domicile it is important to seek legal advice.

Forced Marriages

A forced marriage is where one or both people do not, or cannot, consent to the marriage and pressure or abuse is used. If you think you have been forced into a marriage, or you want to know more about forced marriage.

A forced marriage is a voidable marriage, which means it can be declared not to exist.

A marriage which is voidable is still a marriage in law until it is annulled (declared to not exist). The process of getting an annulment is similar to that of divorce but, unlike divorce, once a marriage is annulled it puts the parties back into their original position as if the marriage had never taken place.

Unlike divorce, it is not necessary to wait one year from the date of the marriage before applying for annulment. It is important to note, however, that you must start the annulment process within three years of the date of the marriage.

If three years have passed since the marriage and you have not started the annulment process then you will need to get permission from the court to start your application.

Benefits and consequences

Upon death of one's spouse, bequests to the other spouse do not incur inheritance tax. Intestate property by default will go to the spouse. Also, there is partial inheritance of pensions. In courts, one spouse may not be compelled to testify against the other. Non-British spouses of British citizens may obtain residence permits if the British spouse meets a minimum income requirement of £18,600 per year. This rises to £22,400 for families with a child, and a further £2,400 for each further child. Spouses are considered to have a duty of care towards each other, and certain social security benefits are calculated differently from those for single people.

Foreign citizens wishing to marry in the UK

From 1 February 2005, visitors who wish to be married in the UK that are a citizen of a country that is not a member of the European Economic Area (EEA), must apply for a visa before they travel. Without the visa, the registrar will not be able to accept the notice of marriage and will not be able to perform the marriage ceremony.

If one of the people wanting to marry is subject to immigration control, notice of marriage can only be done at a designated register office, which both parties must attend together. Marriage must be between two people neither of whom is in a Civil Partnership or separate marriage (foreign divorces are generally recognised; but an existing foreign marriage would prevent a marriage in the UK as this would be treated as bigamy).

DIVORCE

Unhappily married couples in England and Wales can now dissolve their marriage without blaming each other, according to a significant change in divorce law. The bill, which was passed in June 2020, became law.

The "no-fault" divorce is regarded as the most significant change in divorce law in nearly 50 years, as it eliminates the necessity for divorcing couples to assign blame for their marriage's demise. Instead, the law permits spouses to concentrate on important issues such as children, finances, and the future.

Divorce is allowed when it has been determined that the marriage has irretrievably broken down. Grounds for this must be evidenced in one or more of the five possible facts as stated in the Matrimonial Causes Act 1973:

- Adultery
- Unreasonable behaviour, which pertains to physical violence, verbal abuse such as insults or threats, drunkenness or drug-taking, and refusing to pay towards shared living expenses
- Desertion (two years)
- Separation, agreed divorce (two years)
- Separation, contested divorce (five years)

The Civil remarriage is allowed. Religions and denominations differ on whether they permit religious remarriage.

In England and Wales, divorce is allowed on the ground that the marriage has irretrievably broken down. The Matrimonial Causes Act 1973 specifies that the marriage may be found to have irretrievably broken down if one of the following is established:

- Adultery
- Unreasonable behaviour
- Desertion (two years)
- Separation, agreed divorce (two years)
- Separation, contested divorce (five years)

Civil remarriage is allowed. Religions and denominations differ on whether they permit religious remarriage.

A divorce in England and Wales is only possible for marriages of more than one year and when the marriage has irretrievably broken down. Whilst it is possible to defend a divorce, the vast majority proceed on an undefended basis. A decree of divorce is initially granted 'nisi', i.e. (unless cause is later shown), before it is made 'absolute'.

Historically, divorce was not administered as such by the barristers who practised in the common law courts but by the "advocates" and "proctors" who practised civil law from Doctors' Commons, adding to the obscurity of the proceedings. Divorce was de facto restricted to the very wealthy as it demanded either a complex annulment process or a private bill leading to an Act of Parliament, with great costs for either. The latter entailed sometimes lengthy debates about a couple's intimate marital relationship in public in the House of Commons.

The Matrimonial Causes Act 1857 moved litigation from the jurisdiction of the ecclesiastical courts to the civil courts, establishing a model of marriage based on contract rather than sacrament and widening the availability of divorce beyond those who could afford to bring proceedings for annulment or to promote a private Bill.

After World War I, there were reforms made to the divorce law that put men and women on a more equal footing. The Matrimonial Causes Act 1923, made adultery a ground of divorce for either spouse. Previously, only the man had been able to do this; women had to prove additional fault. A further Act in 1937 (the Matrimonial Causes Act 1937) offered additional grounds for divorce: cruelty, desertion and incurable insanity. The need for the reforms was illustrated in the best-selling satirical novel Holy Deadlock (1934).

Regarding the public's reaction to the end of the relationship between never-married Princess Margaret and the divorced Peter Townsend in 1955, The Independent wrote in 1995, "(this) can now be seen to have constituted a watershed in the nation's attitude towards divorce".

The Divorce Reform Act 1969 marked a significant change in that people could end marriages that had "irretrievably broken down" without having to prove fault. They could end marriages after separation of two years, if both parties desired divorce, or five years if only one party desired divorce.

The Matrimonial Causes Act 1973 provided that a marriage had to have lasted for three years before a divorce could be applied for; the Matrimonial and Family Proceedings Act 1984 reduced this period to one year.

The Divorce, Dissolution and Separation Bill 2019-21 was introduced to parliament in January 2020 by the Conservative Government. The bill was a response to the Supreme Court case of Owens (Appellant) v Owens (Respondent), which stated in its conclusion that Parliament may wish to consider replacing the current divorce law. The bill would remove the requirement to provide evidence of fault, or separation; and replace it with a statement from either applicant that the marriage had irretrievably broken down. The legislation received royal assent on 25 June 2020 and was passed as the Divorce, Dissolution and Separation Act 2020.

Laws

Relevant laws are:

- Marriage Act 1949
- Divorce Reform Act 1969
- Matrimonial Causes Act 1973, which sets out the basis for divorce (part i) and how the courts deal with financial issues, known as ancillary relief (part ii)
  - Cruelty has been made irrelevant. See Gollins v Gollins [1964] A.C. 644
- Children Act 1989
- Family Proceedings Courts (Matrimonial Proceedings etc.) Rules 1991
- Marriage Act 1994
- Family Law Act 1996
- Gender Recognition Act 2004
- Divorce, Dissolution and Separation Act 2020

The ground for divorce

There is only one 'ground' for divorce under English law. That is that the marriage has irretrievably broken down.

Until the date on which the Divorce, Dissolution and Separation Act 2020 becomes effective there are five 'facts' that may constitute this ground. They are:

1. Adultery

- often now considered the 'nice' divorce.[by whom?]
- respondents admitting to adultery will not be penalised financially or otherwise.
- cannot be used as a ground for divorce if the couple keeps living together for more than six months after discovering the adulterous act, unless the adulterous relationship is continuing or there are other acts of adultery after the first such act is discovered.

2. Unreasonable behaviour (most common ground for divorce today).

- o the petition must contain a series of allegations proving that the respondent has behaved in such a way that the petitioner cannot reasonably be expected to live with him/her.
- o the allegations may be of a serious nature (e.g. abuse or excessive drinking) but may also be mild such as having no common interests or pursuing a separate social life; the courts will not insist on severe allegations as they adopt a realistic attitude: if one party feels so strongly that a behaviour is "unreasonable" as to issue a divorce petition, it is clear that the marriage has irretrievably broken down and it would be futile to try to prevent the divorce.

3. Two years separation (if both parties consent)

- o both parties must consent
- o the parties must have lived separate lives for at least two years prior to the presentation of the petition
- o this can occur if the parties live in the same household, but the petitioner would need to make clear in the petition such matters as they ate separately, etc.

4. Two years desertion
5. Five years separation (if only one party consents)

Once in force, the Divorce, Dissolution and Separation Act 2020 will provide for no-fault divorce whereby an application for divorce by way of the making of a statement that the marriage has broken down irretrievably disregarding the reasons detailed above. The Act is expected to come into force from Autumn 2021.

UNCONTESTED DIVORCE PROCEDURE

Here is a rough outline of the undefended divorce procedure from start to finish:

1. Filing of Divorce Petition and, if necessary, Statement of Arrangements for the Children
2. Documents issued by Court and posted to the Respondent
3. Respondent returns Acknowledgement of Service to the Court (if he/she does not you will need to consider Bailiff Service, Deemed Service or other options)
4. Petitioner completes affidavit in Support of Petition and Request for directions
5. A Judge will then consider all the divorce papers and if he/she is satisfied issue a Certificate of Entitlement to a Decree and Section 41 Certificate (confirming he/she is content with arrangements for any children)
6. Decree nisi is granted. This is a court order which confirms that the grounds for divorce have been accepted and that the court believes the marriage has irretrievably broken down.

7. Six weeks later the application can be made by the Petitioner for the decree absolute.

From beginning to end, if there are no further issues and Court permitting, it takes around six months. If there are any outstanding financial issues between the parties, most solicitors would advise resolving these by way of a 'Clean Break' Court order prior to obtaining the Decree Absolute.

10

MARRIAGE AND DIVORCE LAWS IN AUSTRALIA

Marriage in Australia is regulated by the federal government, which is granted the power to make laws regarding marriage by section 51(xxi) of the constitution. The Marriage Act 1961 applies uniformly throughout Australia (including its external territories) to the exclusion of all state laws on the subject.

Australian law recognises only monogamous marriages, being marriages of two people, including same-sex marriages, and does not recognise any other forms of union, including traditional Aboriginal marriages, polygamous marriages or concubinage. The marriage age for marriage in Australia is 18 years, but in "unusual and exceptional circumstances" a person aged 16 or 17 can marry with parental consent and authorisation by a court. A Notice of Intended Marriage is required to be lodged with the chosen marriage celebrant at least one month before the wedding. There is no citizenship or residency requirement for marriage in Australia, so that casual visitors can lawfully marry in Australia, provided that a domestic marriage celebrant is employed, the requisite notice given, and other domestic requirements satisfied.

Marriages performed abroad are normally recognised in Australia if entered into in accordance with the applicable foreign law, and do not require to be registered in Australia. It is not uncommon for Australian citizens or Australian residents to go abroad to marry. This may be to the family's ancestral home country, to a destination wedding location or because they would not be permitted to marry in Australia.

As was the case for other Western countries, marriage in Australia for most of the 20th century was done early and near-universally, particularly in the period after World War II to the early 1970s. Marriage at a young age was most often associated with pregnancy prior to marriage. Marriage was once seen as necessary for couples who cohabited. While some couples did cohabit before marriage, it was relatively uncommon until the 1950s in much of the Western world.

According to a 2008 Relationships Australia survey love, companionship and signifying a lifelong commitment were the top reasons for marriage.

NATURE OF MARRIAGE

Australian law recognises only monogamous marriages, being marriages of two people, including same-sex marriages, and does not recognise any other forms of union, including traditional Aboriginal marriages, polygamous marriages or concubinage. A person who goes through a marriage ceremony in Australia when still legally married to another person, whether under Australian law or a law of another country, commits an offence of bigamy, which is subject to a maximum 5 years imprisonment, and the marriage is void.

Since December 2017, Australian law has recognised same-sex marriage in Australia whether entered into in Australia or abroad. The original 1961 Marriage Act did not include a definition of marriage, leaving it to the courts to apply the common law definition. The Marriage Amendment Act 2004 defined, for the first time by statute, marriage as "the union of a man and a woman to the exclusion of all others, voluntarily entered into for life." The 2004 Act also expressly declared same-sex marriages entered into abroad were not to be recognised in Australia. This was in response to a lesbian couple getting married in Canada and applying for their marriage to be recognised in Australia. In 2017, the definition of "marriage" was changed, replacing the words "a man and a woman" with "2 people" and therefore allowing monogamous same-sex marriages. The changes also retrospectively recognised same-sex marriages performed in a foreign country, provided that such marriages were permitted under the laws of that foreign country.

A marriage must be entered into with the full consent of both parties, and it is an offence to force someone to marry them or another person, by the use of coercion, threat or deception, and whether in Australia or abroad. Full consent assumes a mental capacity to understand the nature of a marriage.

Most federal, state and territory laws also recognise de facto relationships, often on an equal basis to formal marital relationships.

Marriageable age

The marriageable age for marriage in Australia is 18 years, which is the age of majority in Australia in all states, but in "unusual and exceptional circumstances" a person aged 16 or 17 can marry with parental consent and authorisation by a Magistrates Court. The application to the court must be filed by a parent. For many years, courts have refused to accept a minor's pregnancy as a pressing consideration in deciding whether to allow an early marriage. In addition, the older partner must be over 18.

Until 1991, the marriage age was 16 for females and 18 for males, but a female 14 or 15 years (wanting to marry a male aged 18 or above) or a male 16 or 17 years (wanting to marry a female aged 16 or above) could apply to the court for permission to marry. The ages were equalised in 1991, with the relevant ages applying to females being raised to those applying to males.

Void marriages

A marriage entered into in Australia is void if:

- either party is already married (bigamy, polygamy).
- the parties are in a prohibited relationship: direct ancestor or descendant or sibling (whether full sibling or half sibling), including those arising from a legal adoption.
- the marriage was not solemnised by an authorised celebrant.
- there is no consent, for example due to duress, fraud, mistake as to identity, mistake as to the nature of ceremony, mental incapacity, or being below the marriageable age.

MARRIAGES OF NON-CITIZENS

Australian citizenship is not a requirement for marriage in Australia, nor for the recognition of a foreign marriage.

When one of the parties to a marriage is a non-citizen of Australia and the other is an Australian or New Zealand citizen or a permanent resident, the non-citizen may apply for an Australian "partner visa" to remain in Australia.

When marriages are entered into, whether in Australia or elsewhere, for the purpose of enabling the non-citizen to obtain an Australian visa to enter or stay in Australia, Australian authorities may investigate whether such a marriage is a sham. If found to be a sham, they may cancel the visa. Such behaviour also carries a possible 10 year jail sentence. Nevertheless, this does not effect the validity of the marriage itself.

Solemnisation of marriages in Australia

A marriage entered into Australia is void (invalid) if it has not been "solemnised" by an authorised marriage celebrant. Only authorised marriage celebrants are allowed to solemnise marriages in Australia. There are three types of celebrants: ministers of religion, state and territory registry officers, and civil marriage celebrants. The only requirements for registration of a minister of religion is that he or she is nominated by a proclaimed "recognised denomination", is a resident in Australia, and is at least 21 years old. The Sex Discrimination Act 1984 (Cth) was amended with the 2017 recognition of same-sex marriages to exempt a minister of religion or religious marriage celebrant or chaplain from the prohibition of sex discrimination by refusing to marry same-sex couples. It is illegal to marry your sibling (brother or sister).

State and territory officers who are allowed to register marriages (under a state law) can also solemnise marriages (i.e. registry marriages).

Civil marriage celebrants are authorised to conduct and solemnise civil wedding ceremonies. For registration, they must meet a number of requirements, in addition to being at least 18 years old and "fit and proper" persons. The register will take into account knowledge of the law, commitment to advising couples about relationship counselling, community standing, criminal record, the existence of a conflict of interest or benefit to business, and "any other matter", which includes professional development and an adherence to a code of practice. Most marriages in Australia are solemnised by civil celebrants.

Notice of Intended Marriage

Couples must give their marriage celebrant a Notice of Intended Marriage at least one month before the intended wedding ceremony. The Notice is valid for 18 months. In exceptional circumstances, the couple can apply for a waiver of the one-month waiting period,

This Notice is not a marriage licence, as a couple does not normally require an official authorisation to marry, but a person under the age of 18 wishing to marry requires parental consent and the authorisation of a judge.

WEDDING CEREMONY

The couple must wait at least one month after giving their marriage celebrant the Notice of Intended Marriage before the wedding ceremony. Both parties to the marriage must be present at the ceremony, with proxy marriages not permitted. The marriage celebrant and two witnesses over the age of 18 years must also be present, besides other guests. The witnesses must sign the certificate prepared by the celebrant.

The celebrant is required to recite the prescribed words to solemnise the marriage. Otherwise, almost anything is permitted. For example, it can be at any venue, indoors or outdoors, at any day or time, and follow any tradition or custom, or none at all.

Recognition of foreign marriages

It is not uncommon for Australian citizens or Australian residents to go abroad to marry. This may be to the family's ancestral home country, to a destination wedding location or because they would not be permitted to marry in Australia. However, if a party to the marriage is not an Australian citizen, issues may arise with plans for the couple to move to and live in Australia. Marriage by itself to a non-citizen does not, for example, guarantee an Australian visa, let alone citizenship.

The Department of Foreign Affairs and Trade (DFAT) can legalise signatures or seals that appear on Australian public documents (apostilles and authentications) and issues Certificates of No Impediment to Marriage (including witnessing the signature on the form).

In general, marriages entered into abroad are normally recognised in Australia as valid if they are valid according to the laws of the country in which the marriage took place, except that a marriage is not recognised as valid in Australia if:

- either person is still married, that is, if it is a polygamous marriage,
- either person is not of marriageable age,
- the parties are within a prohibited relationship, or
- there was no real consent.

So, for example, even though it may be legal for a person under the age of 18 to marry abroad, such a marriage will not be recognised as valid under Australian law, even when the underage partner turns 18.

Marriages performed abroad do not require to be registered in Australia, and it is advisable that the couple obtain and retain the marriage certificate from the relevant authority in the country in which the marriage took place.

Registration

It is compulsory for marriages entered into in Australia to be registered in the appropriate state or territory registry. In Australia, after the marriage ceremony, the marriage celebrant will send a certified copy of Notice to the Registrar of Births, Deaths and Marriages of the state or territory in which the marriage took place. The Registrar uses the information in the Notice to register the marriage. A failure to register does not invalidate the marriage, but the registrar cannot issue a marriage certificate until the marriage is registered.

Marriages entered into abroad do not need to be registered in Australia.

Proof of marriage

In Australia, the marriage celebrant will at the time of marriage prepare three copies of a certificate, one for forwarding to the appropriate state or territory registry, one for the couple and one retained by the celebrant. While legally valid as proof of marriage, the couple's copy is not generally acceptable as an official document.

The state or territory registrars will, on application by either spouse, issue a marriage certificate which is considered to be an acceptable and secure secondary identity document especially for the purposes of change of name, and needs to be obtained separately, for a fee, generally some time after the marriage. This document can be verified electronically by the Attorney-General of Australia's Document Verification Service. States and territories sometimes market commemorative marriage certificates, which generally have no official document status.

Marriage certificates are generally not used in Australia, other than to prove change-of-name, and proof of marital status for probate purposes or in a divorce application. Some visa categories require a certificate (where a partner is to be associated with a primary applicant), however there are similar categories of partner visas that do not.

In the case of foreign marriages, the foreign marriage certificate is normally adequate proof of marriage.

Social change

In 2009, the Australian Bureau of Statistics noted that "The proportion of adults living with a partner has declined during the last two decades, from 65% in 1986, to 61% in 2006". The proportion of Australians who are married fell from 62% to 52% over the same period.

Common-law marriages have increased significantly in recent decades, from 4% to 9% between 1986 and 2006. Cohabitation is often a prelude to marriage and reflects an increasing desire to attain financial independence before having children. In 2015, 81% of all those marrying were already living together.

Civil celebrants have conducted the majority of marriages since 1999. In 2018, they conducted 79.7% of marriages.

On its inception, the Commonwealth Public Service placed a bar on the employment of married women, so that married women could only be employed as temporary staff. Any female employee was required to resign upon marrying. This bar restricted women's opportunities for promotion. After a long campaign the bar was lifted in 1966.

In 1971, more than three quarters of women surveyed placed being a mother before their career. By 1991 this figure had dropped to one quarter.

By the 1980s there was a clear trend towards delaying first marriage. In 1989, more than one woman in five had not married by the age of 30. Between 1990 and 2010, the median age at first marriage increased by more than three years for both women and men (from 24.3 years to 27.9 years for women, and from 26.5 years to 29.6 years for men).

MARRIAGE ACT 1961 (AUSTRALIA)

In Australia, the Marriage Act 1961 is an Act of the Australian Parliament to regulate marriage law in Australia. The Act was passed by the Australian Parliament in 1961 and has been amended on numerous occasions. It applies uniformly throughout Australia (including its external territories); and any law made by a state or territory inconsistent with the Act is invalid. The Act was made pursuant to power granted to the federal parliament under s.51(xxi) of the Australian Constitution. Although the federal parliament was given the power to pass laws about marriage at federation in 1901, it did not use this power until the 1961 Act, while before 1961, each Australian state and territory had its own marriage laws. The Act recognises only marriages of two people and does not recognise any other forms of union, including traditional Aboriginal unions.

An amendment to the Act to legalise same-sex marriage passed into law on 8 December 2017. The Family Law Act 1975 treats de facto relationships and polygamous marriages as marriages for the purpose of recognising the rights of parties at a breakup. Since 2009, the Family Law Act 2009 has also recognised the property rights of each partner of de facto relationships on separation.

Marriageable age

Part II (s.10-21) deals with the marriageable age and the marriage of minors. In the original 1961 Act, marriageable age was set at 16 for females and 18 for males. However, under section 12 of the original 1961 Act a female 14 or 15 years or a male 16 or 17 years could apply to the court for permission to marry. The marriageable age was equalised in 1991 by the Sex Discrimination Amendment Act 1991, which raised the marriageable age of females to 18.

The marriage of a person aged 16 or 17 to another aged over 18 is permitted in "unusual and exceptional circumstances", which requires the consent of the younger person's parents and authorisation by a court. Prior to the 1991 changes, the "unusual and exceptional circumstances" procedures applied to a girl aged 14 or 15 (wanting to marry a male aged 18 or above) or a male aged 16 or 17 (wanting to marry a female aged 16 or above). For many years, courts have refused to accept a minor's pregnancy as a pressing consideration in deciding whether to allow an early marriage.

Void marriages

Part III entitled "void marriages" establishes the circumstances in which a marriage is void. To preserve the validity of past marriages, this part is divided into periods based on when amendments to the Act were introduced. A purported marriage is void if:

- either party is already married (bigamy, polygamy).
- the parties are in a prohibited relationship: direct descendants or siblings, including by legal adoption.
- the marriage was not solemnised by an authorised celebrant (as in Part IV, Division 2).
- there is no consent, for example due to duress, fraud, mistake as to identity, mistake as to the nature of ceremony, mental incapacity, or being below the marriageable age set out in Part II.

Solemnisation of marriages in Australia

Part IV, entitled "Solemnisation of Marriages in Australia", deals with who is authorised to be a wedding celebrant, and the procedures to be followed. It also contains a division on marriages by foreign diplomatic or consular officers.

AUTHORISED CELEBRANTS

Division 1 deals with authorised celebrants. Under the current Act three types of celebrants are allowed: ministers of religion, state and territory officers, and civil marriage celebrants.

Religious ministers

Under Subdivision A, a register is kept of ministers of religion (s.27) of "recognised" denominations (s26). The only requirements for registration is that the person is a minister of religion who is nominated by their denomination, is resident in Australia, and is at least 21 years old (s29). A minister will be registered (s30) unless the registrar refuses registration because there are sufficient ministers of that denomination, or if the minister is "not a fit and proper person" or will not devote sufficient time to the functions of a minister of religion (s31).

Ministers of religion are not bound to solemnise any marriage. Nothing in Part IV of the Marriage Act imposes an obligation on an authorised celebrant, being a minister of religion, to solemnise any marriage (s47).

Registry office marriages

Subdivision B (s.39) preserves the power of "state and territory officers", allowing people who register marriages (under a state law) to also solemnise marriages (i.e. registry marriages).

Civil celebrants

Subdivision C deals with "marriage celebrants", or the authorisation of people to conduct civil ceremonies. Section 39B allows the register to be kept and sections 39D-E are procedural and seek to set up processes to control the number of celebrants.

This section was introduced by the Marriage Amendment Act 2002, after an attorney-general inquiry into the Civil Celebrants Program. Prior to the passage of this amendment the authorisation of celebrants was entirely contained in s39, which in s39(2) allowed the recognition of other "fit and proper persons" as civil marriage celebrants, religious celebrants outside a recognised denomination, and celebrants with special community needs.

The original 1961 Act therefore allowed civil ceremonies, and the first civil celebrants were authorised in 1973. By the time the 2002 amendments were introduced, civil celebrants performed over 50% of marriages. The changes therefore provide legislative recognition to civil celebrants, and prescribe a regime beyond being "fit and proper" in order to control the quality and number of celebrants.

Section 39C now lists a number of requirements to be registered as civil celebrant, in addition to being at least 18 years old and "fit and proper". The register will take into account: knowledge of the law; commitment to advising couples about relationship counselling; community standing; criminal record, the existence of a conflict of interest or benefit to business; and "any other matter".

Section 39G imposes "obligations" on civil celebrants. These include professional development and an adherence to a code of practice.

Sections 39H, I, and J set up a review of celebrants and a disciplinary system.

Significantly, Subdivision C deals only with marriage celebrants (civil or not from a recognised religion), not with ministers of religion, who are governed by Subdivision A. As a result, ministers of religion are not necessarily subject to the same obligations or code of practice.

Recognition of foreign marriages

Part VA deals with recognition of foreign marriages.

This division reflects the Act's tendency to seek to uphold the validity of marriages. Marriages will be recognised if they were valid in the country where they were performed and if the marriage would be legal under Australian law. The foreign marriage certificate is proof of marriage and such marriages need not be registered in Australia.

As a marriage must be legal under Australian law, a foreign marriage will not be recognised if, for example, a person was already married (or the overseas divorce is not recognised in Australia), a person was aged under 18 (subject to some exceptions), the persons were direct descendants or siblings, or there was duress or fraud.

Other sections

- Marriages by Foreign Diplomatic or Consular Officers (Division 3 of Part IV): there are currently no Australian diplomatic or consular officers appointed to solemnise marriages overseas under Australian law.
- Marriages of Members of the Defence Force Overseas: Part V of the Act deals with marriages of members of the Defence Force overseas.
- Legitimation of Children (Part VI): The Act legitimises children if their parents marry, including in some cases the children of foreign marriages and in certain situations the children of void marriages.
- Offences (Part VII): covers various offences including bigamy, marrying a person below the marriageable age (child marriage), and (for celebrants) solemnising a marriage where they believed there to be a legal impediment.
- Miscellaneous provisions in Part IX: covers the role of interpreters, the publication of lists of celebrants, and other matters.

- Section 111A removed the ability to seek to recover damages for breach of contract where a promise to marry (an engagement) did not lead to marriage.

MARRIAGE EDUCATION

Part IA authorises the government to make grants to approved organisations for marriage counselling.

Amendments to the Marriage Act

Two amendments of note to the Act have been made with respect to the legal definition of marriage in Australia, both of which relate to same-sex marriage.

Marriage Amendment Act 2004

Before 2004, there was no definition of marriage in the 1961 Act, and instead the common law definition used in the English case Hyde v Hyde (1866) was considered supreme. Though s.46(1) of the Act required celebrants to explain the legal nature of marriage in Australia to a couple as "the union of a man and a woman to the exclusion of all others, voluntarily entered into for life", these words were descriptive or explanatory, rather than outlining what constituted a legally valid marriage in Australia.

On 27 May 2004 the then federal attorney-general Philip Ruddock introduced the Marriage Amendment Bill 2004 to incorporate a definition of marriage into the Marriage Act 1961 and to outlaw the recognition of same-sex marriages lawfully entered into in foreign jurisdictions. In June 2004, the bill passed the House of Representatives. On 12 August 2004, the amendment passed the Parliament. The bill subsequently received royal assent, becoming the Marriage Amendment Act 2004.

The amendment incorporated a definition of marriage into section 5 of the Act, known as the Interpretation section:

marriage means the union of a man and a woman to the exclusion of all others, voluntarily entered into for life.

and inserted a new section:

88EA Certain unions are not marriages

A union solemnised in a foreign country between:

(a) a man and another man; or

(b) a woman and another woman;

must not be recognised as a marriage in Australia.

The amendment was argued by Ruddock and Liberal MPs to be necessary to protect the institution of marriage, and to ensure that the definition would be beyond legal challenge through the application of common law. Several years later, then-prime minister John Howard admitted that the government was motivated by the prospect of overseas same-sex marriages being recognised under Australian law via the judiciary. Labor Party shadow attorney-general Nicola Roxon said that the Labor Party would not oppose the amendment, arguing that the amendment did not affect the legal situation of same-sex relationships, merely putting into statute law what was already common law. Likewise minor parties Family First and the Christian Democrats supported the bill, as did the junior party in the Coalition government, the National Party.

The Australian Greens opposed the bill, calling it the "Marriage Discrimination Act". The Australian Democrats also opposed the bill. Democrats Senator Andrew Bartlett stated that the legislation devalued his marriage, and Greens Senator Bob Brown referred to John Howard and the legislation as "hateful".

Not all of Labor was in support of the bill. During the bill's second reading, Labor MP Anthony Albanese said, "what has caused offence is why the government has rushed in this legislation in what is possibly the last fortnight of parliamentary sittings. This bill is a result of 30 bigoted backbenchers who want to press buttons out there in the community."

Marriage Amendment (Definition and Religious Freedoms) Act 2017

Ahead of both the 2007 and 2010 federal elections, the Labor Party re-asserted its official opposition to amending the Act to legalise same-sex marriage, but by 2011 a clear majority of the party at the national conference succeeded in changing party policy in favour of the practice. Prime Minister Julia Gillard (opposed to same-sex marriage at the time) successfully moved for Labor Party MPs to be granted a conscience vote on same-sex marriage legislation. This, along with the Coalition's uniform opposition to same-sex marriage while in opposition, prevented two bills which would have legalised same-sex marriage in Australia from passing the House of Representatives and the Senate in September 2012.

The Abbott Government (2013–15) initially opposed same-sex marriage, but in August 2015 resolved to put the matter to the people at a plebiscite after the 2016 federal election. This policy was retained by the Turnbull Government (2015–18), though due to the refusal of the Senate to support the legislation to establish a plebiscite, the government conducted a voluntary postal survey on the matter from September to November 2017. The survey returned 61.6% 'Yes' vote in favour of same-sex marriage. The government subsequently committed to facilitating the passage of a private member's bill to amend the Act, and legalise same-sex marriage, by the end of 2017.

The bill in question, the Marriage Amendment (Definition and Religious Freedoms) Bill 2017, was introduced by Liberal Party Senator Dean Smith on 15 November 2017. The bill amends the definition of "marriage" in the Act, omitting the words "man and a woman" and replacing it with the gender-neutral "2 people". The bill passed the Senate by 43 votes to 12 on 29 November 2017 and passed the House of Representatives on 7 December 2017, with only four votes against. It was given royal assent by the governor-general, Sir Peter Cosgrove, on 8 December 2017.

The Act had the effect of amending the definition of marriage in Section 5 of the Marriage Act: marriage means the union of 2 people to the exclusion of all others, voluntarily entered into for life.

It also repealed Section 88EA, which banned the recognition of overseas same-sex marriages. Consequently, when the Act went into effect on 9 December 2017, such couples became automatically recognised as married under the law.

The original Act and the amendment also applies to Australia's external territories.

DIVORCE IN AUSTRALIA

The crude divorce rate was 2.0 divorces per 1,000 estimated resident population in 2014 and 2015, down from 2.1 in 2013. The median duration from marriage to divorce in 2015 was 12.1 years. The median age at divorce was 45.3 years for men and 42.7 years for women.

Australian family law is principally found in the federal Family Law Act 1975 and the Federal Circuit and Family Court of Australia (Family Law) Rules 2021 as well as in other laws and the common law and laws of equity, which affect the family and the relationship between those people, including when those relationships end. Most family law is practised in the Federal Circuit and Family Court of Australia and the Family Court of Western Australia. Australia recognises marriages entered into overseas as well as divorces obtained overseas if they were effected in accordance with the laws of that country.

Australian marriage and "matrimonial causes" are recognised by sections 51(xxi) and (xxii) of the Constitution of Australia and internationally by marriage law and conventions, such as the Hague Convention on Marriages (1978).

Australia's laws on divorce and other legal family matters were overhauled in 1975 with the enactment of the Family Law Act 1975, which established no-fault divorce in Australia. Since 1975, the only ground for divorce has been irretrievable breakdown of marriage, evidenced by a twelve-month separation. However, a residual "fault" element remains in relation to child custody and property settlement issues. The federal Family Law Act 1975 covers divorce, children's orders, property division, spousal maintenance and related matters.

Same-sex marriage

The Marriage Act 1961 was amended in December 2017 by the Marriage Amendment (Definition and Religious Freedoms) Act 2017 to amend the definition of marriage and to recognise same-sex marriage in Australia whether entered into in Australia or abroad. The original Marriage Act did not include a definition of marriage, leaving it to the courts to apply the common law definition. The Marriage Amendment Act 2004 defined, for the first time by statute, marriage as "the union of a man and a woman to the exclusion of all others, voluntarily entered into for life."

The 2004 Act also expressly declared same-sex marriages entered into abroad were not to be recognised in Australia. This was in response to a lesbian couple getting married in Canada and applying for their marriage to be recognised in Australia.

Since 2009, same-sex couples were included in Australia's de facto relationship laws, unions which provide couples with most, though not all, of the same rights as married couples. Same-sex and opposite-sex de facto couples can continue to access domestic partnership registries in New South Wales, Tasmania, South Australia and Victoria. Civil partnerships/unions are performed in Queensland and the Australian Capital Territory. Western Australia and the Northern Territory do not recognise civil unions, civil partnerships or a relationship register, but do recognise the unregistered cohabitation of de facto couples under their laws.

Annulment

Under the Family Law Act 1975, a decree of nullity can be made if a marriage is void. Annulment does not involve termination of a marriage, but rather a declaration the purported marriage is in-fact void.

What constitutes a void marriage is determined by section 23 of the Marriage Act 1961 The distinction that existed before 1975 between void and voidable marriages no longer exists. In addition, the 1975 Act also abolished the legal concept of non-consummation of marriage as a ground for annulment, so that a divorce application would need to be made.

A marriage is void if:

- one or both of the parties were already married at the time (i.e. bigamy)
- the parties are in a prohibited relationship (i.e. closely related such as siblings)
- the parties did not comply with the marriage laws in the jurisdiction where they were married (note that although a marriage contracted abroad is in general considered valid in Australia, in certain cases, such as when there are serious contradictions with the marriage laws of Australia, the marriage is void)
- one or both of the parties were under-age and did not have the necessary approvals, (minimum marriageable age is 16, but 16 and 17 years-olds need special court approval) or
- one or both of the parties were forced into the marriage.

An application for a decree of nullity takes precedence over an application for divorce, so that if it is found that a marriage is void, then divorce application becomes irrelevant, though other remedies may still be available.

RECENT CASES

Kallestad v Brodie

In Kallestad v Brodie, the husband (Mr Kallestad) sought declaration that his marriage was void on the grounds that his wife (Ms Brodie) had previously been married to another person with that marriage still being live at the time Mr Kallestad was married to Ms Brodie. The Family Court of Australia found the marriage was void on the grounds Ms Brodie's original marriage was still valid at the time the second marriage was made.

Bown v Jalloh

In Bown v Jalloh, the wife (Ms Bown) sought declaration that her marriage was void on the grounds that her husband (Mr Jalloh) had not disclosed his full past to her and so she had married him on grounds of mistaken identity because his name was slightly different. Ms Bown had located a drivers licence issued in the county from where Mr Jalloh originated, which had his name written as 'Jalloph'. Ms Bown sought to end the marriage due to other personal matters about her husband he had not disclosed to her.

However, the Family Court of Australia noted that misrepresentations that could induce consent to marriage relating to age, wealth, social status or other background were not relevant to whether or not Ms Brown consented to marry Mr Jalloh on the day she did, and so the application was dismissed.

Divorce

No-fault divorce

Australia has no-fault divorce with the only ground for divorce being a claim of an irretrievable breakdown of marriage, evidenced by a twelve-month separation. Sometimes the couple may still be living together in the same home and be considered separated. If that is the case for any part of the twelve months before filing the application.

A sole applicant will need to file an affidavit providing evidence that there has been such separation. As well as an affidavit from an independent third party.

For a joint application both parties should file an affidavit, a third party affidavit is NOT needed in this case.

If the parties have reconciled for 3 months or more, then the 12-month qualification period has to start anew.

Though the Commonwealth had the power since federation in 1901 to make laws affecting divorce and related matters such as custody and maintenance, it did not enact uniform national laws until 1961, when the Matrimonial Causes Act 1959 came into operation. The Act continued the fault-based system operating under state authority. Under the Commonwealth law a spouse had to establish one of the 14 grounds for divorce set out in the Act, including adultery, desertion, cruelty, habitual drunkenness, imprisonment and insanity.

In reality, the system was very expensive and humiliating for the spouses, necessitating appointment of barristers, often private detectives, collection of evidence, obtaining witness statements, photographs and hotel receipts, etc. Failure to prove a spouse's guilt or wrongdoing would result in a judge refusing to grant a divorce. The Matrimonial Causes Act 1959 was replaced by no-fault divorce system of the Family Law Act 1975.

Divorce application

Either party to a marriage may apply to the Federal Circuit and Family Court of Australia for a divorce, or both parties may apply jointly. However, an application for divorce cannot be filed before the expiration of at least two years since the marriage had been entered into. The application can be lodged online or using a hard copy form. A fee is payable. If the application is made by one spouse (called a "sole application"), the divorce documents must be served on the other spouse, at least 28 days before the court hearing if the spouse is in Australia or 42 days if overseas.

The spouse can challenge the application in a "response", claiming, for example, that the timeframes set out in the Act have not been satisfied, or that the applicant is not an Australian citizen or resident, etc. The response must also be served on the applicant and filed in court. If both spouses agree to divorce a "joint application" is filed, which does not need to be served and no response can be made.

An application for divorce can be made in Australia if either spouse:

- regards Australia as their home and intends to live indefinitely in Australia and is an Australian citizen or resident, or
- is an Australian citizen by birth or descent or is a naturalised Australian citizen (in which case a citizenship certificate will be required), or
- ordinarily lives in Australia and has done so for 12 months immediately before filing for divorce.

Neither spouse can remarry before the divorce becomes final, which is usually one month and one day after the divorce is granted in court. Such a marriage would constitute bigamy and would be illegal and void.

If there are children of the marriage aged under 18, a court can only grant a divorce if it is satisfied that proper arrangements have been made for them. A child of the marriage includes:

- any child of either spouse, including a child born before the marriage or after separation,
- any child adopted by the spouses or either of them, or

- any child who was treated as a member of the family prior to the final separation; for example, a step-child or foster child.

A copy of the marriage certificate must be provided with the application. The same rules apply if the marriage was entered into overseas, except that if the marriage certificate is not in English, an English translation must be provided, with an affidavit from the translator.

After the divorce is finalised, each party can apply to the Federal Circuit and Family Court of Australia (or the Federal Circuit and Family Court of Western Australia for residents of that state) for a proof of divorce certificate.

PROPERTY AND FINANCIAL OUTCOMES

Australia is an equitable distribution country, meaning that on divorce or death of a spouse net wealth is not split evenly (50/50) as community property. Instead courts have wide powers, taking into account 27 or so statutory factors, to determine what a "just and equitable" division of wealth would be. The vast majority of outcomes result in a division of 55-65% in favour of the wife, or economically weaker spouse, before payment of legal fees. This process is not without its critics: on average the wealth re-allocation process takes between 2 years, or for the more wealthy, up to 4 years.

Property Settlement

Under the Family Law Act a court can make orders dividing the assets, liabilities and superannuation of spouses, and other related orders. The court must approach the decision according to the "4 step process":

1. ascertain the assets, liabilities and superannuation of the parties;
2. assess the contributions that each party made to the asset pool;
3. assess the relevant factors set out in section 75(2), often referred to as the "future needs" factors;
4. consider whether the outcome is "just and equitable" and make any relevant adjustments.

The relevant date to ascertain the property "pool" is at the time of trial, not the time of separation.

Contributions made to the relationship include financial contributions (eg. income, inheritances, assets held at the commencement of the relationship), non-financial contributions (eg. unpaid labour, assistance running a business) and parenting and homemaker contributions (eg. domestic duties and care of children). Contributions as homemaker and parent are not presumed to be of lesser value than financial contributions. Section 75(2) ("future needs") factors allow an adjustment to be made between the parties to take account of particular circumstances. Common relevant circumstances include the care of children, a disparity of income, and the impact on the relationship of time out of the workforce.

Under the Family Law Act, a court has the power to "split" superannuation from one spouse to another. A court can make orders for property settlement or spousal maintenance after the death of a party, but only if proceedings were commenced prior to the death of that party.

The court may decline to make any orders, leaving the legal and equitable interests of the parties as they were.

Spousal Maintenance

Parties to a marriage or a de facto relationship have the right to apply for spousal maintenance from the other party. The party making an application must demonstrate:

1. his or her need for spousal maintenance, and
2. that the other party has the capacity to pay spousal maintenance.

If made, an order for spousal maintenance is usually for a limited period to allow a party to retrain, return to the workforce or care for young children.

Binding Financial Agreements

Under Part VIIIA of the Family Law Act (for de facto couples: Division 4 of Part VIIIAB), parties may opt-out of the ability of the court to make orders in respect of property settlement or spousal maintenance by use of a valid Binding Financial Agreement. The effect of a valid Binding Financial Agreement is to prevent a Court making orders under Part VIII of the Family Law Act (or the corresponding de facto provisions), meaning that property will be divided and/or spousal maintenance will be dealt with in accordance with the provisions of the agreement. A Binding Financial Agreement can only be valid if both parties have received independent legal advice before the agreement was signed.

However, a recent Canstar study found that only 6% of Australian Couples have a Binding Financial Agreement in place, meaning over 90% of Australian couples once separated are still required to divide wealth according to what the family law act sees as "just and equitable".

A Binding Financial Agreement that attempts to limit a person's ability to claim for spousal maintenance will be invalid if the party was unable to support himself or herself without a pension when the agreement came into effect.

A Binding Financial Agreement may be set aside in limited circumstances.

BIBLIOGRAPHY

- Bullough, Vern L. (3 June 2014). Adolescence, Sexuality, and the Criminal Law: Multidisciplinary Perspectives. p. 37. ISBN 978-1-317-95499-6. Retrieved 18 October 2015.
- Chen, Victor Tan (August 20, 2017). America, Home of the Transactional Marriage: The country's exceptionally thin safety net prompts residents—especially those with less-steady employment—to view partnership in more economic terms. The Atlantic.
- Coontz, Stephanie. (2005). Marriage, a History: From Obedience to Intimacy, or How Love Conquered Marriage. New York: Viking Press, Penguin Group Inc. pp. 125–29, ISBN 0-14-303667-X.
- Cudis, Christine (2019-02-14). PH divorce bill status: It's complicated. Philippine News Agency. Retrieved 2020-06-22.
- Culver Bernardo Alford, Jus civile matrimoniale in statibus foederatis americae septentrionalis cum jure canonico comparatum, Kenedy & Sons, 1938
- De Moor, Tine; Van Zanden, Jan Luiten (2010). Girl power: The European marriage pattern and labour markets in the North Sea region in the late medieval and early modern period. The Economic History Review. 63: 1–33 (17). doi:10.1111/j.1468-0289.2009.00483.x.
- Dethier, M.; Counerotte, C.; Blairy, S. (2011). Marital satisfaction in couples with an alcoholic husband. Journal of Family Violence. 26 (2): 151–162. doi:10.1007/s10896-010-9355-z. S2CID 11098947.
- Dew, J.; Wilcox, B. (2011). If momma aint happy, no one is. Journal of Marriage and Family. 73 (1): 1–12. doi:10.1111/j.1741-3737.2010.00782.x.
- Divorce is increasingly common. USC US-China Institute. Archived from the original on 2014-02-19. Retrieved 2009-10-11.

- Divorce. Sveriges Domstolar - Domstolsverket, Swedish National Courts Administration. 2007-03-07. Retrieved 2008-09-29.
- Eby, Clare Virginia (2014). Until Choice Do Us Part: Marriage Reform in the Progressive Era. Chicago: University of Chicago Press.
- Esguerra, Christian V. (2019-09-25). It's complicated: The battle for divorce law in Catholic Philippines. ABS-CBN News. Retrieved 2020-06-22.
- EU Directive on a Community framework for electronic signatures accessed on April 26, 2008.
- Family Code of the Philippines. Archived from the original on 2000-08-19. Retrieved 2006-09-06.
- Family Law in the Fifty States, Chart 4: Grounds for Divorce and Residency Requirements (PDF). Family Law Quarterly. 45 (4): 500. Winter 2012. Retrieved September 19, 2017.
- Fernandez, Butch (2019-10-21). Senators cool to divorce bill, eye dissolution of marriage. BusinessMirror. Retrieved 2020-06-22.
- Gatdula, Jemy (2019-05-16). The May elections, democracy, and the biggest losers. BusinessWorld. Retrieved 2020-06-22.
- Gillis, John R. (1985). For Better, for Worse: British Marriages, 1600 to the Present. Oxford University Press. p. 92. ISBN 978-0-19-503614-5.
- Glorieux, I.; Minnen, J.; Tienoven, T. P. (2011). Spouse together time: Quality time within the household. Social Indicators Research. 101 (2): 281–287. doi:10.1007/s11205-010-9648-x. S2CID 143520009.
- Gordon, C.; Arnetter, R.; Smith, R. (2011). Have you thanked your spouse today?: Felt and expressed gratitude among married couples. Personality and Individual Differences. 50 (3): 339–343. doi:10.1016/j.paid.2010.10.012.
- Helms, H.; Walls, J.; Crouter, A.; Susan, M. (2010). Provider role attitudes, marital satisfaction, role overload, and housework: A dyadic approach. Journal of Family Psychology. 24 (5): 568–577. doi:10.1037/a0020637. PMC 2958678. PMID 20954767.
- Herbermann, Charles, ed. (1913). History of Marriage . Catholic Encyclopedia. New York: Robert Appleton Company.
- Hernandez, K.; Mahoney, A.; Pargament, K. (2011). Sanctification of sexuality: Implications for newlyweds' marital and sexual quality. Journal of Family Psychology. 25 (5): 775–780. doi:10.1037/a0025103. PMID 21875197.
- Japan's First Sperm Bank Aims to Reduce Black Market Sperm Trades. 23 September 2021.

- Kertzer, David I and Marzio Barbagli. (2001). The history of the European family. New Haven: Yale University Press. p. xxii, ISBN 0-300-09090-0.
- Lalu, Gabriel Pabico (2020-02-05). Divorce bill gets House panel's nod; group formed to combine proposals. Philippine Daily Inquirer. Retrieved 2020-06-22.
- Lehmberg, Stanford E. and Samantha A. Meigs. (2008). The Peoples of the British Isles: A New History: From Prehistoric Times to 1688. Lyceum Books. p. 117, ISBN 1-933478-01-2.
- Leneman, Leah (1999). The Scottish Case That Led to Hardwicke's Marriage Act. Law and History Review. Archived from the original on 25 May 2012.
- Licaros vs. Licaros, G.R. No. 150656. April 29, 2003. Archived from the original on 2005-01-02. Retrieved 2006-09-06.
- Llorente vs. Court of Appeals and Llorente, G.R. No. 124371. November 23, 2000. Archived from the original on 2004-12-29. Retrieved 2006-09-06.
- Marriage|LII / Legal Information Institute. Topics.law.cornell.edu. 19 August 2010. Archived from the original on 25 March 2011.
- Nevada Revised Statutes, Sec. 125.020. Nevada Legislature. Retrieved September 19, 2017.
- SD House Votes Down Unilateral No-Fault Divorce Proposal | KDLT.com South Dakota News - News, Sports, and Weather Sioux Falls South Dakota. Kdlt.com. March 10, 2015. Archived from the original on February 27, 2015. Retrieved April 12, 2015.
- Section 32-701 – Idaho State Legislature. legislature.idaho.gov. Retrieved September 19, 2017.
- Tomacruz, Sofia (March 10, 2018). 53% of Filipinos agree to legalize divorce – SWS. Rappler. Retrieved March 12, 2018.
- Van Dorn vs. Romillo, G.R. No. L-68470 October 8, 1985. Retrieved 2006-09-06.
- West's Encyclopedia of American Law, 2nd Edition. Thomson Gale, 2005. ISBN 0-7876-6367-0
- Wibawa, Tasha (2018-10-08). Trapped in an abusive marriage in one of the last places on Earth where divorce is illegal. Australian Broadcasting Corporation. Retrieved 2020-06-22.

INDEX

www.ingramcontent.com/pod-product-compliance
Lightning Source LLC
Chambersburg PA
CBHW071244230926
51849CB00001B/222
* 9 7 8 8 1 9 7 5 5 9 4 0 2 *